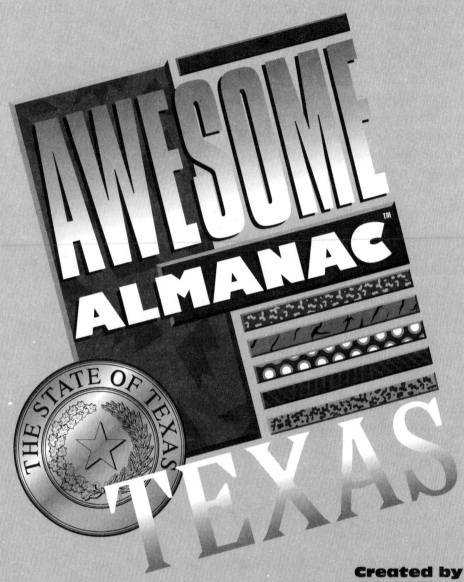

AWESOME ALMANAC™
TEXAS

THE STATE OF TEXAS

Created by
Jean F. Blashfield

Compiled and Written by
Suzanne Martin

B&B Publishing, Inc.

B & B Publishing, Inc.
820 Wisconsin Street
P. O. Box 96
Walworth, Wisconsin 53184

Additional Materials – **Margie Benson**
Editor – **Margie Benson**
Photo Researcher – **Ramona Uhlenhake**
Production Manager - **Katy O'Shea**
Computer Production – **Katy O'Shea and Ramona Uhlenhake**
Original Cover Design – **Gary Hurst**

Publisher's Cataloging in Publication
Martin, Suzanne.
      Awesome almanac: Texas / Suzanne Martin.
      p. cm.
      Includes bibliographical references and index.
      Preassigned LCCN: 92-074714.
      ISBN 1-880190-22-2

1. Texas—History—Miscellanea. 2. Almanacs, American—Texas.
I. Title.

F386.5.M37 1995   976.4
                                  QBI95-20031

Printed in the United States of America

95 96 97 98   5 4 3 2 1

AWESOME ALMANAC is a trademark of B&B Publishing, Inc.

TABLE OF CONTENTS

The Alamo

THE LONE STAR STATE

Welcome to Texas, the Lone Star State, where chili is the official dish and more miles of road crisscross the land than in any other state.

Some people call the sprawling state big and bold. Others say it's brash. Clearly, Texas and Texans inherited an independent and willful streak. Not so many years ago, the people fought a dramatic revolution against Mexico … and won. Presidents governed a great republic before governors ever ruled the state.

No single city or historical figure defines the state. Instead, Texas is better recognized as a place with a peculiar shape, a place with a spaciousness where legends can loom larger than life—and still seem to be born every day. There's room to roam in Texas. Come tour the state.

- Texas by the Numbers
- Naming the State
- The People
- Population
- Texas Government
- The Shape of the State
- Presidents and Governors
- Texas Flags
- Texas Symbols and Songs
- Capitals and Capitols
- Texas County Almanac

TEXAS BY THE NUMBERS

The land
Land area – 262,017 square miles
Water area – 4,790 square miles of inland water
Coast line – 367 miles
Longest point from north to south – 801 miles
Widest point from east to west – 733 miles
Geographic center – Northern part of McCulloch County, about 15 miles northeast of Brady
Highest elevation – Guadalupe Peak at 8,749 feet
Lowest elevation – sea level along the Gulf Coast
Road miles – 305,951 (most of any state)

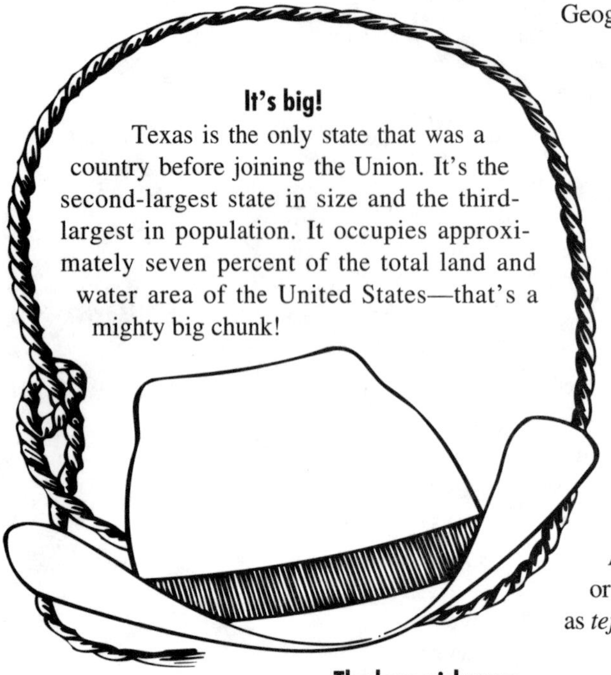

It's big!

Texas is the only state that was a country before joining the Union. It's the second-largest state in size and the third-largest in population. It occupies approximately seven percent of the total land and water area of the United States—that's a mighty big chunk!

NAMING THE STATE

Historic translation

Texas owes its name to the Caddo tribe—and the Spaniards. During the Spanish exploration of Texas in the 1540s, the Spaniards met the Hasnai Caddo tribe in present-day East Texas. The Native Americans used the word *tayshas* for "friends" or "allies." In Spanish, the translation came out as *tejas*. Eventually, Tejas became Texas.

The lone nickname

Texas is also known as the Lone Star State, in reference to the state flag. The flag displays a single, five-point white star on a field of blue with an upper white horizontal stripe and a lower red horizontal stripe.

THE PEOPLE

1990 Resident Census Population – 16,986,510

Race
White – 8,425,309 (49.6%)
Hispanic – 4,348,547 (25.6%)
Black – 2,021,394 (11.9%)
Asian or Pacific Islander – 322,744 (1.9%)
American Indian, Eskimo, or Aleut – 67,946 (0.4%)
Other – 1,800,570 (10.6%)

Gender
Female – 8,620,547
Male – 8,365,963
Median age – 30.8 years

Age
Under 18 – 28.5%
65 and over – 10.1%

POPULATION

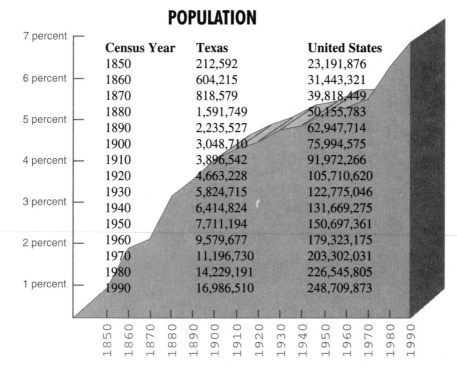

	Census Year	Texas	United States
7 percent			
	1850	212,592	23,191,876
6 percent	1860	604,215	31,443,321
	1870	818,579	39,818,449
	1880	1,591,749	50,155,783
5 percent	1890	2,235,527	62,947,714
	1900	3,048,710	75,994,575
4 percent	1910	3,896,542	91,972,266
	1920	4,663,228	105,710,620
	1930	5,824,715	122,775,046
3 percent	1940	6,414,824	131,669,275
	1950	7,711,194	150,697,361
2 percent	1960	9,579,677	179,323,175
	1970	11,196,730	203,302,031
	1980	14,229,191	226,545,805
1 percent	1990	16,986,510	248,709,873

(x-axis years: 1850 1860 1870 1880 1890 1900 1910 1920 1930 1940 1950 1960 1970 1980 1990)

Graph shows the population of Texas as a percentage of the United States population.

TEXAS GOVERNMENT

Gained independence from Mexico on March 2, 1836, to become the Republic of Texas

A republic

Admitted to the Union on December 29, 1845, as the 28th state

Admitted to the Union

State government is divided into executive, legislative, and judicial branches. The governor is chief executive of the state and is elected for a four-year term of office.

State government

The Texas Legislature includes 31 members in the Senate and 150 members in the House of Representatives. State senators are elected for four-year terms. Representatives are elected for two-year terms. Legislators are paid $600 per month plus $30 per diem during regular and special sessions. The lieutenant governor serves as the president of the Senate. At the beginning of each regular session, members of the House of Representatives elect a Speaker of the House who serves as presiding officer. The Legislature convenes for regular sessions on the second Tuesday of January during odd-numbered years. The governor may call special sessions. Although not a frequent occurrence, special sessions have been called for major issues such as the state budget and educational school tax reform.

To the nation's capital

Texas sends two senators and 30 representatives to the U.S. Congress (up three from the 1980 census), for a total of 32 electoral votes.

The Cabinet until 1999

Governor – George W. Bush (Republican)
Lt. Governor – Bob Bullock (Democrat)
Secretary of State – Tony Garza (Republican)
Attorney General – Dan Morales (Democrat)
State Treasurer – Martha Whitehead (Democrat)
Comptroller – John Sharp (Democrat)

The courts

The judiciary of the state consists of the Supreme Court, with nine members elected to six-year terms, nine members of the State Court of Criminal Appeals elected to six-year terms, and the Courts of Appeals with 80 judges elected to serve six-year terms. In addition, 386 State District Courts judges are elected to four-year terms. The Texas court system also includes 10 Criminal District Courts, 174 County Courts at Law, 434 County Courts, 884 Justice of the Peace Courts, and 853 Municipal Courts.

THE SHAPE OF THE STATE

The shaded area represents Texas in 1836.

Far-reaching republic

When Texas declared independence from Mexico in 1836, the land grab was on and Texans quickly claimed territory for their new republic. From the headwaters of the Rio Grande in the San Juan Mountains of Colorado, the western boundary stretched north to the 42° parallel in Wyoming and followed the Rio Grande south through New Mexico to the Gulf of Mexico. The Sabine River set the eastern boundary. The northern border meandered along the Red River to the 100° meridian, then extended into present-day Kansas. From there, the Arkansas River set the boundary into central Colorado. A long arm of territory reached into Wyoming.

Trading territory

When Texas joined the Union in 1845, the vast territory of the republic was mostly unsettled and was considered public land. The state did not turn over ownership of those public lands to the federal government upon joining the Union. Instead, the classic, if peculiar, shape of Texas known today was determined as part of the Compromise of 1850. For a $10-million price tag, Texas sold 98,300 square miles of that public land to the United States. The land included parts of Colorado, Kansas, New Mexico, Oklahoma, and Wyoming.

The shape of things to come

In February 1845, Texas approved the resolution to enter the Union. Part of that resolution, which came to be known as the Constitution of 1845, stated that Texas would retain its right to divide into four states in addition to the original Texas. Although most Texans can't imagine splitting up the Lone Star State, the legal right to do so still remains.

PRESIDENTS AND GOVERNORS

Presidents of the Republic of Texas

On March 2, 1836, 59 delegates from the largest settlements in Texas convened at Washington-on-the-Brazos and wrote the Declaration of Independence from Mexico. They signed the historic document the next day. Of those signers, only two were native Texans. On March 17, the delegates swore in David G. Burnet as president. More than a month would pass before Texans won the decisive Battle of San Jacinto that promised the new republic freedom to elect more presidents in years to come. The presidents of the Republic were:

David G. Burnet – March 17, 1836, to October 22, 1836
Sam Houston – October 22, 1836, to December 10, 1838
Mirabeau Lamar – December 10, 1838, to December 13, 1841
Sam Houston – December 13, 1841, to December 9, 1844
Anson Jones – December 9, 1844, to February 19, 1846

Better late than never

When U.S. President Polk signed the act that annexed Texas to the Union on December 29, 1845, Republic of Texas President Anson Jones called for a meeting of the Legislature. The meeting date was set for February 19, 1846, for the purpose of organizing a state government. On that day, citizens gathered in front of the Capitol in Austin as the Lone Star flag fluttered down from the flagpole, replaced by the Stars and Stripes. A cannon fired, and Jones, the last president of the Republic of Texas, said, "The final act in this great drama is now performed. The Republic of Texas is no more."

Sculpted by Elisabet Ney, this statue of Sam Houston is in Statuary Hall in Washington, D.C.

After Texas joined the Union, James Pinckney Henderson was the first man to take the governor's seat. Henderson, a North Carolina native, didn't arrive in Texas until 1836, and he didn't stay long after he became governor. He took office on February 19, 1846. Three months later, on May 19, 1846, Henderson left Texas to command troops in Mexico during the war between that country and the United States. During Henderson's absence, Lt. Governor Albert C. Horton served as chief executive of the state. In November 1846, Henderson returned to Texas and served out his term as governor.

First governor of the state

First native-born governor

James Stephen Hogg, born near Rusk in 1851, became the state's first native-born governor on January 20, 1891. One of his most notable accomplishments while in office was creation of the Texas Railroad Commission. Hogg retired in 1895 after serving two 2-year terms as governor. Ironically, Hogg was injured in a train wreck while traveling to Houston on January 26, 1905. Complications from the accident resulted in his death on March 3, 1906.

Short timer

On November 23, 1853, Lt. Gov. James W. Henderson became governor when Governor P. Hansborough Bell resigned to take a seat in Congress. Henderson served only 28 days, the shortest term of any governor. Elisha M. Pease was elected to office and inaugurated on December 21, 1853.

TEXAS FLAGS

Spanish – 1519-1685
Spanish – 1690-1821

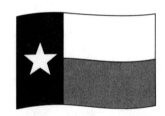

Republic of Texas – 1836-1845

French – 1685-1690

United States – 1845-1861
United States – 1865-present

Mexican – 1821-1836

Confederate States – 1861-1865

Six flags over Texas

During its history, Texas has had eight changes of sovereignty, and six flags have flown over the state. The generally accepted sequence of the flags is shown at left.

Waving other banners

The Lone Star symbol has flown above many historic events. When fighting began in Gonzales in October 1835, the star was outlined on a white banner above a cannon barrel and the daring words "Come And Take It." The challenge referred to a small, brass cannon that Mexico had issued to Texans for defense against Native Americans. Mexico wanted the cannon returned and it wanted the upstart Texans to submit to governmental rule. In December 1835, Texans fought at San Antonio de Béxar under a flag sewn by Sarah Dodson, who made the banner for her husband and his fighting compatriots. A long, tricolor banner of red, white, and blue displayed the familiar five-point star on the blue field.

At the Battle of Goliad in December 1835, volunteers from Georgia arrived waving a white silk flag stitched by Joanna Troutman, an 18-year-old Georgian who had never been to Texas. Her flag featured a blue, five-point star with the words "LIBERTY OR DEATH" inscribed beneath the star. On February 13, 1913, the Texas Legislature named her the "Betsy Ross of Texas" for her Lone Star flag.

A flag for the Republic

In May 1836, the "Lorenzo de Zavala flag" was adopted as the banner for the fledgling Republic of Texas. It featured a blue background with a centered white star circled by the letters T-E-X-A-S. Later that

same year, on December 10, the Republic opted for a different flag. The "David G. Burnet flag" also featured a blue background, but with a gold, five-point star in the center. Neither flag gained support from citizens. Finally, on January 25, 1839, the Third Congress of the Republic officially accepted a flag designed by Dr. Charles Stewart. That Lone Star flag (left) of the Republic still waves today over the Lone Star state.

Exchange of the flags?

At the Battle of the Alamo in 1836, Mexican forces captured a Lone Star flag. Since then, the banner has been displayed at Chapultepec Castle in Mexico City. The cotton "Alamo Flag" is trimmed in gold and embroidered with an eagle. In its beak, the eagle holds a banner that reads "God and Liberty." Texans, in turn, captured three Mexican flags when they defeated General Antonio López de Santa Anna on April 21, 1836, at the Battle of San Jacinto. The Mexican banners were preserved in storage vaults in Austin. The North American Free Trade Agreement has prompted officials in both countries to exchange these flags. As of August 1994, discussions were ongoing and may lead to a trade of the banners.

TEXAS SYMBOLS AND SONGS

State Seal

Article IV, Section 19, of the Texas State Constitution states that the Great Seal of the State of Texas consists of "a star of five points, encircled by olive and live oak branches, and the words, 'The State of Texas'."

The Confederate Air Force

After World War II, a group of former service pilots took to the air as crop-dusters in Texas' Lower Rio Grande Valley. A handful of them pooled their money in 1957 to purchase a P-51D Mustang, one of the few surplus airplanes that had survived the war. As the pilots searched for other aircraft from the war era, they discovered that most had been destroyed. They vowed to find and preserve more WWII airplanes for future generations, and the Confederate Air Force was born. Today, those pilots have amassed more than 140 aircraft in what has become the nation's most complete collection of flyable WWII combat aircraft. In 1989, the state recognized their historic contribution by naming the Confederate Air Force the official Air Force of Texas.

State Tree – pecan, adopted in 1919

Other state symbols

State Flower – bluebonnet, adopted in 1901
State Bird – mockingbird, adopted in 1927
State Motto – Friendship, adopted in 1930
State Stone – petrified palmwood, adopted in 1969
State Gem – Texas blue topaz, adopted in 1969
State Grass – Sideoats grama, adopted in 1971
State Dish – chili, adopted in 1977
State Fish – Guadalupe bass, adopted in 1989
State Folk Dance – square dance, adopted in 1991
State Fruit – Texas red grapefruit, adopted in 1993
State Seashell – lightning whelk, adopted in 1987

The official state song

In 1929, the Texas Legislature adopted "Texas, Our Texas" as the official state song. The music was written by William J. Marsh, who died in Fort Worth on February 1, 1971, at the age of 90. Gladys Yoakum Wright, of Fort Worth, collaborated with Marsh on the lyrics. The words have been changed only once. In the third line, the word "Boldest" replaced "Largest" shortly after Alaska became a state.

Texas, Our Texas

Texas, our Texas! All hail the mighty State!
Texas, our Texas! So wonderful, so great!
Boldest and grandest, withstanding every test;
O empire wide and glorious you stand supremely blest. (Chorus)

Texas, O Texas! Your freeborn single star,
Sends out its radiance to nations near and far.
Emblem of freedom! It sets our hearts aglow.
With thoughts of San Jacinto and glorious Alamo. (Chorus)

Texas, dear Texas! From tyrant grip now free.
Shines forth in splendor your star of destiny!
Mother of Heroes! We come your children true.
Proclaiming our allegiance, our faith, our love for you. (Chorus)

Chorus: God bless you, Texas! And keep you brave and strong.
That you may grow in power and worth, throughout the ages long.

The unofficial state song

As a student at Washington and Lee University, William Lamdin Prather often heard General Robert E. Lee making the statement, "Young men, the eyes of the South are upon you." When Prather later served as president of the University of Texas between 1899 and 1906, he modified that message for his students by saying, "The eyes of Texas are upon you." The phrase caught the fancy of student John Lang Sinclair, and he set the words to the tune of "I've Been Working on the Railroad." On May 12, 1903, the University of Texas Glee Club performed the tune for Prather. The president was duly impressed, and "The Eyes of Texas" soon became the university's alma mater song. Although the stanzas have been lost in memory, the chorus is the unofficial state song.

State Holidays

Martin Luther King Jr.'s birthday –
 Third Monday in January
Texas Independence Day –
 March 2
San Jacinto Day – April 21
Emancipation Day – June 19
Lyndon B. Johnson's birthday –
 August 27

CAPITALS AND CAPITOLS

A Texas capital under Mexican rule

When 27-year-old Stephen Austin inherited a land grant from his father, Moses, he quite by accident began his journey to becoming the "father of Texas." Austin worked for more than a year in Mexico to secure the right to colonize Texas territory then belonging to the Mexican government. His determination was rewarded, and San Felipe de Austin at Atascosito Crossing on the Brazos River was established as the seat of government for the colonists. So began the Anglo-American settlement of Texas. During 1823 and 1824, land titles were given to families settling in the area. Those original Texas colonists became known as "The Old 300." Families engaged in farming received a *labor* of land, or about 177 acres. Those raising livestock were given a *league* of land, about 4,428 acres—Austin laid claim to about 22 leagues. He died on December 27, 1836, only eight months after Texas won its independence from Mexico.

Although San Felipe de Austin (see map on p. 14) is known as the first capital of Texas, Washington-on-the-Brazos is considered the birthplace of the Republic of Texas. Located just 150 miles east of San Antonio de Béxar in March 1836, the tiny town was ill prepared to serve the representatives who arrived to draft the Declaration of Independence. The town began in 1822 as a ferry crossing on the Brazos River. When the delegates arrived, the place barely offered the necessities of life, much less any luxuries. William Fairfax Gray looked on as events unfolded and described the town as having "only one well defined street" and "about a dozen wretched cabins or shanties." A single tavern offered meager lodging that consisted of a single room with two fireplaces. During their 17-day stay in the capital, the delegates endured the same menu for breakfast, lunch, and dinner—beans, cornbread, and fried pork.

Humble beginnings

Unstately Capitol

The crude meeting hall that served as the republic's first Capitol burned in the mid-1800s. Today a replica stands at Washington-on-the-Brazos State Historical Park. Known as Independence Hall, the unfinished frame structure offered only the protection of a roof, four walls, and a wooden floor. Window openings in the framework were covered by simple cotton sheets that blew with the wind. No doors hung on the entranceway, and no fireplace furnished heat during that cold March. The delegates sat on wooden chairs and worked at long, rough-hewn wooden tables as they wrote the freedom words for the new republic.

The run for the capitals

When delegates hastily departed Washington-on-the-Brazos on March 17, 1836, the Alamo had fallen and Mexican forces were only a few days march away. To escape capture by Santa Anna and other Mexican generals, the government relocated temporarily at Harrisburg, and then Galveston Island. After the republic's victory at San Jacinto, President Burnet moved the capital to Velasco. There, on May 14, 1836, Santa Anna signed two treaties that ended the Texas Revolution.

But the search for a permanent capital didn't end. In October 1836, the seat of government moved to Columbia, where Texas' only legitimate newspaper, the *Telegraph and Texas Register*, was published. Sam Houston took over as president that same month. In April 1837, the capital moved once again—this time to his namesake town of Houston on Buffalo Bayou. At the time, the town was little more than a muddy tract of land with two saloons, a few log cabins, and tents. A two-story, unfinished building housed the government.

In October 1839, with Mirabeau B. Lamar as president, the government chose as a capital a town more centrally located in the republic's territory. The community of Waterloo, settled by four families on the north bank of the Colorado River, was renamed Austin in honor of Stephen F. Austin and became the permanent capital of the republic. Furniture and archives of the government were moved from Houston by 50 covered wagons in the fall of 1839.

Austin **Washington-on-the-Brazos** **San Felipe** **Harrisburg** **Houston** **Columbia** **Galveston** **Velasco**

The Archive War

The capital issue appeared to be settled in 1839. But when Sam Houston assumed the presidency of the republic again in 1841, he attempted to move the government's headquarters from Austin back to Houston. He secretly ordered the republic's official records removed from Austin. The attempted late-night record theft was thwarted when Mrs. Angelina Eberly fired a cannon and alerted Austin citizens to the shenanigans. A party of Austin residents retrieved the records, and the seat of government was saved in Austin. The historical farce has become known as the "Archive War."

The biggest trade in Texas

🤎When Texas needed a new capitol building in 1882, the state was cash-poor and land-rich. So the legislature agreed to accept bids from anyone willing to construct the building in exchange for 3 million acres of Panhandle land. A syndicate of four Chicago businessmen got the bid, the 3 million acres, and an extra 50,000 acres for surveying the West Texas soil. The deal created the 3,050,000-acre XIT ranch—a 30-

mile-wide piece of land stretching 200 miles along the Texas-New Mexico border through 10 counties. The cattle herd averaged about 150,000 head. The ranch lasted until 1912 when the last cow was sold. Crops such as wheat and cotton made the property more valuable as farmland and the XIT ranch was sold off piece by piece for about $2.50 per acre.

🏴 The State Capitol that stands today on an Austin hilltop opened on May 16, 1888, amid a week of celebration. The building, designed by Michigan architect Elijah E. Myers, resembles the National Capitol, with a similar dome and separate wings for the state Senate and House.

A Capitol of granite

There is one notable exception to the similarities. The Texas Capitol is about 7 feet higher than the National Capitol. It is the tallest capitol in the United States today, rising 309 feet 8 inches from the basement floor to the top of the Goddess of Liberty statue.

The distinctive pink granite used for the exterior walls wasn't the first choice of state officials or the building contractors. Originally, the plan called for decorative limestone walls to be erected on a base of granite stones brought from Granite Mountain near Burnet. But in March 1884, when the first load of native limestone arrived, building superintendent R.L. Walker rejected the entire 60-ton shipment. Walker found traces of iron pyrites, or fool's gold, in the limestone. When exposed to the atmosphere, iron pyrites rusted, streaked, and marred the light limestone. Since Governor John Ireland insisted that native building materials be used in the Capitol's construction, native pink granite was substituted for the limestone. Residents of Austin were happy with the choice when they got their first look at the granite cornerstone during an unveiling on March 2, 1885. The massive granite statehouse was officially transferred to the citizens of Texas on December 8, 1888. At the time, it was the largest state Capitol Building in the nation.

🏴 In 1989, Texas began a six-year project to restore the Capitol to its original beauty. Costing $192 million, the statehouse was given an interior and exterior face-lift for the first time. The land office and the oldest state office building were also restored, and a new 165,000-square-foot underground building was built just north of the Capitol.

A Capitol face-lift

TEXAS COUNTY ALMANAC

Total counties – 254 (most of any state)
Highest population – Harris, 2,818,199
Lowest population – Loving, 107
Smallest land area – Rockwall, 128 square miles
Largest land area – Brewster, 6,169 square miles
County with most surface water – Calhoun, 519 square miles
Last county organized – Loving, 1931
Only county named for a Civil War battle –
    Val Verde (means "green valley")

TEXAS COUNTIES

County	Population	County Seat	Sq. Miles	Founded	Named after
1-Anderson	48,024	Palestine	1,078	3/24/1846	K.L. Anderson
2-Andrews	14,338	Andrews	1,501	8/21/1876	Richard Andrews, Rev. soldier
3-Angelina	69,884	Lufkin	807	4/22/1846	Angelina, Indian woman
4-Aransas	17,892	Rockport	280	9/18/1871	Spanish palace
5-Archer	7,973	Archer City	907	1/22/1858	Dr. B.T. Archer
6-Armstrong	2,021	Claude	910	8/21/1876	Name of pioneer family
7-Atascosa	30,533	Jourdanton	1,218	1/25/1856	Spanish for "boggy"
8-Austin	19,832	Bellville	656	3/17/1837	Stephen F. Austin
9-Bailey	7,064	Muleshoe	827	8/21/1876	Alamo hero Peter Bailey
10-Bandera	10,562	Bandera	793	1/26/1856	Bandera Mountains
11-Bastrop	38,263	Bastrop	895	3/17/1836	Baron de Bastrop
12-Baylor	4,385	Seymour	862	2/1/1858	H.W. Baylor, Texas Ranger
13-Bee	25,135	Beeville	880	12/8/1857	Gen. Barnard Bee
14-Bell	191,088	Belton	1,055	1/22/1850	Gov. P.H. Bell
15-Bexar	1,185,394	San Antonio	1,248	3/17/1836	Duke de Béxar
16-Blanco	5,972	Johnson City	714	2/12/1858	Blanco River
17-Borden	799	Gail	900	8/21/1876	Gail Borden
18-Bosque	15,125	Meridian	989	2/4/1854	Bosque River
19-Bowie	81,665	Boston	891	12/17/1840	Alamo hero James Bowie
20-Brazoria	191,707	Angleton	1,407	3/17/1836	From Brazos River
21-Brazos	121,862	Bryan	588	2/30/1841	From Brazos River
22-Brewster	8,681	Alpine	6,169	2/2/1887	Henry Brewster, R.O.T.* official
23-Briscoe	1,071	Silverton	887	8/21/1876	Andrew Briscoe, R.O.T. soldier
24-Brooks	8,204	Falfurrias	942	3/11/1911	J.A. Brooks, Texas Ranger
25-Brown	34,371	Brownwood	936	8/27/1856	Henry S. Brown, Indian fighter
26-Burleson	13,625	Caldwell	668	3/24/1846	Edward Burleson, Tex. Rev. hero
27-Burnet	22,677	Burnet	994	2/5/1852	David G. Burnet
28-Caldwell	26,392	Lockhart	546	3/6/1848	Mathew Caldwell, Indian fighter
29-Calhoun	19,053	Port Lavaca	540	4/4/1846	John C. Calhoun
30-Callahan	11,859	Baird	899	2/1/1858	J.H. Callahan, Texas Ranger
31-Cameron	260,120	Brownsville	905	2/12/1848	Capt. Ewen Cameron
32-Camp	9,904	Pittsburg	203	4/6/1874	J.L. Camp, legislator
33-Carson	6,576	Panhandle	924	8/21/1888	S.P. Carson, R.O.T. official
34-Cass	29,982	Linden	937	4/25/1846	Sen. Lewis Cass
35-Castro	9,070	Dimmitt	899	8/21/1876	Henri Castro, Tex. colonizer
36-Chambers	20,088	Anahuac	616	2/12/1858	T.J. Chambers, surveyor
37-Cherokee	41,049	Rusk	1,052	4/11/1846	Cherokee Indians
38-Childress	5,953	Childress	707	8/21/1857	George C. Childress
39-Clay	10,024	Henrietta	1,085	12/24/1857	Henry Clay, U.S. statesman
40-Cochran	4,377	Morton	775	8/21/1876	Robert Cochran, Alamo hero
41-Coke	3,424	Robert Lee	908	3/19/1889	Gov. Richard Coke
42-Coleman	9,710	Coleman	1,277	2/1/1858	R.M. Coleman, Sam Houston aide
43-Collin	264,036	McKinney	851	4/3/1846	Collin McKinney, settler
44-Collingsworth	3,573	Wellington	909	8/21/1876	James Collingsworth
45-Colorado	18,383	Columbus	964	3/17/1836	Colorado River
46-Comal	51,832	New Braunfels	555	3/24/1846	Comal River
47-Comanche	13,381	Comanche	930	1/25/1856	Plains Indians
48-Concho	3,044	Paint Rock	992	2/1/1858	Concho River
49-Cooke	30,777	Gainesville	893	3/20/1848	Capt. W.G. Cooke
50-Coryell	64,213	Gatesville	1,057	2/4/1854	James Coryell, pioneer
51-Cottle	2,247	Paducah	895	8/21/1876	George W. Cottle, Alamo hero
52-Crane	4,652	Crane	782	2/26/1887	W. Crane, Baylor Univ. president
53-Crockett	4,078	Ozona	2,806	1/22/1875	David Crockett, Alamo hero
54-Crosby	7,304	Crosbyton	898	8/21/1876	Stephen Crosby
55-Culberson	3,407	Van Horn	3,185	3/10/1911	D.B. Culberson, Tex. congressman
56-Dallam	5,461	Dalhart	1,505	8/21/1876	James W. Dallam, lawyer & editor
57-Dallas	1,852,810	Dallas	880	3/30/1846	George Mifflin Dallas
58-Dawson	14,349	Lamesa	903	8/21/1876	Nicholas M. Dawson
59-Deaf Smith	19,153	Hereford	1,497	8/21/1876	Erastus (Deaf) Smith, famous scout
60-Delta	4,857	Cooper	278	7/29/1870	Shape of county resembles Greek letter *delta*
61-Denton	273,515	Denton	911	4/11/1846	John B. Denton, pioneer minister
62-De Witt	18,840	Cuero	910	3/24/1846	Green De Witt, colonizer
63-Dickens	2,571	Dickens	907	8/21/1876	J. Dickens, Alamo hero
64-Dimmit	10,433	Carrizo Springs	1,307	2/1/1858	Philip Dimitt, Tex. Revolution
65-Donley	3,696	Clarendon	929	8/21/1876	S.P. Donley, Tex. Supreme Court Justice
66-Duval	12,918	San Diego	1,795	2/1/1858	B.H. Duval
67-Eastland	19,211	Eastland	932	2/1/1858	W.M. Eastland, member of Mier Expedition
68-Ector	118,934	Odessa	903	2/26/1887	M.D. Ector, legislator
69-Edwards	2,266	Rocksprings	2,120	2/1/1858	Hayden Edwards
70-Ellis	85,167	Waxahachie	939	12/20/1850	Richard Ellis, president of 1836 Convention
71-El Paso	591,610	El Paso	1,014	1/3/1849	Paso del Norte

*R.O.T. – Republic of Texas

County	Population	County Seat	Sq. Miles	Founded	Named after
72-Erath	27,991	Stephenville	1,080	1/25/1856	George B. Erath, Tex. Revolution
73-Falls	17,712	Marlin	770	1/28/1850	Brazos River Falls
74-Fannin	24,804	Bonham	895	12/14/1837	James W. Fannin
75-Fayette	20,095	La Grange	950	12/14/1838	Marquis de Lafayette, U.S. Revolution hero
76-Fisher	4,842	Roby	897	8/21/1876	S.R. Fisher, R.O.T. sec. of navy
77-Floyd	8,497	Floydada	992	8/21/1876	D.W. Floyd, Alamo hero
78-Foard	1,794	Crowell	703	3/3/1891	Maj. Robert L. Foard, Confederate Army
79-Fort Bend	225,421	Richmond	876	12/29/1837	River bend where colonists settled
80-Franklin	7,802	Mount Vernon	294	3/6/1875	Judge B.C. Franklin
81-Freestone	15,818	Fairfield	888	9/6/1850	Indigenous stone
82-Frio	13,472	Pearsall	1,133	2/1/1871	Frio River
83-Gaines	14,123	Seminole	1,504	8/21/1876	James Gaines
84-Galveston	217,396	Galveston	399	5/5/1838	Count Bernardo de Galvez, Spanish Gov. of Louisiana
85-Garza	5,143	Post	895	8/21/1876	Pioneer Texas family
86-Gillespie	17,204	Fredericksburg	1,061	2/23/1848	Capt. R. Gillespie, Texas Ranger
87-Glasscock	1,447	Garden City	900	4/4/1887	George W. Glasscock, pioneer
88-Goliad	5,980	Goliad	859	3/17/1836	Anagram of (H)idalgo
89-Gonzales	17,205	Gonzales	1,068	3/17/1836	Gov. Rafael Gonzales
90-Gray	23,967	Pampa	921	8/21/1876	Peter W. Gray, member of first State Legislature
91-Grayson	95,021	Sherman	934	3/17/1846	Peter W. Grayson, R.O.T. Attorney General
92-Gregg	104,948	Longview	273	4/12/1873	John Gregg, Confederate Gen.
93-Grimes	18,828	Anderson	799	4/6/1846	Jesse Grimes
94-Guadalupe	64,873	Seguin	713	3/30/1846	Guadalupe River
95-Hale	34,671	Plainview	1,005	8/21/1876	Lt. J.C. Hale, died at San Jacinto
96-Hall	3,905	Memphis	876	8/21/1876	W.D.C. Hall, R.O.T. sec. of war
97-Hamilton	7,733	Hamilton	836	2/2/1842	James Hamilton, South Carolina governor
98-Hansford	5,848	Spearman	921	8/21/1876	Judge J.M. Hansford
99-Hardeman	5,283	Quanah	688	2/1/1858	Brothers Bailey & T.J. Hardeman
100-Hardin	41,320	Kountze	898	1/22/1858	William Hardin
101-Harris	2,818,199	Houston		3/17/1836	John R. Harris, founder of Harrisburg
102-Harrison	57,483	Marshall	908	2/28/1839	Jonas Harrison, Tex. Rev. advocate
103-Hartley	3,634	Channing	1,462	8/21/1876	O.C. & R.K. Hartley, pioneers
104-Haskell	6,820	Haskell	901	2/1/1858	C.R. Haskell, died at Goliad
105-Hays	65,614	San Marcos	678	3/1/1843	Capt. Jack Hays, Texas Ranger
106-Hemphill	3,720	Canadian	903	8/21/1876	John Hemphill, R.O.T. justice
107-Henderson	58,543	Athens	888	4/27/1846	Gov. J. Pinckney Henderson
108-Hidalgo	383,545	Edinburg	1,569	1/24/1852	Miguel Hidalgo y Costillo, Mex. Independence leader
109-Hill	27,146	Hillsboro	968	2/7/1853	G.W. Hill, R.O.T. official
110-Hockley	24,199	Levelland	908	8/21/1876	Gen. G.W. Hockley, R.O.T. sec. of war
111-Hood	28,981	Granbury	425	11/3/1866	John B. Hood, Confederate Gen.
112-Hopkins	28,833	Sulphur Springs	789	3/25/1846	Hopkins family, pioneers
113-Houston	21,375	Crockett	901	6/12/1837	Sam Houston
114-Howard	32,343	Big Spring	901	8/21/1876	V.E. Howard, Tex. legislator
115-Hudspeth	2,915	Sierra Blanca	4,566	2/16/1917	Claude Hudspeth, political leader
116-Hunt	64,343	Greenville	840	4/11/1846	Memucan Hunt, R.O.T. sec. of navy
117-Hutchinson	25,689	Stinnett	871	8/21/1876	Anderson Hutchinson
118-Irion	1,629	Mertzon	1,052	3/7/1889	R.A. Irion, R.O.T. leader
119-Jack	6,981	Jacksboro	920	8/27/1856	Brothers P.C. & W.H. Jack
120-Jackson	13,039	Edna	844	3/17/1836	U.S. President Andrew Jackson
121-Jasper	31,102	Jasper	921	3/17/1836	Sgt. William Jasper, U.S. Revolution
122-Jeff Davis	1,946	Fort Davis	2,258	3/15/1887	Jefferson Davis, Confederate President
123-Jefferson	239,389	Port Arthur	937	3/17/1836	President Thomas Jefferson
124-Jim Hogg	5,109	Hebbronville	1,136	3/31/1913	Gov. James Stephen Hogg
125-Jim Wells	37,679	Alice	867	3/25/1911	J.B. Wells, developer
126-Johnson	97,165	Cleburne	731	2/13/1854	Col. M.T. Johnson, Mexican War
127-Jones	16,490	Anson	931	2/1/1858	Anson Jones, last president of R.O.T.
128-Karnes	12,455	Karnes City	753	2/4/1854	Henry W. Karnes, Tex. Revolutionary figure
129-Kaufman	52,220	Kaufman	788	2/26/1848	D.S. Kaufman, Tex. & U.S. congressman
130-Kendall	14,589	Boerne	663	1/10/1862	George W. Kendall, journalist
131-Kenedy	460	Sarita	1,389	4/2/1921	Capt. Mifflin Kenedy, steamboat operator

County	Population	County Seat	Sq. Miles	Founded	Named after
165-Midland	106,611	Midland	902	3/4/1885	Midpoint of railroad between El Paso & Fort Worth
166-Milam	22,946	Cameron	1,022	3/17/1836	Ben Milam
167-Mills	4,531	Goldthwaite	750	3/15/1887	John T. Mills, pioneer jurist
168-Mitchell	8,016	Colorado City	916	8/21/1876	Asa and Eli Mitchell, pioneer brothers
169-Montague	17,274	Montague	38	12/24/1857	Daniel Montague, pioneer
170-Montgomery	182,201	Conroe	1,077	12/14/1837	Gen. Richard Montgomery
171-Moore	17,865	Dumas	910	8/21/1867	E.W. Moore, R.O.T.
172-Morris	13,200	Daingerfield	259	3/6/1875	W.W. Morris, jurist & legislator
173-Motley	1,532	Matador	990	8/21/1876	Dr. J.W. Motley, signer of Tex. Dec. of Independence
174-Nacogdoches	54,753	Nacogdoches	981	3/17/1836	Nacogdoches Indians
175-Navarro	39,926	Corsicana	1,086	4/25/1846	Jose Navarro, R.O.T. leader
176-Newton	13,569	Newton	939	4/22/1846	John Newton, U.S. Revolutionary soldier
177-Nolan	16,594	Sweetwater	914	8/21/1876	Philip Nolan, adventurer
178-Nueces	291,145	Corpus Christi	1,166	4/18/1846	Spanish for "nuts"
179-Ochiltree	9,128	Perryton	918	8/21/1876	W.B. Ochiltree, R.O.T. leader
180-Oldham	2,278	Vega	1,501	8/21/1876	W.S. Oldham, Confederate senator
181-Orange	80,509	Orange	379	2/5/1852	Early orange grove
182-Palo Pinto	25,055	Palo Pinto	985	8/27/1856	Named for Palo Pinto Creek
183-Panola	22,035	Carthage	821	3/30/1846	Indian word for "cotton"
184-Parker	64,785	Weatherford	910	12/12/1855	Isaac Parker, pioneer legislator
185-Parmer	9,863	Farwell	882	8/21/1876	Martin Parmer, R.O.T. leader
186-Pecos	14,675	Fort Stockton	4,765	5/3/1871	Pecos River
187-Polk	30,687	Livingston	1,110	3/30/1846	U.S. President James K. Polk
188-Potter	97,841	Amarillo	922	8/21/1876	Robert Potter, R.O.T. leader
189-Presidio	6,637	Marfa	3,856	1/3/1850	Spanish Presidio del Norte
190-Rains	6,715	Emory	259	6/9/1870	Emory Rains, R.O.T. leader
191-Randall	89,673	Canyon	922	8/21/1876	Horace Randall, Confederate Gen
192-Reagan	4,514	Big Lake	1,176	3/7/1903	Sen. John H. Reagan
193-Real	2,412	Leakey	700	4/3/1913	Julius Real, legislator & rancher
194-Red River	14,317	Clarksville	1,058	3/17/1837	Red River
195-Reeves	15,852	Pecos	2,642	8/14/1883	George Reeves, Confederate Col.
196-Refugio	7,976	Refugio	819	3/17/1836	Mission of Our Lady of Refuge
197-Roberts	1,025	Miami	924	8/21/1876	John S. Roberts & Gov. O.M. Roberts, Tex. leaders

County	Population	County Seat	Sq. Miles	Founded	Named after
132-Kent	1,010	Jayton	878	8/21/1876	Andrew Kent, died at Alamo
133-Kerr	36,304	Kerrville	1,107	1/26/1856	James Kerr, member of Austin's Colony
134-Kimble	4,122	Junction	1,250	1/22/1858	George C. Kimble, died at Alamo
135-King	354	Guthrie	914	8/21/1876	William P. King, died at Alamo
136-Kinney	3,119	Brackettville	1,359	1/28/1850	H.L. Kinney, founder of Corpus Christi
137-Kleberg	30,274	Kingsville	853	2/27/1913	Robert Kleberg
138-Knox	4,837	Benjamin	845	2/1/1858	Gen. Henry Knox
139-Lamar	43,949	Paris	919	12/17/1840	Mirabeau B. Lamar, second pres. of R.O.T.
140-Lamb	15,072	Littlefield	1,013	8/21/1876	Lt. G.A. Lamb, died at San Jacinto
141-Lampasas	13,521	Lampasas	714	2/1/1856	Spanish for "lilies"
142-La Salle	5,254	Cotulla	1,517	2/1/1858	La Salle, French explorer
143-Lavaca	18,690	Hallettsville	971	4/6/1846	Lavaca River
144-Lee	12,854	Giddings	631	4/14/1874	Gen. Robert E. Lee
143-Leon	12,665	Centerville	1,078	3/17/1846	Martin de Leon, founder of Victoria
146-Liberty	52,726	Liberty	1,174	3/17/1836	Libertad, Spanish municipality
147-Limestone	20,946	Groesbeck	931	4/11/1846	Indigenous rock
148-Lipscomb	3,143	Lipscomb	933	8/21/1876	A.S. Lipscomb, R.O.T. leader
149-Live Oak	9,556	George West	1,057	2/2/1856	Native tree
150-Llano	11,631	Llano	939	2/1/1856	Spanish for "plains"
151-Loving	107	Mentone	671	2/26/1887	Oliver Loving, trail driver
152-Lubbock	222,636	Lubbock	900	8/21/1876	Col. Tom S. Lubbock, Confederate officer
153-Lynn	6,758	Tahoka	888	8/21/1876	W. Lynn, died at Alamo
154-McCulloch	8,778	Brady	1,071	8/27/1856	Gen. Ben McCulloch, pioneer
155-McLennan	189,823	Waco	1,031	1/22/1850	Neil McLennan, Sr., settler
156-McMullen	817	Tilden	1,163	2/1/1858	John McMullen, Irish impresario
157-Madison	10,931	Madisonville	473	2/2/1853	U.S. President James Madison
158-Marion	9,984	Jefferson	385	2/8/1860	Francis Marion, U.S. Gen.
159-Martin	4,956	Stanton	902	8/21/1876	Wylie Martin, R.O.T. senator
160-Mason	3,423	Mason	934	1/22/1858	Lt. G.T. Mason, died in Mexican War
161-Matagorda	36,928	Bay City	1,127	3/17/1836	Named for canebreak
162-Maverick	36,378	Eagle Pass	1,287	2/2/1856	Sam A. Maverick, pioneer
163-Medina	27,312	Hondo	1,334	2/12/1848	Medina River
164-Menard	2,252	Menard	902	1/22/1858	Michel B. Menard, Galveston's founder

County	Population	County Seat	Sq. Miles	Founded	Named after
198-Robertson	15,511	Franklin	866	12/14/1837	Sterling Clark Robertson, pioneer
199-Rockwall	25,604	Rockwall	149	3/1/1873	Wall-like rock formation
200-Runnels	11,294	Ballinger	1,057	2/1/1858	H.G. Runnels, legislator
201-Rusk	43,735	Henderson	939	2/16/1843	Thomas J. Rusk, state leader
202-Sabine	9,586	Hemphill	577	3/17/1836	Spanish for "cypress"
203-San Augustine	7,999	San Augustine	592	3/17/1836	Mexican municipality
204-San Jacinto	16,372	Coldspring	628	8/3/1869	Battle of San Jacinto
205-San Patricio	58,749	Sinton	707	3/17/1836	Spanish for St. Patrick
206-San Saba	5,401	San Saba	1,138	2/1/1856	San Saba River
207-Schleicher	2,990	Eldorado	1,311	4/1/1887	Gustav Schleicher
208-Scurry	18,634	Snyder	908	8/21/1876	W.R. Scurry, Confederate Gen.
209-Shackelford	3,316	Albany	916	2/1/1858	Dr. Jack Shackelford, Tex. Revolutionary hero
210-Shelby	22,034	Center	835	3/17/1836	Isaac Shelby, American Revolutionary figure
211-Sherman	2,858	Stratford	923	8/21/1876	Sidney Sherman, Tex. Gen.
212-Smith	151,309	Tyler	949	4/11/1846	James Smith, Tex. Rev. Gen.
213-Somervell	5,360	Glen Rose	192	3/13/1875	Alexander Somervell, R.O.T. Gen.
214-Starr	40,518	Rio Grande City	1,299	2/10/1848	Dr. J.H. Starr, R.O.T. official
215-Stephens	9,010	Breckenridge	921	1/22/1858	Confederate Vice President Alexander H. Stephens
216-Sterling	1,438	Sterling City	923	3/4/1891	W.S. Sterling, buffalo hunter
217-Stonewall	2,013	Aspermont	920	8/21/1876	Confederate Gen. T.J. (Stonewall) Jackson
218-Sutton	4,135	Sonora	1,454	4/1/1887	Col. John S. Sutton, Confederate officer
219-Swisher	8,133	Tulia	901	8/21/1876	J.G. Swisher, Tex. Rev. figure
220-Tarrant	1,170,103	Fort Worth	898	12/20/1849	Gen. Edward T. Tarrant
221-Taylor	119,655	Abilene	919	2/1/1858	Brothers Edward, James, George Taylor, Alamo heroes
222-Terrell	1,410	Sanderson	2,358	4/8/1905	A.W. Terrell, Confederate Gen.
223-Terry	13,218	Brownfield	891	8/21/1876	Col. B.F. Terry, head of Texas Ranger troop
224-Throckmorton	1,880	Throckmorton	916	1/13/1858	Dr. W.E. Throckmorton
225-Titus	24,009	Mount Pleasant	426	5/11/1846	A.J. Titus, pioneer settler
226-Tom Green	98,458	San Angelo	1,541	3/13/1874	Tex. Rev. Gen. Tom Green
227-Travis	576,407	Austin	1,022	2/25/1840	Col. William B. Travis
228-Trinity	11,445	Groveton	714	2/11/1850	Trinity River
229-Tyler	16,646	Woodville	936	4/3/1846	U.S. President John Tyler

County	Population	County Seat	Sq. Miles	Founded	Named after
230-Upshur	31,370	Gilmer	593	4/27/1846	A.P. Upshur, U.S. Sec. of State
231-Upton	4,447	Rankin	1,242	2/26/1887	Brothers John & William Upton, Confederate colonels
232-Uvalde	23,340	Uvalde	1,559	2/8/1850	Juan de Uvalde, Indian fighter
233-Val Verde	38,721	Del Rio	3,233	2/20/1885	Civil War battle, Spanish for "green valley"
234-Van Zandt	37,944	Canton	860	3/30/1848	Isaac Van Zandt, R.O.T. leader
235-Victoria	74,361	Victoria	889	3/17/1836	Mexican President Guadalupe Victoria
236-Walker	50,917	Huntsville	801	4/6/1846	R.J. Walker, first U.S. Sec. of Treasury
237-Waller	23,389	Hempstead	518	4/25/1873	Edwin Waller, R.O.T. leader
238-Ward	13,115	Monahans	836	2/26/1887	Thomas W. Ward, R.O.T. leader
239-Washington	26,154	Brenham	621	3/17/1836	George Washington
240-Webb	133,239	Laredo	3,376	2/28/1848	James Webb, R.O.T. leader
241-Wharton	39,955	Wharton	1,095	4/3/1846	Tex. Rev. brothers John A. & William H. Wharton
242-Wheeler	5,879	Wheeler	915	8/21/1876	R.T. Wheeler, pioneer jurist
243-Wichita	122,378	Wichita Falls	633	2/1/1858	Indian tribe
244-Wilbarger	15,121	Vernon	978	2/1/1858	Josiah and Mathias Wilbarger, pioneers
245-Willacy	17,705	Raymondville	784	3/11/1911	John G. Willacy, Texas legislator
246-Williamson	139,551	Georgetown	1,136	3/13/1848	Robert M. Williamson, pioneer leader
247-Wilson	22,650	Floresville	809	2/13/1860	James C. Wilson of Mier Expedition
248-Winkler	8,626	Kermit	841	2/26/1887	C.M. Winkler, Confederate Col.
249-Wise	34,679	Decatur	923	1/23/1856	U.S. Sen. Henry A. Wise
250-Wood	29,380	Quitman	696	2/5/1850	Gov. George T. Wood
251-Yoakum	8,786	Plains	800	8/21/1876	Henderson Yoakum, pioneer historian
252-Young	18,126	Graham	931	2/2/1856	Col. W.C. Young, early Texan
253-Zapata	9,279	Zapata	1,058	1/22/1858	Col. Antonio Zapata, pioneer Mexican rancher
254-Zavala	12,162	Crystal City	1,302	2/1/1858	Lorenzo de Zavala, Tex. Revolutionary leader

TEXAS NATURALLY

Texas offers a more intriguing variety of vegetation, landforms, and climates than any other state. The verdant southeastern forests encroach into the East Texas Piney Woods. Dry southwestern deserts creep into West Texas. From the north, the Great Plains spill into the state. The Rocky Mountain system extends into the state's western arm, and the coastal plains spread along the Gulf of Mexico.

Ten distinctive vegetational regions and 20 major land-resource areas, or soil subdivisions, divide the state. Each celebrates its own unique gathering of plant and animal life, making Texas a meeting place of contrasts.

Although much of Texas has been tamed and settled, much remains wild. Previously unknown plants and animals still reveal themselves, to the surprise and delight of nature lovers. Some of the state's most impressive natural wonders have been preserved for future generations, and that challenging endeavor continues today.

Step inside and discover Texas naturally.

- Exploring Ancient Texas
- Wild Places for the Nation
- The State of Parks
- Water Notes
- Weather Watch
- Unique Wildlife
- Texas Greenery
- Endangered Species
- Tending to Texas
- Superfund Sites

EXPLORING ANCIENT TEXAS

Famous flint

Native Americans made arrowheads and other weapons from Alibates flint.

Twelve thousand years ago, people took flint from the Alibates Flint Quarries. Perched on the bluffs above today's man-made Lake Meredith in the Staked Plains, the quarries supplied the highest-quality flint in North America for making arrowheads, spear points, and tools. Evidence shows that the fame of Alibates flint spread. Weapons and tools made of the multicolored flint have been discovered as far as 1,000 miles from the quarries. About 500 years ago, people built pueblos along the Canadian River to be close to the valuable source of flint. Theirs is the only documented pueblo culture in Texas. Today, the Alibates Flint Quarries National Monument—named for rancher Allie Bates who settled near the flint quarries in about 1880—is part of the Lake Meredith National Recreation Area.

What are staked plains?

A flat, extremely dry area in the High Plains of West Texas is called *Llano Estacado*, meaning "Staked Plains." According to an old story, when Spanish explorer Francisco Vásquez de Coronado moved through this region, he put down wooden stakes—hence, Staked Plains—so that he could find his way back on his return. Most Native Americans didn't like to go into this area because blinding sandstorms decreased visibility to zero. Today, these storms strip the paint off cars!

The big, old rock

Rising 450 feet above the surrounding ranchland in Central Texas, Enchanted Rock's dome is the second-largest mountain in the nation comprised of a single rock. The distinctive pink granite dates back more than 1 billion years, making it some of the state's oldest rock. Its exposed surface area covers nearly 130 square miles and provides more than 300 different routes for thrill-seeking rock climbers.

Where dinosaurs roamed

It seems that dinosaurs liked Texas. The bed of the Paluxy River near Glen Rose bears tracks made by the enormous creatures more than 100 million years ago. When the Blackland Prairie region was nothing more than ocean bottom, giant sea lizards known as mososaurs swam in the waters there. People still find bits of their bones in creek beds even though the lizards lived 70 million years ago. The desert area of Big Bend was once occupied by tidal flats and lagoons, a perfect habitat for the *Deinocheirus mirificus*, meaning "terrible crocodile." A skull from one of the 75-million-year-old crocodiles is now displayed at the American Museum of Natural History in New York City. The head measures 6-1/2 feet, with 6-inch-long teeth. The Big Bend beast is one of the largest crocodilians ever found—52-1/2 feet long. Big Bend country also hosted the largest pterosaur, *Quetzalcoatlus northropi*, meaning "feathered serpent," ever discovered. The 65-million-year-old reptilian flying creature had a wingspan of 36 to 40 feet and a long toothless beak.

☛ At Seminole State Historical Park, paintings etched into canyon walls tell the stories of prehistoric Native Americans. Open, brushy terrain surrounds the canyon, and Indians took refuge in rock shelters that had eroded into the sheer canyon walls. Inside the shelters, colorful rock art paintings, called pictographs, have survived for thousands of years on limestone walls. Fate Bell Shelter, a hollow set into the canyon wall, runs 450 feet long. Inside, angular pictographs depict animals, human figures, and weapons. These are some of North America's oldest pictographs, painted an estimated 4,000 to 8,000 years ago.

Ancient artists

A fossilized reef

About 250 million years ago, a 400-mile-long, horseshoe-shaped limestone reef called Capitan Reef (right) formed beneath a tropical sea that covered far West Texas. After millions of years, the sea evaporated and the Guadalupe Mountains were lifted up, exposing part of the fossilized reef. This range is the best-preserved fossil reef in the world today. Part of the Guadalupe Mountains National Park (below), the highest peaks of the range now rise more than 8,000 feet above sea level and are embedded with fossilized plants and animals. If you visit this park, be prepared for high winds, especially in spring when hurricane-force winds have actually blown trucks off the roads! Texas' Apache, Guadalupe and Glass mountain ranges also contain exposed reef.

Guadalupe
Mountains
(exposed reef)

Carlsbad

NEW MEXICO

Dell City ●

● El Paso

Carlsbad
Caverns
National Park

Guadalupe Mountains
National Park

TEXAS

MEXICO

buried reef

Apache
Mountains
(exposed reef)

Glass Mountains
(exposed reef)

Alpine ●

WILD PLACES FOR THE NATION

The Thicket ... always and forever

🦃 When President Gerald R. Ford signed legislation on October 11, 1974, to create the Big Thicket National Preserve, he established the first national preserve in America. Since then, the 12 separate areas that constitute the preserve have been designated an "International Biosphere Reserve" by the United Nations Educational, Scientific and Cultural Organization (UNESCO).

The preserve itself occupies 84,550 acres of the Big Thicket region in southeast Texas. Before settlers and lumberjacks and boomtowns moved in, the Thicket boasted 3.5 million acres of Lone Star wilderness. Today less than one-tenth of the original, primitive Big Thicket still stands. The immensely diverse region displays 1,000 species of wildflowers, and almost 200 species of shrubs and trees. Two stretches of wild river run through it, and eight major ecological systems flow together. But there is also the unkind mark of human foolishness—Kaiser's Burnout.

Writing in the February 1988 issue of *Texas Highways*, Howard Peacock tells the story of Kaiser's Burnout. "During the Civil War, some Thicket youths rushed to the Confederate banner while others, taking to the woods where none could follow, refused to associate with any government. A jackass Confederate captain named Kaiser set fire to the woods, hoping to corner and capture a group of Thicketeers who had ignored his recruiting threats. He succeeded only in burning several thousand acres of idyllic forest. Near Honey Island, a scar is still known as Kaiser's Burnout."

The Texas treasure

🦃 The first national park created in Texas was carved out of the southern section of Brewster County. No place could have captured the eclectic spirit of the state more vividly. Canyons, mountain ranges, deserts, and the great Rio Grande share more than 800,000 untamed acres in Big Bend National Park. The Chihuahuan Desert creates the setting for the park. This desert is the wettest and highest in North America. It rises to elevations of 6,500 feet in Mexico and 5,000 feet in the United States and receives between 8 and 12 inches of rain per year. The Chisos Mountains serve as the centerpiece. And the "big bend" of the Rio Grande sets the mood as it swings southward through Santa Elena, Mariscal, and Boquillas canyons.

No other national park has the number or variety of cacti seen at Big Bend. About 70 different kinds have been recorded. And no other national park hosts more bird species—at last count, they totaled more than 400. Each spring, as if to remind Texans that preserving Big Bend was the right thing to do, the Colima warblers return. The little grayish birds with the white breasts and yellow rumps breed only in the Chisos Mountains of Big Bend—and nowhere else in the country.

About 416,000 acres are protected in 18 existing or planned national wildlife refuges throughout the state. Known as the "gem of the National Wildlife Refuge System," tiny Santa Ana National Wildlife Refuge (NWR) sits on the north bank of the Rio Grande in Hidalgo County. Established in 1943, it covers over 2,000 acres of dense, subtropical forest and native brushland in the lower Rio Grande Valley. Most of the border area between Texas and Mexico used to look like this area, but urban sprawl and agriculture changed that. Santa Ana is the northern limit of native habitat for many exotic Mexican birds. Thirty-one of Santa Ana's bird species can be found nowhere else in the country outside of the Rio Grande Valley. The refuge also serves as a haven for ocelots (only known place in the country where an ocelot has denned) and jaguarundi, endangered members of the cat family. Plant species also make the area special. Several national champion trees, including a Texas lignum vitae and a saffron plum, can be found in Santa Ana. The refuge also had the biggest Texas ebony tree in the state, measuring 131 inches in diameter, until it died in the 1980s.

For the birds ... and other creatures

Two major migration flyways converge in south Texas—the Central and Mississippi Valley flyways—carrying thousands and thousands of birds south in the winter and north in the spring. Most of Texas' national wildlife refuges play a vital role in maintaining healthy bird populations.

Laguna Atascosa NWR

Largest number of bird species of any U.S. refuge at 396 in 1994. Aransas NWR and Santa Ana NWR are very close with 389 and 380, respectively.

Anahuac NWR

Last area of the country where the rare red wolf is found in the wild. All were captured for a captive breeding program.

Aransas NWR

The refuge is the wintering ground for the endangered whooping crane. It played an important part in saving the bird from extinction.

Attwater Prairie Chicken NWR

The endangered Attwater prairie chicken is protected here. Hunting prairie chickens has been illegal since 1937. There are probably less than 500 in Texas today.

Brazoria/San Bernard NWR

Two refuges administered by the same office in Angleton. Some Texans claim this region has "the best birding in the state."

Hagerman NWR

Most waterfowl species traversing the Central Flyway stop here. Especially known for sparrows—and oil wells that pump over 5,000 barrels of oil per day!

Linking habitat islands

🦃 In 1980, the Lower Rio Grande Valley National Wildlife Refuge was established, linking Santa Ana NWR with valuable Rio Grande habitat. Today, about 64,000 acres along the Rio Grande have been purchased as a protected wildlife corridor, a place where animals can travel between "islands of habitat." Santa Ana is one of those islands of habitat through which the corridor, composed of private, state, and national lands, passes. Refuge managers would like to protect about 100,000 acres of corridor, but that might be difficult. Thirteen new bridges have been proposed for the Rio Grande to accommodate increased trade as a result of NAFTA and that might complicate the creation of an unbroken corridor.

Aquatic blooms

The Flower Garden Banks are the northernmost coral reefs on the North American continental shelf. They rest in the Gulf of Mexico about 110 miles southeast of Galveston. These banks probably began forming during the last Ice Age—10,000 to 15,000 years ago. However, their official proclamation as a marine sanctuary didn't come about until March 9, 1992, under the signature of then-President George Bush. The Flower Garden Banks were the 10th marine sanctuary designated by the National Oceanic and Atmospheric Administration (NOAA). The "flowers" are actually wildly colored corals, along with strikingly bright marine animals and stunning plants that all live more than 50 feet below the surface of the Gulf. The "banks" are really twin gardens set atop salt domes about 12 miles apart. The West Flower Garden runs about 6.8 miles long and 5 miles wide. The coral reef fills a bit more than 100 acres. The pear-shaped East Flower Garden measures 3.1 miles in diameter with approximately 250 acres of reef.

The Padre paradox

🦃 Consider Padre Island National Seashore (below) a paradox. It is the longest strip of undeveloped barrier island remaining in the nation.

But because two currents converge here, more trash washes ashore at Padre than on any other beach in the country. The government opened the national seashore in 1968 after buying the land from ranching families. Yet in keeping with the Texas ranching tradition, cattle grazed on the grass flats and drank from the freshwater ponds in the middle of the island until 1972. Oil and gas exploration continues today amid the serene setting.

The island is named in honor of Padre Nicolas

Balli, who was granted the island in 1800 by the Spanish Crown. Previously, it had been known by a more poetic name. Early Spanish navigators called it *La Isla Blanca*, or "White Island." From their ships they saw only the immense white sand dunes and white shell beaches, much as they appear today.

The white sand dunes and coastal grasses stretch for 67.5 miles without ever getting more than three miles wide. Eight distinct habitats co-exist within the park, providing shelter for 350 bird species and sustenance for 400 plant species. The national seashore contains 130,355 acres in Kenedy, Kleberg, and Willacy counties and draws about 1 million visitors annually. While the northern part of the island is preserved as national seashore, the southern part is known for its schlock. Filled with multi-story condos, seafood restaurants, and other tourist amusements, it's famous as the site of spring-break festivities for college students from across the Southwest.

🦃 During the 1930s, the beating winds of the Dust Bowl days swept away topsoil across millions of acres of U.S. land. The federal government decided to help restore part of that lost land, and in the mid-1930s, the national grasslands program began. Today, scattered pockets of grasslands from Texas to Montana grow where there was once only wasteland. Texas devotes almost 120,000 acres to national grasslands in five different areas.

Green grow the grasses

Black Kettle National Grassland – 576 acres in Hemphill County
Caddo National Grassland –17,785 acres in Fannin County
LBJ National Grassland (formerly Cross Timbers National
    Grassland) –20,313 total acres, with 61 acres in Montague
    County and 20,252 in Wise County
McClellan Creek National Grassland – 1,449 acres in Gray County
Rita Blanca National Grassland – 78,027 acres in Dallam County

THE STATE OF PARKS

🦃 When Isabella Eleanor Shepherd Neff settled in Central Texas in the mid-1850s, she offered such hospitality to neighbors that they came to call her "Mother." She even offered a shady spot on the Leon River as a community gathering place. When Mother Neff died, her hospitality continued in spirit. She gave the state a six-acre tract along the Leon River that later became the foundation for the first state park in Texas. One of Mother Neff's son's, Pat Morris Neff, was elected Texas' governor in 1921. He championed the cause of a state park system and persuaded others to share his vision. Then he arranged to make his mother's six acres part of the first state park in Texas. In 1938, Mother Neff State Park was dedicated in Coryell County. Today, the state has more than 130 state parks for all Texans to enjoy.

The mother of all parks

🦃 When Big Bend Ranch State Natural Area opened on January 19, 1991, it literally doubled the size of the existing state park system. The natural area covers more than 250,000 acres and contains colorful geologic formations, such as the vent crater of an ancient volcano.

Double the pleasure

Record-setting swimming hole

Balmorhea State Park in the foothills of the Davis Mountains boasts the world's largest spring-fed swimming pool. The Civilian Conservation Corps built the 1.75-acre pool in the 1930s and rimmed it with concrete. The concrete ends four feet below the surface of the water, and the natural underwater world begins.

The circular pool offers 80-foot visibility for swimmers, scuba divers, and snorkelers. The water maintains a constant temperature of 74°F to 76°F and reaches a depth of 30 feet. At the bottom, San Solomon Springs bubble forth, releasing 26 million gallons of crystalline water every day.

Happy trails

The longest trail in any state park winds through Lake Somerville State Park near Brenham. The main trail connects the Nails Creek and Birch Creek Units of the park. Other trails loop off the main course. In all, the trail system wanders for about 22 miles. Hikers, backpackers, mountain bikers, and any other strong-legged nature lover can tackle the trail. Equestrians are welcome, too. Two wells along the route provide hand-pumped water for horses. Humans need to bring their own.

The old mill stream

One of Texas' newer state parks runs for a mere 5-1/2 acres along the San Marcos River. The John J. Stokes, Sr., San Marcos River Park was donated to the Texas Parks and Wildlife Department in 1994 by Stokes and his wife. Locals know the park site as Thompson's Island, named for William Alexander Thompson. In 1850, Thompson constructed a millhouse and wheelhouse along the river to provide corn meal and flour for settlers. Thompson's son built a new dam in 1867 using stones that were transported by oxcart from the Blanco River. The stones are still in place, and the waterfall created by the old mill figures prominently in the park.

WATER NOTES

Sharing the wealth

Amistad Reservoir—called Lake Amistad by Texans—straddles the United States and Mexican border. With more than 67,000 acres of surface water and 860 miles of shoreline, Amistad (Spanish for "friendship") ranks as one of the world's largest international reservoirs. It serves its neighbor nations well, providing hydroelectric power, irrigation, flood control, and recreation for citizens in both countries. Presidents Richard Nixon and Gustavo Díaz Ordaz dedicated the 6-mile-long Amistad Dam on September 8, 1969. The Amistad National Recreation Area encompasses Lake Amistad, which local folks have appropriately nicknamed the "Big Friendly."

Water Resources

- Texas has 80,000 miles of rivers in 23 river basins
- The state has about 4 million acres of salt water in bays, estuaries, lagoons—and the Gulf of Mexico out to 9 nautical miles

🦃 Caddo Lake in Harrison County is the only natural lake of any significant size in the state, covering 26,800 acres. Native Americans believed the lake was formed by "powerful shaking earth spirits" angered by a Caddo chief. The lake may have actually been formed by "shaking" from the great New Madrid, Missouri, earthquake of 1811. This scenic lake is surrounded by dense, tangled forests with Spanish moss hanging from tree branches. The trees often extend into the lake waters causing a maze of water channels. Forty-two miles of boat roads have been marked to aid boaters. In the early 1900s, divers explored the lake in search of freshwater mussels that produced pearls. Today, people come for the gorgeous "southern" scenery and good fishing.

"Pearl" of a lake

🦃 The Pueblo Indians knew the Rio Grande as the *P'osoge*, meaning "river of great water." Antonio de Espejo of Mexico called it the *Río del Norte* (River of the North) in 1582. Explorer Juan de Oñate landed on the river's banks in 1598 near present-day El Paso and gave the river the name *Rio Grande*. A combination of those Mexican names resulted, with the river being called Río Grande del Norte. Folks still have trouble with the name. *Rio Grande* means "big river," yet some people insist on saying "Rio Grande river." That's equivalent to saying "big river river." By any name, the Rio Grande is still the longest river in Texas (889 miles) and the second-longest river entirely within or bordering the United States. A 191-mile protected strip along the U.S. shore of the river has been nationally designated as "Wild and Scenic." In contrast, the the tiny Comal River—at 2.5 miles long—in central Texas hill country is the state's smallest river.

Name that river

🦃 Since the 1850s, life in Wimberley has revolved around Cypress Creek, the stream that winds through the downtown area. The main source of water for Cypress Creek comes from Jacob's Well, a spring five miles upstream from where the creek meets the Blanco River. Although located on private property, Jacob's Well has enticed divers for years with its submerged caverns. The caverns reach at least 120 feet deep, and at last count had claimed the lives of 10 divers.

Dive carefully

🦃 Dolan Falls is championed as the largest waterfall in Texas that spans the entire width of a river. But not many people get the opportunity to admire the scenic wonder. The waterfall is part of Dolan Falls Preserve—18,500 acres that were purchased by The Nature Conservancy of Texas in 1991. Not much is yet known about the ecosystem in the preserve, so until studies can be completed, the area will be open only for educational and research field trips.

Preservation neighbors

The devil's canyons 🦃 Adjacent to Dolan Falls lies Devils River State Natural Area, the largest natural area in the state park system. Its 20,303 acres are managed by the Texas Parks and Wildlife Department, and access is limited to only a few visitors at a time. Deep canyons in the area cut across flat tableland and channel water that eventually flows into Devils River.

Gone fishin' 🦃 Since Texans appreciate big things, the Port Lavaca State Fishing Pier should evoke pride and joy. The 3,200-foot pier was created from the former causeway across Lavaca Bay and acquired from the state highway department in 1963. The only other designated state fishing pier is Copano Bay in Aransas County. It was acquired from the state highway department in 1967.

WEATHER WATCH

The worst weather ever 🦃 On September 8, 1900, a hurricane like none before slammed into Galveston Island. It killed 6,000 to 8,000 people and became known as the Great Galveston Storm, the worst natural disaster in U.S. history. The massive hurricane spun winds up to 120 miles per hour and sent 15-foot storm tides surging into the city. Not a single structure escaped damage. Mountains of debris, some as high as 50 feet, accumulated inland, with property damage at $30 million to $40 million. Although some residents heeded warnings and left the island, many stayed—and died. One young boy jumped into a trunk and floated 20 miles until landing on safe ground the next day. A soldier clinging to debris drifted to the mainland 40 miles away. Clara Barton, founder of the Red Cross, came to the city's rescue. She was 78 years old and in frail health, but she directed the relief efforts for two months and established a local Red Cross chapter. The exact number of survivors was never determined, nor was the exact number of dead.

Just the stats

Highest temperature – 120°F in Seymour on August 12, 1936

Lowest temperature – –23°F in Tulia on February 12, 1899, and in Seminole on February 8, 1933

Most annual rainfall – Clarksville in 1873 with 109.38 inches

Most rainfall in a month – Alvin in July 1979 with 35.7 inches

Most rainfall in 24 hours – Thrall on September 9 and 10, 1921, with 38.2 inches

Least annual rainfall – Wink in 1956 with 1.76 inches

Greatest seasonal snowfall – Romero in 1923-1924 with 65.0 inches

Greatest snowfall in 24 hours – Plainview on February 3-4, 1956, with 24 inches

🖝 One of the most destructive hailstorms ever to hit Texas brewed up on a sizzling, late-summer afternoon in the High Plains region. On August 24, 1979, a single, towering thunderhead began to drop small hailstones near Hereford. As the storm continued, it bombarded hundreds of thousands of cropland acres with hailstones as big as softballs. Hail pummeled parts of Hockley County for 40 minutes and made Highway 385 impassable near Dimmit. When the barrage ended, the 40-mile-wide path of destruction extended for 200 miles from Deaf Smith County south to Glasscock County. Damage to crops, such as cotton and corn, amounted to an astronomical $200 million.

The sky is falling

Beulah's babies

Texas holds the dubious honor of being the state with the most tornadoes recorded in a single year. In 1967, 232 twisters hit the Lone Star State. About 115 of those unpredictable storms ripped through the southern half of Texas between September 19 and 23, spawned by Hurricane Beulah. The storm blew ashore on September 20 near Brownsville and still holds the state record as the hurricane that generated the greatest number of tornadoes.

Chilled to the bone

Texas folklore claims that if you count more than 13 blackbirds landing on a fence, then prepare for a "norther" to descend. No one reported seeing that sight before an epic norther blasted across Texas in February 1899. Lasting two cold days, the storm spared no part of the state. The Arctic air rolled into West Texas like a milky fog on February 11, carrying with it a blizzard that dumped snow all the way into South Texas. In Dallas, a 35-mile-per-hour wind slung sleet that left behind an icy glaze. City firemen started a fire around a hydrant just to get the water flowing. Cattle as far south as Houston moved along with the cruel winter storm until many drifted into fences and froze to death. Six to seven inches of snow blanketed the ground from just south of San Antonio to the Rio Grande. The water in the bays at Galveston and Corpus Christi froze solid, halting all water traffic. On February 12, Panhandle residents in Tulia shook and shivered as the mercury dropped to –23°F, the state's coldest recorded temperature ever.

Whirling dervish
On April 2, 1958, in Wichita Falls, the winds of one tornado were clocked at 280 miles per hour. It is still the fastest tornado speed ever measured in the world.

🖝 On September 9, 1921, a gray day dawned in Thrall. Mist fell early on the Williamson County town and slowly turned into a steady rain. By mid-afternoon, blinding rain deluged pastures about two miles north of Thrall. Water runoff cut wide gullies through fields and transformed lowlands into lakes. When the storm finally subsided about 24 hours later, Thrall laid claim to one of the greatest recorded rainfalls in U.S. history. Within 18 hours, Thrall and the surrounding area received 36.4 inches of precipitation, according to the official measurement. The unofficial total was 38.2 inches.

Rain, rain go away

Killer heat wave

🐦 Most Texans have become accustomed to the hot summers that bake the state during June, July, and August. But in 1980, an unbearable, prolonged heat wave caught residents by surprise. On June 26 and 27, the Dallas-Fort Worth temperature shot up to 113°F. Thermometers in Wichita Falls recorded 117°F on June 28. In much of the northern portion of the state, daytime temperatures climbed above 100°F every day during July. In the southern half of Texas, estimated livestock and crop losses ranged from $250 million to $500 million. Across the state, soil cracked, crops withered, and river levels plunged. One of the hottest summers in Texas history also took a human toll. At least 60 people died of heat stroke.

UNIQUE WILDLIFE

The dog days

At Mackenzie State Park and Muleshoe National Wildlife Refuge, visitors can get a close look at modern-day prairie dog towns. Each is home to about 500 black-tailed prairie dogs. But neither compares to the dog town discovered by Vernon Bailey in 1905. Bailey found a single, continuous prairie dog town that sprawled from Clarendon south to San Angelo, a distance of about 250 miles. The dog town varied in width from 100 to 150 miles. A conservative head count put the population at 400 million prairie dogs. The state properly immortalized these prairie dog homes on the range. The stream that created scenic Palo Duro Canyon was named the Prairie Dog Town Fork of the Red River.

Holy bat cave!

No one knows what makes Bracken Cave near San Antonio so special. But each March, 20 million adult Mexican free-tailed bats (*Tadarida brasiliensis*) arrive to bear and raise their young. The cave becomes the species' largest maternity ward during the summer when each female gives birth to a single bat pup. With approximately 40 million bats "hanging around," the cave houses the world's largest concentration of mammals at a single time.

The big bat cave has both aided and confounded the military over the years. Confederate troops mined the cave's guano (dung) deposits during the Civil War when they needed potassium nitrate, an ingredient of gunpowder. But in the early 1990s, the Air Force wanted to bomb the cave closed. It seems that the bats' nightly flights interfered with radar tracking at nearby airfields. However, the future of Bracken Cave now appears secure under the management and protection of a conservation group called Bat Conservation International, headquartered in Austin.

Sandhill stop-over

On the flat expanse of the Staked Plains in the Panhandle, close to 20,000 shallow basins dot the landscape. Known as *playas*, from a Spanish word meaning "beaches" or "shores," they are barely perceptible across the level, treeless land. But the clay-bottomed playas collect precious rainwater for the region, with many of the larger ones supporting diverse wetland plants. The playas often remain dry for months at a time, and then the rains come just in time for the autumn arrival of sandhill cranes. For decades the playas have served as the second most important habitat for wintering waterfowl on the Central Flyway, surpassed only by the Gulf Coast. In those Panhandle playas, sandhill crane numbers can exceed 450,000 or about 90 percent of the mid-continental population. The playas also offer nesting grounds for various duck species, especially mallards. By some estimates, the playas help produce about 250,000 ducks during a healthy nesting season. Muleshoe NWR and Buffalo Lake NWR are located in this region.

🐦 The largest roundup of wild mustangs happened around 1878 when a herd of about 1,000 was captured near Cotulla in the South Texas county of LaSalle. The whole event took place to fill a mustang order from the Argentine government.

Head 'em up

🐦 Four different species of wildcats—the mountain lion, bobcat, ocelot, and jaguarundi—roam the Texas landscape, giving the Lone Star State the largest collection of wild felines in the United States. Only the snow-loving lynx of the north is absent. The jaguarundi, nicknamed "weasel-cat" for its gait, is considered to be the rarest Texas wildcat and is on the endangered species list. The bobcat ranks as the most common wild feline in the state, taking up residence within some city limits. Mountain lions—also known as cougars, pumas, and panthers—prowl at night and range widely, making population estimates difficult. Only about 100 ocelots now live in the South Texas brush country, protected as an endangered species. Before vanishing, the jaguar and margay also resided in the Texas wilds. A margay-breeding program near Glen Rose may someday return the small cat to its natural environment.

The cat's meow

Tortoise islands

The Texas tortoise is one of only four surviving tortoise species in North America. Designated as "threatened" by the Texas Parks and Wildlife Department, the Texas tortoise is losing its native brushland habitat in the lower Rio Grande Valley. But in Cameron County, on the southern tip of Texas, the Texas tortoise finds refuge on dry "islands" known as *lomas*. Low mounds of clay, or *lomas*, rise above the coastal marshes like islands dotting the sea. The islands are surrounded by dense marsh grasses and separated by barren salt flats. The tortoises live only on the *lomas*, isolated from one another by circles of grass and intervening salt flats.

TEXAS GREENERY

The four forests

🐾 Texas relinquished its sovereignty in 1845 when it joined the Union. But the state held on to its public lands. Not until 1933 did the Texas Legislature give the U.S. government authorization to purchase public land for the creation of national forests. On October 15, 1936, President Franklin D. Roosevelt proclaimed the establishment of four national forests on Texas soil. None have been added since that historic day. All 637,134 acres of those national forests can be found in East Texas. Within the official boundaries of each forest private property still exists, ranging from small tracts to quite sizable acreages.

Angelina National Forest – 153,176 acres in Angelina, Jasper, Nacogdoches, and San Augustine counties

Davy Crockett National Forest – 161,841 acres in Houston and Trinity counties

Sabine National Forest – 160,609 acres in Jasper, Newton, Sabine, San Augustine, and Shelby counties

Sam Houston National Forest – 161,508 acres in Montgomery, San Jacinto, and Walker counties

Lots of phlox

🐾 Scottish botanist Thomas Drummond overcame Indians and illness to explore Texas plant life in the 1830s. While in the state, he collected more than 700 plant species. One, however, blossomed more brilliantly in history than all the others. In 1834, Drummond discovered Texas' native phlox, now known internationally as "Drummond phlox" (scientific name, *Phlox drummondii*). He sent some specimens to his sponsors in England, where the plant thrived and began its spread to gardens across the world. Since then, plant breeders have cultivated, hybridized, and improved on phlox. But the original strain still blooms each spring in shades of purple, pink, and red in the sandy soils of South and Central Texas.

Stars of Starr County

🐾 Finding a ramadero forest requires a trip to Starr County in far south Texas. Dense ribbons of tall trees and tangled vines grow there along narrow channels of water flowing through dry brushland. For years, fertile soil collected in these ramadero strips as it washed off nearby hills. Settlers quickly exploited these "oasis" areas, plowing pastures and creating cropland. By U.S. Soil Conservation estimates, ramaderos once covered 15 percent of Starr County. Today that figure has diminished to less than 8 percent. To help save the vanishing ramaderos, the U.S. Fish and Wildlife Service purchased 1,100 acres north of Rio Grande City. Only one 150-acre tract that never exceeds 50 yards in width contained one of the rare ramadero forests unique to Starr County.

Troublesome tumbleweeds

Midland motorists dodged tumbleweeds in April 1990 when a strong West Texas prairie wind blew the spiny balls into the city. The rolling plants—some the size of basketballs, others as large as compact cars—clogged roads, jammed farm equipment, littered city parks, lodged in fences, and piled into neighborhood front yards. City workers resorted to dump trucks and trailers to remove the vegetative pests. Inconvenienced residents blamed the tumbleweed trouble on Russian thistles, prolific plants that grow along West Texas roadsides and in cultivated fields. Each summer the tumbleweeds die, breaking off at ground level. The skeletal remains of the dead plants live again as tumbleweeds—quite a haunting experience, as the folks in Midland can attest.

Chow time

Four of North America's five genera of prominent carnivorous plants wait patiently for their meals in the Big Thicket. Five species of bladderwort grow in Big Thicket waters. On the surface, innocent-looking flowers bloom. But below the surface, bristles surround small openings that lead to several bladders in the plant. When organisms in the water wiggle by and touch the bristles, the bladder suddenly opens and sucks the prey inside. The tall and elegant pitcher plant uses its long, slender leaves to trap bugs. The plant secretes nectar at the end of each leaf to attract prey. The insect takes the bait, slips down the tube to a waiting pool of water, and drowns. The sundew and butterwort work by emitting a sweet nectar that acts like glue. An insect sticks to the plant when it tries to steal some nectar.

Voila!

In 1987, a ranger at Guadalupe Mountains National Park found yellow violets blooming on a mountain cliff at an altitude of 8,000 feet. A botany professor from Alpine's Sul Ross State University determined that the ranger's discovery was a new species, *guadalupensis*, of the genius *Viola*. It seems the plants descended from violets that grew in the colder climate of 10,000 years ago. The violets survived in the coolness of the high altitude where the limestone mountains retain enough moisture for the plants and a stand of Douglas fir trees offers shade from the Texas sun.

Admirers of Stormie Jones, the world's first heart-and-liver transplant patient, said the yellow violet and the 13-year-old girl shared some common characteristics. Both were small, beautiful, and resilient. She fought seven years to survive, losing her battle on November 11, 1990. The violet is commonly called "the Stormie Jones violet."

ENDANGERED SPECIES

Seeking refuge

🐦 On October 16, 1992, Balcones Canyonlands National Wildlife Refuge was created for a special purpose: to protect two small songbirds and a handful of cave-dwelling invertebrates, or bugs. Located in Williamson and Travis counties, and near the state capital, Balcones Canyonlands stirred up a Texas-sized brouhaha among conservationists, developers, private landowners, and government officials. Conservation groups wanted to protect endangered species. Developers crusaded for urban growth and expansion. Private property owners feared a land grab by government. And local governments squirmed at the sight of a rather large price tag to help finance the project.

Finally, compromises were reached. The area will include 41,000 acres, protecting the nesting habitat of the endangered golden-cheeked warbler and the black-capped vireo. Seven endangered species of invertebrates (some of Texas' smallest residents) are also protected: the Tooth Cave pseudoscorpion, Tooth Cave spider, Tooth Cave ground beetle, Kretschmarr Cave mold beetle, Bee Creek Cave harvestman spider, Coffin Cave mold beetle, and Bone Cave harvestman spider.

Endangered Species

In 1973, the Texas Legislature authorized the Texas Parks and Wildlife Department (TPWD) to establish a list of endangered animals in the state. In 1988, the legislature authorized TPWD to establish a list of endangered plant species in the state. A plant is considered endangered if it is "in danger of extinction throughout all or a significant portion of its range." Listing of endangered plants and animals is coordinated by TPWD's Resource Protection Division. The following list was issued by TPWD in September 1993.

Mammals
Mexican long-nosed bat*
Sperm whale*
Finback whale*
Blue whale*
Black right whale*
Manatee*
Red wolf*
Gray wolf*
Mexican wolf*
Black bear
Louisiana black bear
Coati
Black-footed ferret*
Ocelot*
Margay*
Jaguarundi*
Jaguar

Birds
Brown pelican*
Whooping crane (right)*
Bald eagle*
American peregrine falcon*
Northern aplomado falcon*
Eskimo curlew*

Interior least tern*
Attwater's prairie-chicken*
Red-cockaded woodpecker*
Ivory-billed woodpecker*
Black-capped vireo*
Bachman's warbler*
Golden-cheeked warbler*

Reptiles
Loggerhead sea turtle
Hawksbill sea turtle*
Kemp's ridley turtle*
Leatherback sea turtle*
Chihuahuan mud turtle
Speckled racer
Northern cat-eyed snake
Concho water snake
Smooth green snake
Louisiana pine snake

Amphibians
Texas blind salamander*
Blanco blind salamander
Black-spotted newt
Rio Grande lesser siren
Houston toad*
White-lipped frog

Fishes
Shovelnose sturgeon
Paddlefish
Bluntnose shiner
Phantom shiner
Leon Springs pupfish*
Comanche Springs pupfish*
Big Bend gambusia*
San Marcos gambusia*
Clear Creek gambusia*
Pecos gambusia*
Blotched gambusia
Fountain darter*
Blackfin goby

Spiders
Tooth Cave pseudoscorpion*
Tooth Cave spider*
Bee Creek Cave harvestman*
Bone Cave harvestman*

Insects
Tooth Cave ground beetle*
Kretschmarr Cave mold beetle*
Coffin Cave mold beetle*

and 20 plant species.

*Indicates that the animal is on a federal list of animals protected by the Endangered Species Act.

TENDING TO TEXAS

Lady Bird's legacy

Drivers who pass by roadside parks on Texas highways should give a salute to native Texan Lady Bird Johnson (right). When her husband, the late president Lyndon Baines Johnson, was serving as director of the National Youth Administration's office in Texas, Mrs. Johnson encouraged him to develop the system of roadside parks in the state. These were years of the Depression, between 1935 and 1937. Lady Bird's idea put young people to work, and it was her first public step in a beautification campaign that has lasted a lifetime.

The personal campaign expanded when LBJ was elected president in November 1964. She convinced her husband to take up her cause, and in October 1965, Congress passed the Highway Beautification Act. Even in the post-presidential years, Lady Bird continued her beautification efforts. In 1982 she announced plans to found the National Wildflower Research Center, saying "Wildflowers are the stuff of my heart." In October 1993, she participated in the ground-breaking ceremony for the center's new 42-acre site southwest of Austin. Today the research center is the only national nonprofit environmental organization dedicated exclusively to the study, preservation, and re-establishment of native plants in public and private landscapes.

Patches of prairie

From a narrow slice near San Antonio, the Blackland Prairie extends northward for almost 400 miles to the Red River. Tall grasses as high as a man on a horse once grew here, and bison roamed the open space. The untamed prairie covered 12 million acres of Lone Star land. But plowing and paving destroyed most of the virgin prairie. Today, less than 5,000 acres of native Blackland Prairie remain.

Conservation groups hope to preserve those few patches of prairie. The Nature Conservancy of Texas cares for five Blackland Prairie sites, totaling 588 acres. The Collin County Open Space Program tends to Parkhill Prairie, covering 436 acres, with 60 of those considered native tallgrass prairie. Members of the Native Prairies Association of Texas save pockets of native Blackland Prairie wherever they can find it— beside highways, along railroad tracks, and in parks.

For the birds

The Texas Bird Song Library at Sam Houston State University in Huntsville houses more than 2,000 recordings of individual bird songs and calls. That's a lot of tweets and twitters from the 400 species represented. Established in 1979 by Dr. Ralph Moldenhaur, the library specializes in Texas birds, but also has recordings from other states, Mexico, Canada, and Venezuela. The field of study is called avian bioacoustics, and it means looking at the songs as well as listening to them. Recordings are converted into graphs, known as sonograms or audiospectrographs, and used for research. But the songs themselves have been aired on radio shows and used in natural history exhibits at museums.

SUPERFUND SITES

The Pantex problem

The Pantex plant in Carson County, 17 miles northeast of Amarillo, sits on top of the Ogallala Aquifer. Lying under South Dakota, Wyoming, Nebraska, Colorado, Kansas, New Mexico, Oklahoma, and Texas, the aquifer is the largest in the United States. And that's where the problem may ultimately lie. The Pantex plant is owned by the U.S. Department of Energy and covers 9,100 acres. Begun in 1942 as an ammunition plant for the army, it moved into the nuclear field in 1950. At one point, Pantex was the final assembly point for all nuclear weapons in the country. Now it's the major spot for dismantling the atomic beasts. Improper disposal of waste in unlined ditches and surface ponds has caused concern. Organic solvents, such as barium and arsenic from wastewater and buried waste, may be seeping toward the aquifer, which lies from 390 to 420 feet beneath the site. Amarillo gets about one-third of its water from wells and some contamination has been documented in the area. This superfund site wasn't proposed until 1991 and preliminary studies are now being conducted.

Superfund sites

As of early 1994, 29 sites in Texas were listed on the Environmental Protection Agency's National Priorities List of hazardous-waste sites. That listing qualifies the sites for cleanup under the federal Superfund program. The EPA administers and enforces Texas Superfund sites in cooperation with the Texas Natural Resource Conservation Commission.

Bowie County – Lone Star Ammunition Plant
Bridge City – Triangle Chemical Co.
Calhoun County – ALCOA/Lavaca Bay
Carson County – Pantex
Conroe – United Creosoting
Crystal City – Crystal City Airport
Dallas – RSR Lead Smelter
Galveston County – MOTCO
Grand Prairie – Bio-Ecology
Harris County – Brio Refining, Dixie Oil Processors, French Limited, Highlands
    Acid Pit, Sikes
Harrison County – Longhorn Army Ammunition Plant, Stewco
Houston – Crystal Chemical, Geneva Industries, Industrial Transformers, North and
    South Cavalcade Streets
Liberty County – Petro Chemical
Odessa – Odessa Chromium 1 & 2
Orange County – Bailey Waste Disposal
Tarrant County – Air Force Plant #4, Pesses Chemical
Texarkana – Koppers, Texarkana Wood Preserving
Waller County – Sheridan

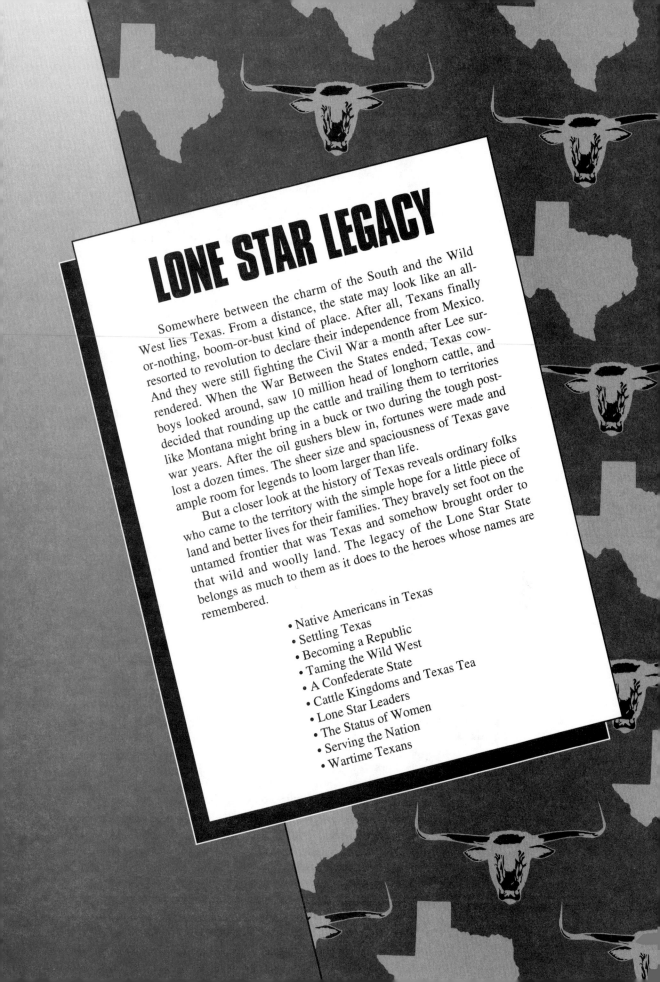

LONE STAR LEGACY

Somewhere between the charm of the South and the Wild West lies Texas. From a distance, the state may look like an all-or-nothing, boom-or-bust kind of place. After all, Texans finally resorted to revolution to declare their independence from Mexico. And they were still fighting the Civil War a month after Lee surrendered. When the War Between the States ended, Texas cowboys looked around, saw 10 million head of longhorn cattle, and decided that rounding up the cattle and trailing them to territories like Montana might bring in a buck or two during the tough post-war years. After the oil gushers blew in, fortunes were made and lost a dozen times. The sheer size and spaciousness of Texas gave ample room for legends to loom larger than life.

But a closer look at the history of Texas reveals ordinary folks who came to the territory with the simple hope for a little piece of land and better lives for their families. They bravely set foot on the untamed frontier that was Texas and somehow brought order to that wild and woolly land. The legacy of the Lone Star State belongs as much to them as it does to the heroes whose names are remembered.

- Native Americans in Texas
- Settling Texas
- Becoming a Republic
- Taming the Wild West
- A Confederate State
- Cattle Kingdoms and Texas Tea
- Lone Star Leaders
- The Status of Women
- Serving the Nation
- Wartime Texans

NATIVE AMERICANS IN TEXAS

Native American tribes in Texas

When Spanish explorers ventured into the territory north of New Spain (now present-day Mexico) in the early 1500s, they found different and varied Native American tribes scattered across the land. The Caddo people occupied East Texas. Karankawas lived along the Gulf Coast. Wichita and Tonkawa tribes shared Central Texas. Apaches dominated the western part of the state, where Comanches and Kiowas often invaded from the northern plains. The great tribes tried to hold their ground for more than 300 years after the first Spaniards arrived. But by the late 1800s, the colonization of Texas overcame the Native American cultures.

Final Cherokee battle

In the Redland community of southeastern Van Zandt County, a single stone marker designates the final Texas battleground between the Cherokee and Texas colonists. On July 16, 1839, along the banks of the Neches River, 800 Cherokee braves fought 500 Texans. Among the many Native Americans who fell was 83-year-old Cherokee Chief Bowles. He was killed brutally by a shot to the head while wearing a sword and a sash that had been given to him by Sam Houston, president of the Republic of Texas. The 70-acre tract of land where Chief Bowles and his followers fought is now the object of the "Renew the Dream" project. Organizers of the project plan to purchase the tract of private property for $175,000 and build an Indian Heritage Center to commemorate Chief Bowles and the Cherokees.

Bittersweet repayment

During the Texas war with Mexico, the Alabama-Coushatta of East Texas voiced a neutral stance, outwardly refusing to take sides. But during the "Runaway Scrape" in April 1836, when Texas settlers fled the advance of Santa Anna's army, the Native Americans cared for settlers. Repayment for their help and kindness was bittersweet. The Alabama-Coushatta were among the few Native Americans allowed to remain in Texas, but during the next few years they were forced from their ancestral lands by white colonists. Not until 1854 did the state purchase 1,110 acres in Polk County for them. In 1928, the federal government added another 3,071 adjacent acres. Today, about 550 Alabama-Coushatta live on a 4,766-acre reservation near the Big Thicket.

Tigua heritage

The Tigua Reservation in southeastern El Paso boasts the oldest mission in Texas, the silver-domed Mission Ysleta. Tigua workers built the structure in 1682. The original mission, named Corpus Christi de los Tihuas de Ysleta del Sur, has been rebuilt. However, some of the old adobe walls still stand on the original foundation.

Satanta's prophecy

★ Comanche Chief Satanta, born about 1820, became known as the "Orator of the Plains" for his wise counsel during the Medicine Lodge Treaty negotiations in 1867. "I don't want to settle," he said. "I love to roam over the prairies. There I feel free and happy, but when I settle down I grow pale and die." Satanta spoke the truth. In 1871 he was sent to prison in Huntsville for his part in the Salt Creek Massacre, a Native American raid on a wagon train in which most of the teamsters were killed or wounded. Although paroled in 1873, he continued his raiding activities in Texas. Satanta returned to prison in October 1874, where he learned that a life sentence would forever keep him confined. In 1878, he committed suicide by jumping from a second-story window at the prison.

Returning to Texas

★ After Texas gained its independence from Mexico, the Kickapoo tribe, who came to Texas from Illinois, split into two groups. One group moved to Indian Territory (Oklahoma). The other group settled in Mexico. But the drought of the 1940s parched the farmland and created a game shortage. The Mexican Kickapoo became migrant farmworkers, laboring from California to New York. In the 1960s, they constructed a squatter village under the international bridge in Eagle Pass, Texas. From there they worked the vegetable harvests in Zavala County. The Mexican government encouraged the Kickapoo to return to their lands in Mexico. The U.S. government urged them to move to Oklahoma. The Kickapoo did neither. In the 1980s, the Texas band of Kickapoo finally gained state and federal recognition. They were given a 125-acre tract of land as a reservation near Eagle Pass.

Quanah Parker

In May 1836, a 9-year-old Anglo girl was captured when a band of Comanche attacked Fort Parker in the Texas Panhandle. Cynthia Ann Parker stayed with the Comanche for 24 years before unwillingly returning to the Anglo culture. During that time, she married Comanche Chief Peta Nocona. They had several children, including a boy Quanah who became the last great Comanche war chief at age 19. Quanah (right) served as a judge, made numerous trips to Washington, D.C., and took part in President Teddy Roosevelt's inauguration. He dressed in "white man's" suits, but he never cut his hair and never learned to write. Quanah died on February 21, 1911, at age 64.

```
┌─────────────────────────────────────────┐
│  Notable Chiefs in Texas                  │
│  •Placido (Tonkawa) – An ally of Texas for more than
│        20 years. Known as a traitor to his people. Boasted
│        that he had "never shed a white man's blood."
│  •Big Tree (Kiowa) – Sentenced to prison for his partici-
│        pation in the Salt Creek Massacre. After being
│        paroled in 1873, he returned to the reservation and
│        died in 1927.
│  •Kicking Bird (Kiowa) – Died under mysterious cir-
│        cumstances on the reservation in 1875.
│  •Satank (Kiowa) – Shot to death in 1871 while on his
│        way to stand trial for his part in the Salt Creek
│        Massacre.
│  •Ten Bears (Comanche) – Lost his standing with his
│        people because he advocated peace with the
│        Anglos. Died among strangers in 1872 at Fort Sill.
│  •Victorio (Apache) – Shot to death in the Candelaria
│        Mountains of Mexico on October 14, 1880, after
│        attempting to lead his followers through Texas to
│        the Mescalero Apache Reservation in New Mexico.
└─────────────────────────────────────────┘
```

SETTLING TEXAS

Tales of gold

★ When Álvar Núñez Cabeza de Vaca was shipwrecked along the Texas coast in 1528, he and three surviving shipmates became the first Spaniards to explore the territory that would become Texas. Cabeza de Vaca and his companions lived among the Native Americans for eight years before returning home to what is now Mexico. They took with them tales of cities of gold that caused great excitement. In 1540, Francisco Vásquez de Coronado set off with an army to find the fabled cities of gold. Coronado searched all the way to present-day Kansas without ever finding the wealth described by Cabeza de Vaca.

Au revoir, Texas!

In 1682, Frenchman René Robert Cavelier, Sieur de La Salle, followed the Mississippi River to its mouth and claimed all of the country that was drained by the great river for France. He called the area Louisiana, which included the territory of Texas. In 1685, La Salle established a crude stockade, Fort St. Louis, on the Texas coast. But in 1690 Spaniard Alonso de León discovered that Native Americans had destroyed the fort and La Salle had been assassinated by one of his own men in 1687. The French flag flew over Texas for only five years, from 1685 until 1690, before the land once again became the property of Spain.

★ With the threat of the French removed, the Spanish immediately began establishing missions in East and Central Texas. Along the San Antonio River, five missions still stand as testament to the Spanish heritage of Texas. Financed by the Spanish government and directed by Franciscan friars between 1680 and 1773, the missions were civil as well as spiritual centers. Each mission was designed as a self-contained village, with a fortified wall surrounding a central plaza. The Alamo is the most famous of the missions. But the Mission San José is the state's largest restored mission. Mission Concepcíon (below), established in 1731, remains virtually untouched by any restoration, and original, slightly faded frescoes adorn the walls. Between Mission Espada and Mission San Juan Capistrano, a water system considered one of the oldest in the United States still carries water. More than 30 missions were established by the Spanish in Texas.

The Spanish missions

★ In 1803, when France sold Louisiana to the United States, and Texas found itself on the border of New Spain (present-day Mexico) and the United States. The Spanish intended to colonize the territory with loyal subjects and keep out the land-hungry Americans. But in 1821, Spain gave Stephen F. Austin permission to bring American families into the territory. That small crack in the border would lead to the Anglo-American settlement of Texas. Austin's colonists began arriving in 1823, only to find that Mexico had won its independence from Spain. The territory was now the Mexican state of Coahuila-Texas.

Texas as a Mexican state

Nuestra Señora de la Purísima de Concepción de Acuña is located in the San Antonio Missions National Historic Park.

BECOMING A REPUBLIC

Moving toward revolution

★ The colonization of Texas as a Mexican state brought Anglos westward from the United States and Mexicans northward. Differences in language and culture led to tension. Most Mexicans were Catholic and most Anglos were Protestant. The Americans felt ties to the United States, not Mexico. Trade grew between Texas and the United States, alarming Mexico. In 1830, the Mexican Congress passed a law that stopped American immigration into Texas. It initiated custom collections as the government tried to stay in control. Dissatisfaction spread among the settlers, and in 1832, skirmishes broke out that signaled the coming revolution.

Start of the war

War broke out in Gonzales on October 2, 1835, when Mexican troops attempted to confiscate a cannon from the Texas settlers. Waving a banner that read "Come and Take It," the Texans defeated the Mexicans. The Texas Revolution lasted from that October until the Battle of San Jacinto on April 21, 1936.

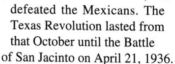

The shrine remains

★ Santa Anna surrounded the Alamo on February 23, 1836. He finally attacked on March 6. All of Texas' 187 men died in the battle, including David Crockett, James Bowie, and William Travis. Toribio Losoya, a 27-year-old who was born at the Alamo compound, was one of eight native-born Mexicans who fought on the side of Texas. The four corners of the church crumbled, and Santa Anna burned the interior. Yet the church's front limestone wall survived with its delicate carvings intact. Over the arched doorway of the Alamo, the keystone still bears the carving of the royal seal of the Spanish Crown.

San Jacinto and the search for Santa Anna

On April 21, 1836, Sam Houston and his Texas forces defeated Mexican troops at the Battle of San Jacinto. It was the Texas Revolution's decisive battle and lasted a short 18 minutes. Houston attacked the Mexicans during the afternoon while Santa Anna, the Mexican president, was taking his siesta. When the smoke cleared, Santa Anna was nowhere in sight, and Houston dispatched patrols to find the Mexican general. While on patrol, James Sylvester spotted a group of deer grazing in the grass. The Kentucky sharpshooter leveled his gun, but a movement nearby spooked the animals. When Sylvester went to investigate, a Mexican in a dirty hat bolted from the grass only to fall flat on his face in front of his captors. As the patrol rode back into camp with their catch, Mexican prisoners began shouting, "El Presidente!" James Sylvester had snared Santa Anna.

Monument to independence

Officials dedicated the San Jacinto Monument (right) on April 21, 1939, to commemorate the battle that finally declared Texas independent from Mexico. The tower of the monument rises 570 feet, taller than either the Washington Monument or the Statue of Liberty. The 35-foot-high star atop the tower is faced with three-inch-thick Texas Cordova shell limestone.

A public political feud with Sam Houston

Sam Houston served two terms as a Tennessee congressman and was elected governor in 1827. Resigning from office after the dissolution of his marriage, he lived with the Cherokee in Indian Territory (Oklahoma) for six years. By 1835, Houston had moved to Texas where he served his adopted home for three decades. He was a military commander, a two-term president of the republic, and a U.S. senator after annexation. Like any person in public life, Houston had enemies. None was quite as irritating as Mirabeau B. Lamar—a man he disagreed with on almost every issue. Houston advocated Native American rights; Lamar worked to eradicate entire native populations. Houston wanted to avoid the Civil War; Lamar favored secession. The political rivalry between the two—never a secret—became glaringly apparent at Lamar's inauguration as president of the Republic of Texas in December 1838. The crowd expected a brief, dignified introduction of the new president. Instead, Houston came dressed in "George Washington" attire, complete with knee britches and white wig. He then began a three-hour speech. When Houston finally stepped down, Lamar was too exhausted to deliver his inaugural address. His private secretary read it to the inattentive audience.

TAMING THE WILD WEST

Border dispute settled

★ When the United States annexed Texas, a dispute arose about the state's southern boundary. The disagreement triggered the war with Mexico in 1846. Most of the fighting took place in Mexico, with about 5,000 Texans actually serving. When the war ended, a treaty was signed in February 1948 establishing the Rio Grande as the boundary. Even though the war was officially ended, the actual boundary dispute wasn't settled until 1963. It seems the Rio Grande shifted after the United States signed the treaty ending the Mexican War. Mexico was ready to settle in 1911, when an arbitration commission gave them land south of the present river channel. The United States said no. Finally, in July 1963, President John Kennedy and President Lopez Mateos signed the Chamizal settlement giving Mexico 437 acres of land and selling some U.S. property to a Mexican bank. Today the Chamizal National Memorial at El Paso commemorates the settlement of the dispute.

Good fences make good neighbors

Before barbed wire came to Texas, German and Norwegian immigrants in Central Texas built dry-laid rock fences to protect their land from free-roaming cattle. Built without mortar, the fences rely on gravity and craftsmanship to hold them together. Hill Country counties had few trees large or straight enough for construction projects. But the soil yielded lots of rocks. So between 1850 and 1900, settlers sometimes enclosed several acres with rock fences that stood five to six feet tall. In Austin, rock fences along Barton Creek were constructed to keep livestock in, rather than out. Known as the Barton Creek Corrals, the structure is listed on the National Register of Historic Places.

The strong arm of the law

★ After the Texas Revolution, bandits roamed the Mexican border, Native Americans controlled the Western Plains, and desperadoes hid out in the countryside. To stem the lawlessness, the Texas government turned to the Texas Rangers, a unique group of lawmen established by Stephen F. Austin in 1826. Men such as "Big Foot" Wallace, John Coffee Hays, and Samuel H. Walker tracked down outlaws, settled feuds, and reconciled land disputes. In 1846, Ranger Walker and Samuel Colt modified the Colt revolver into the Walker Colt, a six-shooter specially adapted for the range. Ranger Jim R. Hughes wore a badge for 28 years between 1887 and 1915, but lived on in legend as the fictional hero in the novel *The Lone Star Ranger*, penned by Zane Grey. Ranger Captain Bill McDonald earned a reputation as "the man who would charge hell with a bucket of water." In 1935, the Rangers became a branch of the Texas Department of Public Safety and today the organization still works for law and order in the state.

Tracks across Texas

Texas got its first railroad in 1853 when tracks were laid from Houston to nearby Stafford's Point. Only 600 miles of rails ran through the entire state by 1870. But beginning in 1873, Texas gave land grants to railroad companies in exchange for putting down tracks. In all, Texas traded about 32 million acres by the year 1882, and by the end of 1890, approximately 8,700 miles of tracks crossed the state.

A CONFEDERATE STATE

Leaving the Union

In 1859, most Texans cared little about secession. But several events swung the pendulum. Native American raids persisted on the frontier and Texas turned to the federal government. When Congress failed to offer aid, Texans lost faith in the government. About 90 percent of Texas' Anglo immigrants were from the South, and with the election of Abraham Lincoln as president, secessionists had more ammunition. On March 2, 1861, exactly 25 years after Texas proclaimed independence from Mexico, the state seceded from the Union. Governor Houston was removed from office when he wouldn't support the action. Lt. Governor Edward Clark served out Houston's term. About 2,000 Texans volunteered to serve in the Union Army.

★ During the Civil War, "cotton roads" led from the Texas interior to Mexican border towns along the Rio Grande. Haulers took bales down the hazardous roads through the brushy South Texas country. Empty cotton wagons were then loaded with guns, ammunition, cloth, nails, sugar, medicine, and other supplies needed by Confederate troops in Texas.

★ The last battle of the Civil War was fought on Texas soil at Palmito Ranch east of Brownsville. About 300 Confederate soldiers led by Colonel John Solomon Ford defeated Union forces that consisted of two African American regiments and a company of unmounted Texas cavalry. The battle took place on May 12–13, 1865, and the Confederates won. But they learned from Union prisoners that General Lee had surrendered at Appomattox more than a month earlier.

The end of slavery in Texas

President Lincoln issued the Emancipation Proclamation on January 1, 1863, and freed an estimated 200,000 slaves. But the news didn't reach Texas until June 19, 1865, when Major General Gordon Granger read the proclamation in Galveston. June 19th, or "Juneteenth," became an anniversary to be remembered and honored by former slaves and Juneteenth celebrations spread across the state. The historic day drew official recognition when Texas State Representative Al Edwards of Houston sponsored House Bill 1016. On January 1, 1980, Juneteenth was made a state holiday, the first state holiday in the nation to honor emancipation.

Making change

In the clamorous days of frontier Texas, small coins were scarce but bullets were plentiful. Settlers frequently used six-gun cartridges, known as "cowboy change," in place of dimes and quarters.

Trails of the bales

Winning the battle and losing the war

Little comfort in Comfort

★ Many German settlers in Central Texas preferred to remain neutral during the Civil War. But Confederate military officials condemned them as traitors. When Texas Partisan Rangers began lynching some of the men and boys, a few settlers tried to flee to Mexico for safety. On August 10, 1862, the rangers caught up with a group in Kinney County, near the Nueces River. The rangers attacked, killing 19. Nine wounded settlers were later executed. Eight escaped, only to be killed on October 18 while trying to cross the Rio Grande. The battle became known as the Nueces River Massacre. The remains of the dead were buried in a mass grave in Comfort in August 1865, and a monument was erected in 1866 in memory of the men who were true to the Union, or *Treue der Union*. Today, a 36-star U.S. flag flies at half-mast in perpetuity at the Treue der Union Monument to honor the slain settlers.

CATTLE KINGDOMS AND TEXAS TEA

How longhorns saved Texas

★ During the Texas Revolution and the Civil War, settlers abandoned their homesteads and their herds of English-bred cattle. Those animals crossbred with free-roaming cattle that had migrated from Mexico. When the Civil War ended, the Texas range had tens of thousands of longhorns, and northern states were willing to pay for beef. As many as 35,000 cowboys rounded up the range cattle and the trail-driving days began. Cowhands pushed 10 million longhorns up the cattle trails from Texas to northern markets. The drives averaged 10 to 15 miles per day over such dusty trails as the Goodnight-Loving to Wyoming, the Chisholm to Kansas, and the Western to Montana. The trail-driving days lasted about 30 years, and sales of tasty Texas cattle rescued the state's post-Confederacy economy.

Cattle rustlers beware

Herds weren't fenced in by barbed wire until the mid-1880s, so the Texas Legislature declared cattle stealing a felony in 1873, but that didn't stop rustlers from rounding up cattle in the wide-open spaces. Ranchers rose up against the rustlers on February 15, 1877, when about 40 cattlemen gathered beneath a spreading oak at the Young County Courthouse in Graham. They formed the Stock-Raisers Association of Northwest Texas, later called the Texas and Southwestern Cattle Raisers Association (TSCRA). In 1883, the organization began encouraging ranchers to register their brands as proof of cattle ownership. Headquartered in Fort Worth today, TSCRA is one of the oldest and largest organizations of its kind in the United States. More than 40 inspectors search for and capture modern-day outlaws who still practice cattle rustling.

Fort Buford

Miles City

Cheyenne   Ogallala

Ellsworth   Kansas City
        Abilene
              St. Louis
Dodge City

Red River Station

Dallas

Houston

San Antonio
        Victoria
        Corpus Christi

Brownsville

CATTLE TRAILS
- - Shawnee Trail
— Chisholm Trail
····· Western Trail
— Goodnight-Loving Trail

Queen of the cattle drive

Lizzie Johnson, better known as the "Cattle Queen of Texas," began her career as a bookkeeper for cattle dealers and wound up a wealthy woman. In 1871, at age 28, she rounded up stray cattle and registered her own brand. Then she drove the herd north, giving rise to the legend that she was the first and only woman to drive her own cattle up the Chisholm Trail. Johnson married at age 38, but kept her business and her money separate from her husband's. When the Cattle Queen died in 1924, she reportedly left diamonds hidden in her home, property scattered across central Texas, and an estate valued at $250,000.

An all-boy herd

★ Samuel Burk Burnett of the enormous Four Sixes Ranch in Wichita County introduced the concept of an all-steer herd to Texas. In 1874, he purchased 2,300 steer for his famous ranch on the Big Wichita River. Neutered bulls (steers) gain weight faster, making them more profitable as a beef product for cattle ranchers.

Experimenting with oil

★ Before the big gushers blew in, oil was a rather mundane commodity put to commercial use in a variety of ways. In the 1860s, oil was spread on Texas roads to settle the dust. In 1878, Martin Meinsinger of Brownwood sold his oil as a lubricant for 50 cents a gallon. He made more profit though selling it as a medicine for 25 cents per 4-ounce bottle. Cattlemen even experimented with the black crude, dipping their cattle in oil to rid the animals of fever ticks. That failed when the cattle overheated during hot summers.

Chasing oil

★ When the state's first major commercial oil well was discovered in Corsicana in 1894, Joseph S. Cullinan wasn't far behind. Arriving in 1897, Cullinan built the first oil refinery in the state. He also constructed Texas' first oil pipeline to transport the crude to his refinery. When the Lucas No. 1 erupted in 1901, Cullinan wasted no time getting to Spindletop. In 1902, he and his partners founded the Texas Fuel Company—the company that became Texaco.

The greatest gusher of them all

In 1900, Texas produced about 836,000 barrels of oil annually, less than one-quarter of the total U.S. oil production. Then on January 10, 1901, a few miles from Beaumont, the Lucas No.1 (named for Anthony Lucas who used a rotary drill and hit oil at 1,000 feet) roared in at Spindletop (right). The oil gushed with such force that within only a few days, Spindletop surpassed the state's total annual production. In 1902, the well produced 94 percent of all the oil in Texas. The great gusher changed Texas forever, and signaled the end of rural life based on an agricultural economy. Spindletop, the first salt dome oil discovery, made news around the world. It brought wildcatters and oil investors scurrying into the state. Spindletop, and the oil fields that followed, fueled Texas into the modern industrial age. Gulf Oil got its start at Spindletop.

LONE STAR LEADERS

First, and only, governor impeached

★ When Governor James E. Ferguson tangled with the University of Texas, he met his match. He often called professors "butterfly chasers" and saw no need for fraternities. In 1916, the university regents selected Robert E. Vinson as president without consulting the governor. Resentful of the snub, Ferguson threatened to veto the entire $1.5-million university appropriation unless Vinson and several faculty members were fired. The regents refused. After the legislature adjourned in June 1917, Ferguson vetoed the university's budget. The action outraged the university's powerful alumni association and the movement to impeach Ferguson grew. A special session of the legislature was called, and the House impeached the governor on 21 articles. The Senate convicted him on 10 of those articles and Ferguson was removed from office on August 25, 1917. He was barred from ever holding elective office in Texas again. Eight years later, however, he returned to the governor's mansion with his wife—Governor Ma Ferguson.

Ma made her mark

Miriam Amanda Ferguson (known as "Ma" for the initials of her first and middle names) was not only the first woman to become a Texas governor, but also the second woman in the country to serve as a state's executive officer. Ferguson took her oath as Texas governor on January 20, 1925. Much to Ma's disappointment, Nellie Tayloe Ross was sworn in 15 days before as Wyoming's governor. Ferguson served a second stint as governor from January 17, 1933, until January 15, 1935. Not until 1990 did Texans elect another woman governor. Ann W. Richards took the reins of the state on January 15, 1991. At a victory celebration, she held up a tee shirt imprinted with an image of the state's Capitol and the words "A Woman's Place Is in the Dome!"

At home in the dome

★ Born in Lakeview on September 1, 1933, as Dorothy Ann Willis, Ann Richards raised four children before embarking on a political career. She was first elected to the county commission of Travis County in 1976, then stepped up to the state treasurer's office in 1982—the first female to hold that position. In 1990, she successfully ran for governor, opening the doors of power to those long locked out. Dozens of Hispanics, blacks, and women were appointed to state commissions and boards. The nation got a look at the future Texas governor in 1988 when Richards delivered a witty keynote address at the Democratic National Convention. In 1994, George W. Bush, son of former president George Bush, soundly defeated Richards in the race for governor.

THE STATUS OF WOMEN

★ Clara Driscoll is best known as "the savior of the Alamo." The daughter of a South Texas millionaire, Driscoll wrote a check for $25,000 in 1903 and purchased the property adjacent to the Alamo. She gave the real estate to the Daughters of the Republic of Texas. That organization protected the Lone Star shrine from commercial exploitation. Less well known about Driscoll is that in 1928, she became the first Texas woman elected to the Democratic National Committee. She served until 1944 and died in 1945 at the age of 64.

A distinguished judicial career

In 1935, Sarah T. Hughes of Dallas was the first woman appointed as a district judge in Texas. She proved herself a popular judge, being re-elected to the judicial position seven times. In 1961, President John F. Kennedy appointed Hughes as the state's first female federal judge. Two years later, when Kennedy was assassinated in Dallas, Hughes swore in Lyndon Baines Johnson as president aboard *Air Force One* in Dallas.

★ The Special Supreme Court of Texas that was appointed by Governor Pat Neff on January 8, 1925, made national history. It was the first State Supreme Court composed entirely of women. In the case of *W.T. Johnson et al v. J.M. Darr et al* the three sitting male justices disqualified themselves because of potential conflict of interest. The governor chose Hortense Ward of Houston as Special Chief Justice. Ruth Brazzil of Galveston and Hattie L. Henenberg of Dallas were appointed Special Associate Justices. The women served until May 23, 1925, when the case was finally decided.

First female to sit on the Supreme Court

On August 19, 1981, President Ronald Reagan nominated Sandra Day O'Connor to the Supreme Court of the United States. The Senate confirmed the appointment on September 19, 1981. On September 25, 1981, the Texas native took her oath and became the first female Associate Justice in the history of the High Court. Although born in El Paso on March 26, 1930, O'Connor built her judicial reputation outside of the state. She graduated from Stanford University Law School in 1952 and began her climb through the courts when she was elected to Arizona's Maricopa County Superior Court. She was appointed to the Arizona Court of Appeals in 1979, where she served until joining the Supreme Court.

Jordan makes political history

★ Barbara Jordan was born in Houston in 1936 the daughter of a Baptist preacher. She prepared for her political career by earning a degree in political science from Texas Southern University and a law degree from Boston University. In 1966, she became the first African American elected to the state Senate since Reconstruction and the first African-American woman ever elected to the state Senate. In 1972, Jordan made political history again, when she became the first Texas woman elected to the U.S. House of Representatives. She was also the first African-American woman from the South to serve in Congress, winning 81 percent of her district's vote. While serving on the House Judiciary Committee, Jordan gained national attention during the impeachment hearings of President Nixon with an impassioned defense of constitutional principles. Today, Jordan teaches public affairs as a professor at the University of Texas. She served as Governor Ann Richards' special advisor on ethics.

More firsts for Texas women

- Mrs. L.P. Carlisle was the first woman to hold office in the state when she was appointed clerk of Hunt County in 1902.
- Elected in 1922, Dallas attorney Edith Therrel Wilmans was the first woman to serve in the Texas House of Representatives and the first woman to preside as Speaker of the House.
- Annie Webb Blanton was the first woman to run for office in Texas after women won the right to vote in 1918. She was elected to the statewide office of State Superintendent of Public Instruction and held the post for eight years.
- In 1910, Hortense Ward of Houston became the first woman admitted to the Texas Bar. As president of the Houston Equal Suffrage Association, Ward was the first woman in Harris County who registered to vote after women won that right in 1918.
- Publisher Margie Neal of Carthage was the first woman elected to the Texas Senate in 1926. She introduced the bill to create the State Board of Education.
- In 1954, Texas women won the right to serve on juries, and Charlye O. Farris became the first African-American woman admitted to the Texas bar.
- During the decade of the 1970s, women moved into mayoral seats of major cities. Austin elected Carole McLellan, Lila Cockrell took over as mayor of San Antonio, and Kathy Whitmire became mayor of Houston.
- In 1972, Irma Rangel of Kingsville became the first Mexican-American woman elected to the Texas Legislature.
- Attorney Sarah Weddington (right) of Austin argued and won a landmark case, *Roe v. Wade*, before the U.S. Supreme Court in 1973, securing a woman's right to abortion.
- In 1974, Dr. Lorene Rogers became the nation's first female president of a major publicly supported university as president of the University of Texas at Austin.
- In 1979, Gabrielle McDonald of Houston became the first African-American federal judge.
- In 1983, Elma Salinas was appointed the state's first Mexican-American female judge.
- In 1984, Myra McDaniel became the first African American appointed to a statewide office as secretary of state.

★ In 1992, former Republican state legislator Kay Bailey Hutchinson of Dallas won the election for state treasurer. The ballot for the race boasted the first all-female slate of candidates for a top executive office in state government. Hutchinson moved from state to national politics in 1993 when she filled the unexpired term of Senator Lloyd Bentsen. In a special election in June 1993, Hutchinson became the first woman to represent the Lone Star State in the U.S. Senate, defeating 24 other candidates. Hutchinson joined Senator Phil Gramm, giving Republicans both Texas Senate seats for the first time since 1875.

A Republican sweep of the Senate

SERVING THE NATION

★ In 1956, Henry B. Gonzalez became the first Mexican American elected to the state Senate since 1846. A few years later, in 1961, Gonzalez became the first Mexican American ever elected from Texas to serve in the U.S. House of Representatives. In 1994, at age 78 and while serving his 33rd year in Congress, the San Antonio native accepted the "Profile of Courage" award. The award is named after President John F. Kennedy's Pulitzer Prize-winning book *Profiles in Courage*. Gonzalez, a long-time Democrat, was the fifth recipient of the annual award and the only Texan ever to claim the prize.

Profile of a public servant

Presidential debt repaid

Dwight David Eisenhower (right) was born on October 14, 1890, in Denison, but lived for only two years in Texas before his impoverished family moved to Abilene, Kansas. Still, President Eisenhower repaid his native state a political debt on May 22, 1953, when he signed the National Tidelands Bill. As a republic, Texas claimed jurisdiction over about 10 miles and 2.5 million acres off the coastline of the state. Until oil was discovered, no one cared. Legal arguments and congressional battles over the land and the oil ensued between the United States and Texas until the election of Eisenhower. Native son Eisenhower carried the Texas vote and won the race for president against Adlai Stevenson. Eisenhower returned the favor by signing legislation that gave the tidelands—and the oil—to Texas.

★ On June 12, 1967, Tom C. Clark retired after serving on the U.S. Supreme Court for 17 years. That same day, his son Ramsey Clark was appointed attorney general of the United States. Clark, born in Dallas in 1899, had once held the national post of attorney general himself. He was appointed to the position in 1945 by President Harry S. Truman. Four years later, on August 2, 1949, Truman again turned to Clark, this time nominating him to the Supreme Court. The Senate confirmed Clark, and on August 24, 1949, he took the oath as an associate justice. Clark retired on June 12, 1967. He then served as the first chairman of the Federal Judicial Center, which was created by Congress to improve federal court administration. He died on June 13, 1977, at the age of 77.

A Supreme Court justice from Dallas

Wright was wrong   ★ James Claude Wright, Jr., born in Fort Worth in 1922, got his start in politics as mayor of Weatherford. He was elected to the U.S. House of Representatives as a Democrat in 1954. In 1977, Wright was chosen House Majority Leader by one vote. He became Speaker of the House in 1987. But two years later, in June 1987, he resigned the speakership and his House seat amid charges of ethics violations and improprieties—some of them involving a book deal. Sound familiar?

From humble beginnings

Lyndon Baines Johnson spent much of his adult life in Washington, D.C. He served as vice president under President Kennedy and as president from November 1963 until January 1969. But three of the biggest events in Johnson's life happened in Texas. He was born on his parents' ranch (above) near Stonewall in rural Gillespie County on August 27, 1908. When Kennedy was assassinated in Dallas, Johnson took the oath of office aboard *Air Force One* at Dallas' Love Field. And on January 22, 1973, Johnson suffered a coronary and died at his ranch in Gillespie County.

After graduating from high school, LBJ worked odd jobs in Texas and California, then returned home and enrolled at Southwest Texas State Teachers College in San Marcos. He taught elementary school in Cotulla and Houston before entering politics as a campaign worker during Richard Mifflin Kleberg's 1931 congressional race. After serving as a congressman, LBJ won the U.S. Senate seat in 1948 thanks to the town of Alice. In a close runoff race against Coke Stevenson, it looked as if Stevenson was ahead by 114 votes on August 28, election day. But on September 3, Jim Wells County reported amended returns. For some reason, ballots in Box 13 in Alice hadn't been counted. When the tally came in, LBJ got 202 votes to Stevenson's 1 from Box 13. LBJ won the race by 87 votes.

After Johnson assumed the presidency in 1963, Congress passed the medicare program in 1964 and civil rights bills such as the Voting Rights Act of 1965. But the controversial Vietnam War and Johnson's policies of escalation overshadowed everything. On March 31, 1968, Johnson announced that he would stop bombing North Vietnam, seek a negotiated peace, and would not run for re-election. Five days after his death in 1973, a treaty agreement arranged for the United States withdrawal from Vietnam.

Cabinet members from Texas

In March 1909, Charles Nagel of Bernardo was appointed secretary of commerce and labor by President William H. Taft. Nagel was the first native-born Texan to serve as a member of a president's Cabinet.

President	Cabinet Post	Appointed
	Secretary of State	
Bush	James A. Baker III	1989
	Secretary of Treasury	
Nixon	John B. Connally	1971
Reagan	James A. Baker III	1985
Clinton	Lloyd M. Bentsen	1993
	Attorney General	
Wilson	Thomas W. Gregory	1914
Truman	Thomas C. Clark	1945
Johnson, L.B.	Ramsey Clark	1967
	Secretary of Labor	
Carter	F. Ray Marshall	1977
	Secretary of Commerce	
Roosevelt, F.D.	Jesse Jones	1940
Bush	Robert A. Mosbacher	1989
	Secretary of HUD	
Clinton	Henry G. Cisneros	1993

The vice president from Uvalde

John Nance Garner, a Democrat from Uvalde in south Texas, once claimed that the office of vice president was "not worth a bucket of warm spit." However, in 1932, he became Franklin Delano Roosevelt's running mate in the presidential election. Garner had first gone to Washington as a representative in 1901. He became Speaker of the U.S. House of Representatives in 1931. When he moved on to the vice presidency, he said that he "gave up the second most important job in the government for one that didn't amount to a hill of beans." Roosevelt and Garner took office in 1933 and were re-elected in 1936. Under Roosevelt, Garner was the first vice president to travel abroad in an official capacity, visiting Japan, Mexico, and the Philippines. In 1940, Garner sought the Democratic nomination for president, but was trounced by the popular FDR. When Garner left the vice-presidential office in 1941, he retired to his Texas ranch.

★ In 1961, Reynaldo Garza of Brownsville became the first Mexican American appointed to the federal bench. In 1966, Irving L. Goldberg became the first Jew appointed to the federal bench in the South. His long-time friend, President Lyndon Johnson, named Goldberg to the Fifth Circuit court of Appeals.

At the federal level

WARTIME TEXANS

First Texan to receive the Medal of Honor

★ Twenty-three black soldiers and sailors received the nation's highest military honor during the Civil War. One of those men was Milton M. Holland, the first native Texan awarded the Medal of Honor. Holland was born August 1, 1844, on a farm near Carthage in Panola County. He went to Athens, Ohio, at an early age for schooling. When African Americans were allowed to join the Union Army in 1863, Holland organized a company of African-American soldiers. During an attack on Richmond, Virginia, in 1864, a wounded Sergeant Major Holland led the charge that enabled a white unit to return to Union lines. Holland's Medal of Honor is credited to the state of Ohio because he enlisted there.

A solemn honor

Many Texans might not recognize the name Hartley B. Edwards. But the native of Denison was asked by General John J. Pershing to blow the last "Tap"s of World War I on his bugle. On November 11, 1918, at 11 A.M., after the signing of the Armistice, Edwards did his duty. The solemn sound echoed through the Compiègne Forest in France. The bugle now rests at the Smithsonian Institution in Washington, D.C.

Texans end World War II

★ Two native Texans were personally involved in the ending of World War II. Denison-native Dwight David Eisenhower, Supreme Allied Commander and later the nation's 34th president, directed the D-Day (June 6, 1944) Allied invasion of Normandy. He accepted the German surrender on May 7, 1945, at Rheims. Admiral Chester W. Nimitz, a native of Fredericksburg and commander-in-chief of the Pacific Fleet, was on board the battleship *Missouri* in Tokyo Bay on September 2, 1945. He signed the agreement of Japanese surrender.

From farm boy to national hero

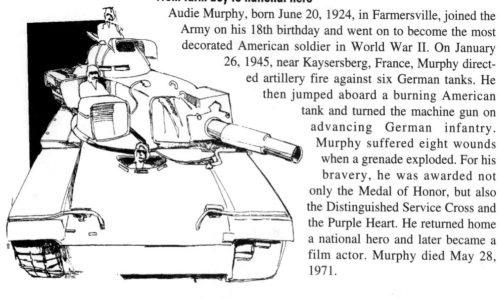

Audie Murphy, born June 20, 1924, in Farmersville, joined the Army on his 18th birthday and went on to become the most decorated American soldier in World War II. On January 26, 1945, near Kaysersberg, France, Murphy directed artillery fire against six German tanks. He then jumped aboard a burning American tank and turned the machine gun on advancing German infantry. Murphy suffered eight wounds when a grenade exploded. For his bravery, he was awarded not only the Medal of Honor, but also the Distinguished Service Cross and the Purple Heart. He returned home a national hero and later became a film actor. Murphy died May 28, 1971.

★ The Women's Airforce Service Pilots, better known as WASPs, earned their wings at Avenger Field in Sweetwater during World War II. It was the only all-women air base in history. In an effort to free more men for combat, the women trained as pilots and prepared to fly military aircraft to stateside bases and embarkation points for shipment overseas. The experimental program began in 1942 and a total of 1,074 women completed six months of training. When the WASP program ended on December 20, 1944, the women pilots had ferried more than 12,000 planes, logged 60 million miles in 78 different types of aircraft, trained pilots, and made 1,000 male pilots available for combat. They did it all as civilians, without military benefits or rank.

Silver wings in Sweetwater

A WAC-ky Hobby

In June 1940, Oveta Culp Hobby of Houston went to Washington as the $1-a-year head of a women's section in the War Department's public relations office. With World War II approaching, a congressional committee suggested the establishment of the Women's Army Auxiliary Corps. Hobby had the word "auxiliary" dropped and in 1942, she became the first director of the WACs. She was the first woman ever to hold the rank of colonel, and the first woman to receive the Army's Distinguished Service Medal. Under President Eisenhower, she became the first secretary of the Department of Health, Education, and Welfare. In 1964, Hobby returned to Houston as publisher of the *Houston Post* after her husband died. She added another first when she was elected director of the American Society of Newspaper Editors.

★ Finnis D. McCleery of Stephenville was the oldest Texan awarded the Medal of Honor in any war. He was just over 41 years old and received the medal for his courageous actions on May 14, 1968, in the Quang Tri province of Vietnam.

The oldest recipient

World War I
David B. Barkeley,
   Laredo*
Daniel R. Edwards,
   Mooreville
David E. Hayden,
   Florence

World War II
Lucian Adams, Laredo
William James Bordelon,
   San Antonio*
Robert G. Cole,
   Fort Sam Houston*
Samuel David Dealey,
   Dallas*
James H. Fields, Caddo
Thomas W. Fowler,
   Wichita Falls*
William George Harrell,
   Rio Grande City
James L. Harris,
   Hillsboro*
Johnnie David Hutchins,
   Florence*
Neel E. Kearby,
   Wichita Falls
George D. Keathley,
   Olney*
Truman Kimbro,
   Madisonville*
Jack L. Knight, Garner
Raymond L. Knight,
   Houston*
T.W. Leonard, Dallas*
James M. Logan, McNeil
José M. Lopez, Mission
Jack Lummus, Ennis*

The Medal of Honor

The Congressional Medal of Honor is America's highest reward for bravery in combat. Only 3,398 people have been given the medal since it originated in the Civil War, and half of those were from that war. President Truman said, "I'd rather have this medal than be president." The action for which it is given must present clear risk to life, be a voluntary act beyond normal duty, and be witnessed by two other people. Those men whose names are followed by an asterisk (*) were honored posthumously. Their place of birth is listed after their names.

World War II
Jack W. Mathis,
   San Angelo*
John C. Morgan,
   Vernon*
Charles Howard Roan,
   Claude*
Cleto Rodriguez,
   San Marcos
Eli Whiteley, Florence

Korea
Benito Martinez, Fort
   Hancock*
Frank N. Mitchell,
   Indian Gap*
Whitt L. Moreland,
   Waco*
George H. O'Brien,
   Fort Worth

Vietnam
Roy P. Benavidez,
   Cuero
Alfredo Gonzalez,
   Edinburg*
Robert D. Law,
   Fort Worth*
Clarence Eugene
   Sasser, Chenango
Russell A. Steindam,
   Austin*
Marvin R. Young,
   Alpine*

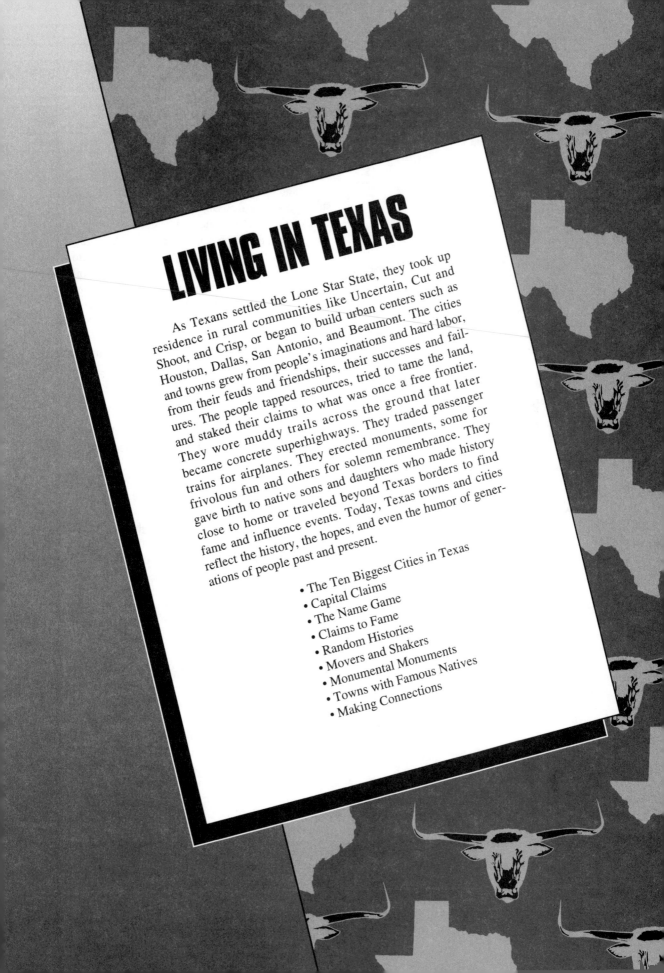

LIVING IN TEXAS

As Texans settled the Lone Star State, they took up residence in rural communities like Uncertain, Cut and Shoot, and Crisp, or began to build urban centers such as Houston, Dallas, San Antonio, and Beaumont. The cities and towns grew from people's imaginations and hard labor, from their feuds and friendships, their successes and failures. The people tapped resources, tried to tame the land, and staked their claims to what was once a free frontier. They wore muddy trails across the ground that later became concrete superhighways. They traded passenger trains for airplanes. They erected monuments, some for frivolous fun and others for solemn remembrance. They gave birth to native sons and daughters who made history close to home or traveled beyond Texas borders to find fame and influence events. Today, Texas towns and cities reflect the history, the hopes, and even the humor of generations of people past and present.

- The Ten Biggest Cities in Texas
- Capital Claims
- The Name Game
- Claims to Fame
- Random Histories
- Movers and Shakers
- Monumental Monuments
- Towns with Famous Natives
- Making Connections

THE TEN BIGGEST CITIES IN TEXAS

It began on the banks of the Trinity

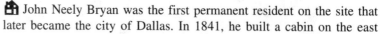

John Neely Bryan was the first permanent resident on the site that later became the city of Dallas. In 1841, he built a cabin on the east bank of the Trinity River. It served as the first courtroom and the first post office in Dallas. Historical stories also say that Bryan plowed his sod with the fork of a *bois d'arc* tree and crossed the river in a dugout canoe. Bryan's wooden cabin (left) can be seen today, surrounded by skyscrapers, in downtown Dallas. The city that Bryan started is now part of the Dallas/Fort Worth Metroplex that covers 100 miles and is home to over 4,000,000 people. Today, Dallas/Fort Worth International Airport serves as one of the world's largest airports, shuffling more than 2,000 international and domestic flights every day to and from more than 200 worldwide destinations. The well-known facility is actually located in Grapevine, Irving, Euless, and Fort Worth.

Washers for rent

Fort Worth is hailed as the birthplace of the washateria. In 1934, as the story goes, J.E. Cantrell installed four washing machines in an empty building. He rented the washers out by the hour to any housewife who couldn't afford an electric washing machine of her own. Cantrell's idea obviously spread to every city and town in the nation.

When cotton was king

Between 1849 and 1850 Texas produced 58,072 bales of cotton, with most of the crop coming from the river valleys of the Coastal Plain and the bottomlands of East Texas. As cotton fields extended into Central Texas, production increased. In 1860 the state recorded 431,463 bales, and by the turn of the century, Galveston had grown into the nation's leading cotton port.

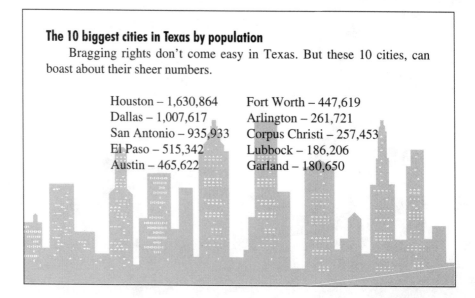

The 10 biggest cities in Texas by population

Bragging rights don't come easy in Texas. But these 10 cities, can boast about their sheer numbers.

Houston – 1,630,864	Fort Worth – 447,619
Dallas – 1,007,617	Arlington – 261,721
San Antonio – 935,933	Corpus Christi – 257,453
El Paso – 515,342	Lubbock – 186,206
Austin – 465,622	Garland – 180,650

William O. Douglas called Austin's Hamilton Pool "the three most beautiful acres in Texas." Most Texans know the place as one of the best swimming holes in the Lone Star State. It comes complete with emerald green water, a 50-foot waterfall, and remnants of a cavern's ceiling. Once owned by the Reimers family, the summer cool spot is now managed by Travis County, gateway to Texas Hill Country.

Beating the Texas heat

The Texas State Cemetery in Austin was officially established in 1879 and provides the final resting place for many illustrious Texans. Folklorist J. Frank Dobie, buried there in 1964, was one of the first exceptions to the Texas Legislature's rules that limited plots to state officials. Founding father Stephen F. Austin, who was buried at Peach Point in Brazoria County in 1836, was disinterred and brought to the State Cemetery on October 18, 1910. Other Texas notables buried there include former governors "Ma" and "Pa" Ferguson and prolific author Walter Prescott Webb. But none of the four presidents of the Republic of Texas are interred at the Texas State Cemetery. David G. Burnet is buried in Galveston, and Sam Houston is interred at Huntsville. Mirabeau B. Lamar is buried at Richmond's Morton Cemetery. Anson Jones rests in Houston.

Rest in peace

Big in any language

Texas' westernmost city, El Paso, is situated in the mountain pass from which it gets its name. Juan Maria Ponce de Leon organized four civilian settlements in the area in 1827, although there were Spanish missions in the area long before. Corpus Christi de La Isleta at El Paso (now called Ysleta Mission, shown at right) is Texas' oldest mission and was built in 1861 for the Tigua Indians. It was south of the Rio Grande then, but because of changes in the river's channel it's in Texas now! *Sierra de Cristo Rey* (the Mountain of Christ) rises high above El Paso (4,576 feet) where Mexico, Texas, and New Mexico meet. A statue at the summit, *Christ on the Cross* by Urbici Soler, is made from Cordova cream limestone from a quarry near Austin. Just across the Rio Grande from El Paso sits its twin city, Ciudad Juárez, Mexico. Together, these two cities reportedly form the largest bilingual, bicultural metropolis on any international border in the world.

Memories of the music

🏠 Quakers settled the region around Lubbock in 1879. But, the community of Lubbock was established in 1890-1891 when the old town of Lubbock and Monterey merged and moved to a nearby location. It is named for Tom S. Lubbock (1817-62), a signer of the Texas Declaration of Independence. Lubbock's favorite son, rock 'n' roller Buddy Holly, was killed in an airplane crash on February 3, 1959. Music historians call it "the day the music died." Holly's contributions and those of other entertainers who hailed from West Texas are remembered at the Buddy Holly Statue and Walk of Fame in Lubbock.

Justice of Garland's peace

Back in the 1840s, Garland was just a small settlement on Duck Creek east of Dallas. In 1886, the Gulf, Colorado & Santa Fe Railroad built a depot about a mile east of the community. The company named it Embree, and citizens quickly moved homes and businesses to be near the depot. When the Missouri, Kansas & Texas Railroad erected a depot about one-half mile north of Duck Creek, other citizens took up residence there, calling it New Duck Creek. A bitter rivalry ensued between the two communities until Judge Thomas F. Nash stepped in to make peace. He persuaded U.S. Congressman Joe Abbott to influence the placement of the post office. The peace-making idea worked. With the post office located halfway between Embree and New Duck Creek, the towns merged in 1891 to become Garland. The city of Garland was named for Augustus Hill Garland, attorney general under President Grover Cleveland.

Then and now

🏠 Forty-two men of Company F, commanded by General Winfield Scott, organized a military camp on June 6, 1849, after the Mexican War. This settlement—Fort Worth—was named for General William Jenkins Worth, an officer in the Mexican War. George Leroy Parker and Harry Longbaugh, better known as Butch Cassidy and the Sundance Kid, took a liking to the city almost 50 years later in 1898. That year they established the headquarters of their "Hole in the Wall Gang" in Hell's Half Acre, located along Main Street near present-day Tenth Street. The saloons and dance halls provided entertainment for the boys before they went to Argentina and died during a shootout. Those hangouts have since been replaced. Today, Sundance Square, named for the trigger-happy kid—and the brainchild of Fort Worth developer Sam Bass—bustles with businesses that attract locals and tourists alike. A luxury hotel, office complex, and specialty shops in restored buildings cater to a more genteel clientele in this century.

Water, water everywhere

🏠 Begun as a trading post in 1839 by Colonel Henry Lawrence Kinney, Corpus Christi is a major international port today—the sixth-busiest in the nation. Located along Nueces Bay, Corpus Christi Bay, and the Gulf of Mexico, the city was named for the pass between St. Joseph and Mustang Islands. Apparently the citizens in Corpus Christi don't have enough water—they want more and more. At the city's Bayfront Arts and Science Park, the Watergarden spouts 150 fountains into the air.

San Antonio's rich past fills the city with history. Native Americans established a village at the southern limit of Texas Hill Country around 1718, in an area of streams and woods. When Spaniards came to the area, they built Mission San Antonio de Valero—today we call it the Alamo. The *presidio* (fort) built near the mission was named San Antonio de Béxar. The first civilian settlement began in 1731 when a Spanish villa was built. Texas settlers came all the way from Spain's Canary Islands and colonized the area.

Much of San Antonio's history can be seen today along a 2.6-mile walking tour that begins and ends at the most historic Texas landmark of all—the Alamo. Blue disks embedded in sidewalks designate the Texas Star Trail, which includes almost 100 historic sites.

A historic walk in San Antonio

A party in any language

Fiesta Texas in San Antonio celebrates Texas cultures and music in a 200-acre theme park that includes railroads and restaurants, theaters and amusement rides. Set in a limestone quarry surrounded by 100-foot cliffs, the park features four themed areas. Los Festivales highlights the state's Mexican and Spanish influences. Crackaxle Canyon remembers the boom towns of the 1920s. Spassburg (*spass* means "fun") pays tribute to German heritage. Rockville recalls the nostalgic days of Texas during the 1950s. It's a Texas-size party for the whole family.

A mortician's favorite town

In Houston, the Funeral Service Museum touts the largest collection of funeral service memorabilia in the nation. Among the horse-drawn hearses and Civil War cast-iron caskets, turn-of-the-century embalming artifacts are also on display. There's even a 1915 Packard "mourning bus" that transported casket, pallbearers, and 20 mourners. It traveled at a top speed of 15 miles per hour.

Bird's Fort was established in 1845 at Mary le Bone Springs in Caddo territory, marking the very beginnings of Arlington. When the railroad came through about 1876, the town relocated to its present site. Things move a lot faster in Arlington these days. At Six Flags Over Texas, the massive wooden roller coaster known as the Texas Giant climbs 143 feet into the air and leaves passengers breathless when it reaches a top speed of 62 miles per hour. The thriller has twice been voted the top roller coaster in the world.

Hang on tight

CAPITAL CLAIMS

How sweet it is

🏠 No one disputes Poteet's claim as the "Strawberry Capital of Texas." Each year the South Texas town produces nearly half of all the sweet red strawberries grown in the state. That amounts to about 500,000 pints of strawberries annually. In honor of the big berry harvest, townsfolk erected the world's largest strawberry. The monument stands six feet tall and weighs 1,600 pounds.

Staking multiple claims

🏠 In Amarillo, a six-story, stainless-steel time column was erected in 1968 to pay tribute to the town's helium heritage. Known as the "Helium Capital of the World," Amarillo does indeed lead the globe with its quantities of the inert gas. The city is also known as home to Texas' largest livestock auction. More than 600,000 head of cattle move through the stockyard ring annually.

Aunt Jemima lived here

🏠 In the small town of Hawkins, Lillian Richard is probably the most famous deceased resident. Richard is better known as one of the numerous women who portrayed Aunt Jemima for the Quaker Oats Company. She was born in Hawkins in 1891 and buried there in 1956. No one knows exactly how she landed the part as Aunt Jemima, but she was cast as the character for more than 40 years. In 1994, when Hawkins residents discovered that Richard had starred in the nationally known role, town leaders began a movement to promote their famous citizen. Aunt Jemima memorabilia found its way onto the shelves at local shops, and the town approached the state to be officially designated the "Pancake Capital of Texas." While some citizens see the opportunity to boost tourism in the rural town and bring in much-needed dollars, others say the mammy stereotype of Aunt Jemima is better left in the past. As of September 1994, the issue still had not been decided. But one of the residents in favor of capitalizing on the Aunt Jemima connection is Jewel McCalla, Richard's niece.

Roses for the world

🏠 The nation's largest rose showplace can be found at the Municipal Rose Garden & Museum in the East Texas city of Tyler. About 38,000 rose bushes flourish in the 22-acre garden, making Tyler the "Rose Capital of the World." Nearly 500 varieties of roses are represented, including the blushing "Lady Bird Johnson" rose introduced in Tyler. The roses around Tyler aren't just for show, however. Commercial growers ship hundreds of thousands of rose bushes to nurseries throughout the United States and 25 foreign countries.

🏠 Terlingua, on the western edge of Big Bend National Park, could be considered the "Quicksilver Capital of Texas," but that was many years ago. In about 1890, a couple of cattle wranglers discovered cinnabar, a brilliant red ore that yields mercury, or quicksilver. In 1917, at the height of the Terlingua mercury boom, mines produced 10,791 three-quart (76-pound) flasks of quicksilver worth millions. The end of the boom spelled the end of Terlingua, too—until 1967. That year, the International Championship Chili Cookoff came to the ghost town. Amid the crumbling rock and adobe buildings, about 5,000 "chili-heads" now gather each autumn to compare and judge "bowls of red." The weekend of hot competition has earned Terlingua the title of "Chili Capital of the World."

Two in one

🏠 City promoters call Beaumont the "Museum Capital of Texas," and they may be right. First, visitors can tour the Babe Didrikson Zaharias Museum & Visitors' Information Center where photos, trophies, and memorabilia honor the most famous sportswoman in Texas history. The Edison Plaza Museum claims to offer the "largest collection of Thomas A. Edison artifacts west of the Mississippi," including a 1905 cylinder phonograph. The Old Central Fire Station built in 1927 houses the Fire Museum of Texas. On display is the search and light truck on which young newspaper reporter Walter Cronkite hitched a ride to the New London School explosion site in 1937. Robotic exhibits liven up the Spindletop Museum that honors the historic oil field, and the Gladys City Museum re-creates the world's first oil boom town, complete with clapboard buildings, saloon, and wooden oil derricks. For the artistic, there's the Art Museum of Southeast Texas and the Dishman Art Gallery. Even the oldest house in the city has been converted into a museum. The John Jay French House Museum dates back to 1845 when the tanner and merchant came to the area.

A museum on every corner

THE NAME GAME

🏠 Judging from the names of many towns, Texas is a heavenly place. There's Elysian Fields, with a blissful population of about 300. There's also the town of Star in Mills County, with an estimated population of 85 residents in 1994. Venus may be known in other states as the most brilliant planet. In Texas, however, it's a town of about 900 in Johnson County. Altair got its name from the largest star in the constellation Alpha Aquilae. But the towns of Eden, Utopia, and Paradise are blessed with the most divine names in the state.

Heaven on earth

Weather phenomena

In the winter of 1850, surveyors accidentally misnamed the little town of Zephyr in Brown County. A blue norther descended with blustery winds as the original land grants were being plotted. Confusing his weather definitions, one surveyor commented on the winter storm, "This is some zephyr we have run into." Zephyr is defined as a soft, gentle breeze or westerly wind, but the surveyor's misnomer made history when the town chose Zephyr as its name.

AWESOME

Translation, please

Native American, Spanish, Aztec, German, even Latin words have contributed to the descriptive naming of Texas towns. Most of the time, the foreign words sound more poetic than the translation.

Anahuac – Aztec for "plain near the water"
Aspermont – Latin words *asper*, meaning "rough," and *mont*, for "mountain"
Concan – Mexican gambling game
Danevang – Dutch for "Danish meadow"
Elmaton – Spanish for "the killer"
Helotes – Native American word for "green roasting ear of corn"
Tahoka – Native American word for "deep water" or "clear water"
Tehuacana – Wichita word for "three canes"
Thalia – Latin for "blooming"
Waka – Shortened version of Native American word *wawaka* for "swampy or wet ground"
Waxahachie – Native American word for "cow creek" or, some say, "cow chip"

It could have been greenbacks

E.H.R. Green, president of the Texas Midland Railroad, wanted to name a Hunt County community in honor of J.A. Money. Money, a railroad promoter, store owner, and modest man, politely declined the offer. He agreed instead to the use of the synonym—Cash.

A toasty town

Cereal magnate C.W. Post, creator of Post Toasties, moved to Texas in 1906. He took up residence near the Cap Rock and amassed some 400,000 acres of land. Post also spent more than $50,000 trying to bring rain to arid West Texas using experiments with dynamite. In July 1907, his namesake town of Post became the county seat of Garza County.

Mistaken identity

Local folks in Brown County thought Cross Out was an appropriate name for their new post office. It was across the county and out of the way of usual travel. But when the town submitted the name for approval, a case of mistaken identity occurred. The "O" in Out became a "C," and so the name turned out to be Cross Cut, which remained when the post office opened on April 9, 1879.

Sunny side up

Texas is famous for its hot summers, so it seems only fitting that half a dozen towns would honor the source of all that heat. There's Sunray, Sun Valley, Sunrise Beach, and Sunset Valley. Of course there's Sunrise and Sunset, too. And since the sun must rise and set somewhere, what better place than Horizon City in El Paso County?

Not the green frog

Kermit, the county seat of Winkler County in West Texas, took its name from Kermit Roosevelt, President Teddy Roosevelt's son.

A literal name

Nogalus in Trinity County got its name because the town lacked money to build a gallows. Horse thieves and other evildoers were put to death by being hanged from a tree limb. The town was known originally as Nogallows. When the post office was established in 1858, the town became Nogallis Prairie. In 1894, the town's modern name of Nogalus finally stuck.

CLAIMS TO FAME

In the 1920s, Niles City occupied only 1-1/2 square miles of real estate, but it was known as the "richest little town in the world." The tiny town boasted a tax base of $30 million from the contributions of such businesses as a petroleum refinery, meat-packing plants, a cottonseed oil company, grain elevators, and the Fort Worth Stockyards. Niles City used every legal maneuver possible to stop the big city of Fort Worth from taking over. In 1923, however, Fort Worth prevailed, incorporating its diminutive neighbor—and the now famous stockyards.

Ill-fated fame

Colonel Theodore Roosevelt rode a horse named "Texas" while charging his Rough Riders into the Spanish-American War. The horse was sired in Seguin and acquired by Roosevelt in 1898 when he was in San Antonio. Northwest of Seguin in Amarillo, the American Quarter Horse Heritage Center & Museum serves as headquarters for the world's largest equine registry. More than 2.6 million quarter horses are registered in 53 countries.

Horse notes

On September 15, 1896, about 30,000 witnesses gathered a few miles south of West for an unusual railroad event—the collision of two full-speed locomotives. William G. Crush, a passenger agent for the Missouri, Kansas and Texas Railroad, conceived the publicity stunt. Spectators were assured that the feat posed no danger, but 200 special deputies were brought in to maintain order. Onlookers still managed to slip past rope barriers for a closer view of the impending action. Finally, two 35-ton locomotives with throttles pre-set rushed toward each other at more than 60 miles per hour. They crashed head-on just as Crush had planned. Upon impact, the steam boilers unexpectedly exploded, hurling metal into the crowd. Two people were killed and many others injured. Crush was fired by the railroad, but rehired the next day. The temporary tent town, which came to be known as Crush City, quickly disappeared after the destructive spectacle. The incident, however, chugged on into Texas history. It inspired ragtime musician and Texarkana native Scott Joplin to compose "The Crash at Crush."

Fleeting fame

During the Civil War, the East Texas town of Marshall was the wartime capital of Missouri. Supplies, such as powder and ammunition, saddles, and clothing, were produced here for the Confederates. It was also headquarters for the Trans-Mississippi Postal Department.

Capital of Missouri in Texas

Oldest Polish hometown   🏠 On December 24, 1854, 800 Polish immigrants from Upper Silesia established a colony in Karnes County and named it *Panna Maria*, meaning "Virgin Mary." The Catholic Poles walked 200 miles from the port of Galveston to arrive at their new home. Today, Panna Maria is recognized as the nation's oldest continuous Polish settlement.

The march of Dime   🏠 The Lee County town of Dime Box, population 313, gained national fame in 1943. It was the first U.S. town to "contribute 100 percent" to the March of Dimes. The town's unusual name, by the way, came from the community mailbox. Freighters and teamsters passing through the town in the late 1800s carried mail to residents, requesting a service charge of 10 cents for each letter delivered.

A few famous firsts

It seems more "firsts" occurred in Galveston than in any other Texas town or city. The city claims to have instituted the first country club and golf course in the state in 1895. On January 21, 1871, the Galveston Chamber of Commerce opened the first public library in Texas. The state's first electrical power plant was erected in the early 1880s in Galveston. And the list goes on: first electric lights, first convent, first private bank, first nursing school, first chamber of commerce, first jewelry store, first telegraph, and first medical school.
But a few firsts did take place in other locales.

- Jefferson in Marion County was the first Texas town to use natural gas for illumination. Legend says that the first beer made in Texas was brewed in Jefferson. The first commercial production of ice in Texas also took place in Jefferson, probably to help keep the beer cold.
- El Paso landed the first cigar factory in the southwest when Ernst and Moritz Kohlberg established the International Cigar Company in 1886.
- At San Antonio's Menger Hotel, Theodore Roosevelt recruited his first Rough Riders. The Roosevelt Bar in the present-day hotel is named in his honor.
- Fort Worth lays claim to the first domed-roof arena built in the United States. Known as Will Rogers Coliseum (below), it was constructed for the 1936 Texas Centennial celebration held in the city. Fort Worth's Herbert Hinckly designed the historic arena.

- Isaac Merritt Singer, inventor of the Singer sewing machine, sent one of his inventions to his niece on Padre Island in 1861. It was the first Singer sewing machine in the state.
- The city of Houston issued its first traffic ticket in 1903. T. Brady was caught exceeding the six-miles-per-hour speed limit on Main Street and fined $10.
- Texas City had the first tin smelter on the North American continent. It was opened during World War II by the federal government and later sold to a private company.

RANDOM HISTORIES

Of camels and presidents

Camels helped the town of Victoria stake a place in history. The War Department sent 34 of the African animals to Texas in April 1856. The idea was to see if the beasts could be used as pack animals in campaigns against the Indians. The camels were caravanning to Camp Verde, south of present-day Kerrville, when they made a stop in Victoria. They were clipped during the stopover, and Mrs. Mary Shirkey spun a pair of socks from the hair. She presented the socks to U.S. President Franklin Pierce, who returned the favor by sending Mrs. Shirkey a silver goblet.

A wave of Czechs from across the Atlantic

In the early 1850s, a wave of Central European emigrants left their homeland in what would eventually become Czechoslovakia and sailed across the Atlantic to Galveston. They stocked up on supplies and moved inland, settling such towns as Cat Spring, Sealy, and Frydek. Fayetteville became known as the cradle of Czech settlement in the state. The terrain was hilly, and fertile soil made for prosperous farming in the lowlands. Letters home enticed more Czechs to immigrate to the new land of Texas by the thousands. Today, Texas boasts the largest rural Czech population in the United States. Folks oom-pa-pa their way through a weekend each May when Ennis hosts the National Polka Festival. Big-band polka groups gather with their brass and accordions, and dancers roam from polka hall to polka hall as everyone celebrates the national dance of Czechoslovakia deep in the heart of Texas.

©Paige Bridges

An entertaining family

Along Highway 80 in Wills Point, the marquee at the Majestic Theatre (above) still shines brightly. It first lit up in 1907 when the Lybrand family opened the movie house. Today Karl Lybrand III keeps the movies rolling, pops the popcorn, and oversees what has become the oldest family-owned theater in Texas. Modern-day Wills Pointers can enjoy the latest blockbuster hits for a mere $3 admission ticket.

End of the line

In cities and towns up and down the Union Pacific Railroad line, cabooses stand idle as testament to a passing time. In the early 1980s, the company began using an electronic end-of-train device that is making the traditional caboose obsolete. The device transmits information to the engine crew—a job once handled by the caboose conductor. With high-tech electronics replacing cabooses, Union Pacific found itself with a surplus of the cars. The company decided to donate the cabooses to civic organizations in cities along the railroad line. The caboose giveaway started in 1987 and ended in 1990 when Union Pacific ran out of free cabooses. East Texas communities, such as Wills Point, Forney, Edgewood, and Mineola, were a few on the long list of towns that latched onto the cars. The cabooses now sit alongside the tracks serving as visitor centers, chambers of commerce, and local souvenir shops.

AWESOME

MOVERS AND SHAKERS

Safe harbor

Between 1907 and 1914, the Galveston Movement brought 10,000 Jewish immigrants to Texas through the port of Galveston. Historians say that Rabbi Henry Cohen met every ship at the pier. Fondly and respectfully known as the "rabbi of Texas," Cohen served as the director of the Jewish Immigrants Information Bureau during those years. He helped the new arrivals find jobs, shelter, and transportation. He helped them locate new homes in other Texas cities and in the Midwest. At the request of the American secretary of state in 1914, Cohen directed aid to American citizens who were victims of the Mexican Revolution. The tide of immigrants stopped when war erupted in 1914, but Cohen's work continued. He persuaded President Woodrow Wilson to appoint Jewish chaplains in the armed forces, and in Texas he worked for prison reform. Cohen retired in 1949. Three years later he died.

Buying time

Residents of Wichita Falls voted a bond issue for civic improvements in 1920, only to find that tax revenues weren't enough to redeem the bonds. Mayor Walter D. Cline thought he solved the problem when he doubled city taxes. The citizens rebelled. In response to the protest, Cline and a buddy offered to purchase the property of every resident in town. The offer impressed Waco citizens and boosted their confidence in the city's future. Without further ado, they accepted the tax increase.

Big bird
Fort Stockton in far West Texas claims the world's largest roadrunner. Known as Paisano Pete, the big bird stretches 20 feet long and stands 11 feet tall.

MONUMENTAL MONUMENTS

Towering replica

The world's tallest windmill stands in the Lamb County town of Littlefield. Actually, it's a replica of a wooden, 132-foot-tall windmill that once stood in *El Canyon de las Casas Amarillas* (The Canyon of the Yellow Houses). The original, constructed on the XIT ranch in 1887, was blown down on Thanksgiving Day, 1926. The replica towers 114 feet to the axis of the 12-foot windmill.

The most famous horned lizard of all

One Texas town made a hero of a Texas horned lizard (also known as a "horny toad"). In 1897, Eastland County built a new courthouse. At the building's dedication, Ernest Wood reputedly placed a live horny toad in the cornerstone. In 1928, word spread that authorities were about to demolish the old courthouse and open the cornerstone. On February 28, 1928, 31 years after the live lizard had been tucked away, 3,000 spectators gathered to watch the cornerstone opening. Oilman Eugene Day reached into the stone and lifted out a dusty horny toad. The lizard twitched to life, or so the stories say, and the legend of "Old Rip" was born. Named in honor of Rip Van Winkle, the horny toad of Eastland County made history. It toured the country, but fell ill with pneumonia and died in January 1929. The remains of Old Rip were laid to rest, but stolen in 1973. Today, a stand-in for the most famous lizard of Texas rests peacefully under glass in a small, open casket in the Eastland County courthouse—a monument to Texas folklore.

TOWNS WITH FAMOUS NATIVES

🏠 Frank "Bring 'Em Back Alive" Buck, the famed adventurer and wild animal trainer, was born in Gainesville on St. Patrick's Day in 1884. In 1911, he made the first of many expeditions to South America. He didn't dawdle when at home either. He often served as ringmaster for the three-ring circus that was founded and produced by Gainesville residents. When fire destroyed the circus big top in 1954, the wild animals formed the beginning of the Frank Buck Zoo. The zoo still operates today in Buck's hometown.

Lions and tigers and bears

Tribute to stubbornness

The residents of Muleshoe in the Texas Panhandle decided tribute should be paid to the hardy animals that helped settle the Wild West. Mules—sterile crosses between female horses and male donkeys—pulled covered wagons, plowed the sod, and worked on the expansion of the railroads. Contributions to help finance the National Mule Memorial came from across the country. A clergyman in Muleshoe made a trip to Russia and returned with a donation from a mule driver in Samarkand, Uzbekistan. The contribution amounted to 21 cents in American money. Although the original plan called for a statue cast in bronze, fiberglass was chosen because donations would cover the cost. On July 3, 1965, at a ceremony that included a mule parade down Main Street, the city unveiled a life-size statue of a mule. It stood five hands high and the accompanying plaque read in part, "Without ancestral pride or hope of offspring, he made history."

🏠 Grand Saline's native son Wiley Post saw his first airplane at a county fair when he was only 14 years old. Before he turned 25, he was barnstorming at fairs and exhibitions. On June 23, 1931, Post took off in his plane, the *Winnie Mae*, and completed an around-the-globe flight in 8 days, 15 hours, and 51 minutes. Four years later, in August 1935, Post and his close friend, humorist Will Rogers, were killed when their plane crashed in Alaska. The plane, piloted by Post, experienced engine failure while trying to take off from a small village.

Flying high

🏠 The Flying Tigers were an elite group of American flyers who battled the Japanese in China before and during World War II. Major General Claire L. Chennault commanded the Tigers in the late 1930s and early 1940s. He was born in Commerce in 1890.

Major native son

🏠 Two Texas governors were born in the city of Rusk in Cherokee County. James Stephen Hogg served as governor from January 20, 1891, to January 15, 1895. Thomas M. Campbell was governor from January 15, 1907, until January 19, 1911.

Big on governors

MAKING CONNECTIONS

The check's in the mail

The Texas Provisional Government established a permanent post office department in December 1835. But few folks could afford the luxury of writing letters. In 1836, it cost 6-1/4 cents to send a letter up to 20 miles; 12-1/2 cents for the next 30 miles; and a whopping 37-1/2 cents for any distance greater than 200 miles. The rates covered a single sheet of paper that was folded and addressed. Those who did pay up were often disappointed with the service. In 1840, on the Houston-to-Austin route, the carrier's mule ran off with the postal bags, which were never recovered.

Working on the railroad

The country around the Lower Pecos River remained an unsettled frontier until the early 1880s. In 1882, the Southern Pacific Railroad completed a bridge across the Pecos River. On January 12 of the next year, the first southern transcontinental railroad was completed. At Dead Man's Gulch, about a mile north of the mouth of the Pecos River, a silver spike joined the east and west sections of the historic railroad.

A station that chugged into history

In 1906, El Paso Union Station opened for business and became the nation's first international union station. The Santa Fe, the Southern Pacific, the Texas and Pacific, and the Nacional de México formed the historic union. During the first year of operation, 22 trains arrived and departed each day. Legendary railroads such as the Apache, the Arizonian, and the Texas Eagle stopped at the station for supplies, water, and passengers. The impressive building design, with its red-brick walls, lofty spire, and green slate roof, drew criticism from many El Paso citizens. So in 1941, a low, red-tiled roof was placed atop the spire and white paint covered the red bricks. The city of El Paso later purchased the station. In 1982 a completed restoration project returned the station to its original beauty and earned the building a listing on the National Register of Historic Places.

Crossing the Brazos River

The Waco Suspension Bridge opened for business in January 1870, 13 years before New York City's Brooklyn Bridge came into being. It was the first suspension bridge in Texas, the only span across the Brazos River at the time, and it changed life in Waco forever. As people migrated west after the Civil War, the bridge was a safe crossing site on the Brazos. Waco businesses expanded with the influx of people. Sales of horses, mules, supplies, and equipment boomed. When the bridge opened, Waco's population was about 3,000 people. In 10 years that figure jumped to more than 7,200. After serving as a toll bridge from 1870 to 1889, McLennan County bought the structure. The county then transferred it to the City of Waco, which let people cross for free. The bridge closed for major reconstruction during 1913, reopening in 1914. When the great bridge retired in 1971, it was placed on the National Register of Historic Places. Today, it serves only pedestrian traffic in a park east of the Waco central business district.

TAKING CARE OF BUSINESS

Step into the corporate offices of Texas business and you're likely to find yourself smack in the middle of a cattle herd, standing next to an oil rig, surrounded by computers, or witness to a leveraged buyout. The industry of the Lone Star State is as varied as the entrepreneurs and wheeler-dealers who built the state and continue to bring in the bucks. From agricultural crops to the newest electronic technology, there's business to be done in Texas.

Come meet the millionaires, the inventors, the financiers, and the folks down on the farm who take care of business in the Lone Star State.

RICHES FROM THE LAND

The big boom in East Texas

💲By 1930, major companies and major drillers had declared East Texas void of oil. But veteran wildcatter Columbus "Dad" Joiner had a vision. He drilled for four years in Rusk County before the Daisy Bradford No. 3 came in on October 3, 1930, near Henderson. Joiner and his backers had discovered the East Texas Oil Field, the world's largest oil field at the time. It was 42 miles long, extending into Kilgore, Longview, and farther north, and covered 200 square miles. Since its discovery, the gigantic field has produced more than 5 billion barrels of oil and supported 32,000 wells. Wells continue to pump today, and some say another billion barrels of black gold still waits beneath the surface.

Too much oil

By mid-1931, the oil production frenzy caused prices to fall to about 10 cents a barrel (a barrel is 42 gallons). Drinking water, however, was selling for 10 cents a gallon.

From boom to bust

The Texas oil patch paid no attention to the national economy's decline in the early 1980s. Crude oil prices continued to rise even after the Arab oil embargo ended in the 1970s. Oil operators, backed by lending institutions, drilled in every conceivable location throughout the state. The price of oil peaked in mid-1980. By 1981, Texas counted 1,317 working rigs, and oil accounted for about 27 percent of the state's gross product. But in early 1982, the national economic slump slid into Texas. By 1986, only 311 rigs were drilling oil, and lending institutions toppled when operators reneged on loan payments. The industry begin to recover from the roller-coaster ride in 1989, and in early 1991, oil was again sitting at the top of Texas as the fastest-growing industry in the state. Today the industry accounts for only about 12 percent of the state's economy, but the boom and bust and boom again oil history continues in Texas.

What's in a name?

To Texans, oil was called Cadillac crude, Texas tea, and black gold. The workers who drilled the wells, usually known as roughnecks, also took on lively monikers. Job titles in the oil fields ranged from stud duck, meaning the big boss, to boll weevil, referring to a newcomer to the operation. In between were the tool pushers, shooters, boomers, and roustabouts.

Oldest cow show in the country

💲Fort Worth's Southwestern Exposition and Livestock Show started in 1896 when a few of North Texas' more notable ranchers gathered to compare their animals. That friendly competition evolved into the oldest continuing annual livestock show in the nation. The show closed its doors during only one year, 1943, when World War II activities required use of all city facilities. Today, the event spreads over 100 acres and fills 17 days with exhibitions of ranch equipment and Western art, chuck-wagon cooking demonstrations, sales of cowhand clothes, 28 rodeos, and traditional livestock judging and auctions. Each year, winners of the livestock competitions and rodeo events pocket more than $600,000 in prize money.

The legend of Monkey lives on

Richard King established his cattle empire in 1853 when he purchased 75,000 acres of a former Spanish land grant called Santa Gertrudis. Today, his descendants manage the largest ranch in the continental United States, 825,000 acres that stretch across four counties. The ranch feedlot alone holds 15,000 head, and 65,000 acres of farmland produce the feed. It was here on the coastal prairies of the King Ranch that Bob Kleberg developed a kind of cattle that wouldn't wilt under the sweltering Texas sun. He crossed Brahman with British Shorthorns. The result was Santa Gertrudis, and in 1940 it was named the first American beef breed. The world supply of Santa Gertrudis can be traced back to Monkey, the foundation sire. His mounted head surveys the offices of the Santa Gertrudis Breeders International, across the road from the King Ranch headquarters. It seems fitting that the famed King Ranch was declared a National Historic Landmark in 1961.

Lumbering along in East Texas

$ After the Civil War, the most abundant and obvious natural resource of East Texas became its best-selling product. The seemingly endless expanse of virgin forest was cut down, sawed up, and shipped out as the region grew into an economic giant. Lumber production became the state's first significant manufacturing industry with new sawmills cropping up every month. In 1899, East Texas lumber production surpassed 1 billion board feet per year, and within a few years, the figure doubled. Beaumont and Orange gained national reputations as sawmill centers by 1900. Production across East Texas peaked in 1907, then faltered. As the 100-year-old pines and ageless hardwoods diminished, the lumber industry shrank along with the forests. Modern-day Texas sawmills now produce about 1 million board feet of lumber annually. Timber consistently ranks among the top four cash crops, with an estimated annual value of $550 million.

Sweet and sour tooth

$ In 1929, nurserymen A.E. Henninger of Mission and J.R. Webb of Donna flipped a coin to see who would claim the patent on a new strain of grapefruit. Henninger won the coin toss and named the grapefruit "Ruby Red" for its rose-colored meat. The now-famous grapefruit evolved from grafting the wood of "Thompson Pink" onto the rootstock of "Sour Orange" grapefruit and growing the plant in the saline-alkaline soil of the Rio Grande Valley.

Six record crop harvests
Wheat – 7,310,000 acres in 1947
Sugar beets – 874,000 tons in 1968
Peanuts – 533,025,000 pounds in 1979
Hay – 6,147,000 tons in 1979
Eggs – 3,014,000,000 in 1944
Cotton – 5,628,000 bales in 1926

Heard through the grapevine

$ Frank Qualia, an immigrant from northern Italy, founded the Val Verde Winery at Del Rio in 1883. By 1910, 225 out of 254 Texas counties reported grape production. But in 1919, the states ratified the 18th Amendment to the U.S. Constitution, prohibiting the manufacture, transport, and sales of intoxicating beverages. Wineries across Texas closed. Only the Val Verde operation survived, growing fruit for table grapes, jams, and jellies. The oldest producing winery in the state, Val Verde has been owned and operated by the Qualia family since its founding.

French wine with a Texas twang

The modern vineyards of France have an unusual and life-saving connection to Texas. Thomas Volney Munson arrived in the northeast Texas town of Denison in April 1876 and discovered wild grapes growing on a patch of wooded land he tended along the Red River. He built a successful nursery business, but more important, he became an authority on native wild grapes in North America. In the 1860s, a devastating disease known as phylloxera caused grape vines in France to die. No one found a solution until Munson grafted French vines onto phylloxera-resistant American rootstock. The combination worked so well that French growers imported massive quantities of Texas and other American rootstock during the 1880s and 1890s. The French wine industry survived thanks to Munson. In honor of his work, Munson was named to the French Legion of Honor in 1888. He was only the second American, after Thomas Edison, to be accorded the honor.

Snap, crackle, pop

David French and his family poked a few rice seeds into the gummy, black soil around Beaumont in 1863. The seeds took root, and French harvested the first documented rice crop in Texas. Today, rice fields spread across about 20 counties on the coastal prairies, and the crop's value hovers around $150 million annually.

Uncle Ben's, Inc.—known for its famous "converted" rice—is headquartered in Houston, Texas.

GREAT EXPECTATIONS

Sweet dreams

Daniel Haynes lived in Austin County in the 1880s when he got an idea for getting a good night's sleep. He invented a process and a machine for producing a cotton mattress, the predecessor of modern bedding. Haynes founded his business and named it after the town where he first produced his cotton bedding. Today, the company is known as Sealy Mattress Company.

The canned dairyman

Gail Borden, Jr., was born in New York and arrived in Texas in 1829. He had only a year and a half of formal education, but his active mind thirsted for knowledge. While in Texas he published the state's first permanent newspaper, the *Telegraph and Texas Register*. Borden also hatched schemes for such inventions as a wind-powered wagon and a portable bathhouse for women. In 1850, he spent his fortune on a meat biscuit. The ill-fated sandwich led him into bankruptcy. Moving to the Northeast, his claim to fame came in 1856 when he received a patent for condensing milk in a vacuum and opened a plant in Connecticut. The invention sputtered financially until the Civil War broke out and Union troops needed milk that wouldn't spoil. Borden's sales soared. Although Borden left Texas for the northeast with his condensed milk plan, he returned after the Civil War. He died on January 11, 1874. Texans named the county of "Borden" and its county seat "Gail" in honor of this famous milk maker.

A sodbuster's idea

Ole Ringness, the son of a Norwegian immigrant, lived near the town of Norse and developed a model for a disk plow and a disk harrow. The farming implements were designed to replace the heavy standard plow used by most early Texas sodbusters. In 1872, Ringness headed to New York to patent his agricultural inventions, but was murdered before he could lay claim to the designs.

A secretary's hero

James Field Smathers of Llano County invented the first electric typewriter between 1909 and 1914. A royalty agreement with the Northeast Electric Company of New York in the 1920s allowed production of the machine through a subsidiary known as Electric Typewriters. In 1933, International Business Machines Corporation bought the typewriter manufacturer. The purchase launched IBM's Office Products Division and secured a career for Smathers. He worked at IBM for the next 15 years as a development engineer and consultant.

$ Others had tried before. But in 1928, John Daniel Rust of Weatherford succeeded in building the first important mechanical cotton picker. The horse-drawn contraption was known appropriately as the Rust Cotton Picker. In 1929, Rust redesigned the machine into a self-propelled model powered by a Model T motor. He built a tractor model in 1935 and made additional improvements in 1937. That year, his invention managed to pick a whopping 13 bales of cotton in a single day.

The mechanics of picking cotton

$ After experimenting with different formulas in her kitchen, Dallas artist Bette Graham finally found a paint mixture that would cover typing mistakes almost invisibly. In 1951, the working mother developed Liquid Paper and founded the multimillion-dollar corporation. She used her wealth to endow two private foundations that were devoted primarily to helping women. Graham died in 1980.

From the kitchen to the boardroom

Let's do the twist

$ Engineers at the Texas Department of Transportation can take credit for at least one highway safety feature. Where guardrails join the ground, they slope into the soil and are anchored in concrete beneath the surface. Known as the "Texas Twist," the guardrail design has been adopted worldwide as a life-saving measure. Vehicles that run off the road are steered along the rail's twist, reducing the severity of impact.

Thanks for the snack

Fritos, the original corn chips, were introduced in 1932 by Elmer Doolin of San Antonio. Frito Company and H.W. Lay & Company became Frito-Lay in 1961, with headquarters in Dallas. In 1965 Frito-Lay joined with Pepsi to become the giant PepsiCo.

Moving right along

The first-ever two-way moving sidewalk started operation at Dallas' Love Field Air Terminal on January 30, 1958. The passenger convoy, as it was called, consisted of three loops totaling 1,435 feet. Folks at today's Dallas Love Field airport can still hop a ride on a two-way moving walkway. It carries them between the main terminal and the airline gates.

BUSINESS, TEXAS-STYLE

Back in the saddle

$ The nation's largest hatmaker, Hat Brands of Garland, lassoed the famous saddle-making firm of Edward H. Bohlin Company through a buyout in 1994. Founded 70 years ago by a Swedish immigrant, Bohlin is best known for its expensive and high-profile Western saddles. Hollywood's matinee cowboy idols of the 1920s rode tall in Bohlin saddles as did television's Western heroes of the 1960s. Tom Mix, Gene Autry, Roy Rogers, and John Wayne all mounted up on Bohlin saddles. The company's handiwork also showed up on such television classics as "Rawhide" and "Have Gun, Will Travel."

Still on the air

On September 15, 1938, Texas State Networks (TSN) hit the airwaves with radio broadcasts live from Fort Worth. That gives TSN bragging rights as the oldest state radio network in the country. Elliot Roosevelt, son of Franklin Roosevelt—U.S. president at the time—founded the network on August 2, 1938. The historic first broadcast took place at the old Casa Mañana Theater, where 500 people attended. These days, TSN programming goes to 123 affiliates, making it the largest, as well as the oldest, state radio network in the United States. Owned by Command Communications, TSN is now based in Dallas.

Attention chili lovers

A Corsicana company introduced Wolf Brand Chili to Texans in 1921 with a rather unusual product promotion. Salesmen toured the state in modified Model T Ford roadsters. Passenger compartments were designed to look like oversized cans of chili, and each auto carried a live wolf confined in a steel cage.

Double the java

The Fertitta family founded the Texas Coffee Company in Beaumont in 1921. Today it remains the only family-owned coffee-manufacturing company in the state. Its Seaport brand packs a punch that can compete with any of the better-known national coffee names. Seaport magnifies the oils because it's roasted longer, a process that gives the Texas coffee twice the kick of major brands. A mail-order business serves all 50 states, and Seaport can be found in major grocery chains along the Texas and Louisiana Gulf coast.

Hotels across Texas

(💲) The name "Hilton" has become synonymous with the word "hotel" thanks to the luck of Conrad Hilton. His hotel empire began in 1919 by sheer chance when he arrived in the small town of Cisco seeking a loan to go into the oil business. The bank reneged on the loan. But when Hilton checked in at the local Mobley Hotel (right), he found business so brisk that the owner was renting rooms by the hour. He bought the hotel for $40,000 and described it as a "cross between a gold mine and a flophouse." Hilton followed his success in Cisco by opening nine more hotels in the cities of Fort Worth, Dallas, Abilene, Waco, Marlin, Plainview, San Angelo, Lubbock, and El Paso.

True blue

(💲) Levi Strauss opened its first El Paso blue jeans plant in 1966. The Wrangler Western-wear division followed in 1969. Today, Levi Strauss is the city's third-largest employer, putting more than 4,000 people to work. Wrangler employs another 2,100 workers. Every week, more than 2 million pairs of blue jeans roll off assembly lines in El Paso. No wonder the city's been called the "Blue Jeans Capital of the Universe."

Hats off to Resistol

Resistol Western hats have been made famous by such illustrious wearers as John Wayne, country music star George Strait, and the late actor Dan Blocker who played Hoss on the television show "Bonanza." Even Pope John Paul II was presented with a Resistol during a visit to San Antonio. The company got its start in the 1930s when hatmaker Harry Rolnick and his partner Ed Byer patented an interior leather headband that expanded and conformed to the wearer's head. The pair opened the Byer-Rolnick Hat Manufacturing Company on Jackson Street in downtown Dallas. By World War II, the factory had moved to its present location in Garland, just outside of Dallas. The company has changed ownership several times over the years. But the Garland plant still manufactures about a million hats each year. Nearly three-quarters of those are Western-style felt and straw hats.

Just what the pharmacist ordered

The oldest nationwide soft drink is a genuine Texas product. Dr Pepper was first sold in 1885 at Morrison's Old Corner Drug Store in Waco. Charles Alderton, the store's pharmacist concocted the syrup, and Robert Lazenby bottled the drink. Today the soda is the fifth most popular soft drink in the country and a product of the Dallas corporation Dr Pepper/Seven-Up Companies.

She seldom wore cowboy boots

$ H.J. Justin came to Texas in the 1870s and catered to cowboys by opening a boot shop in the small town of Burlington. In 1889, Justin moved his boot company to Nocona. Justin's daughter Enid was born in 1894. She grew up loving to dance, and school officials suspended her in the eighth grade for shaking a leg at one of her brother's birthday parties. Indignant, Enid went to work full-time for her father. She learned the boot business and never returned to school.

In 1925, the Justin brothers took their boot business to Fort Worth. Enid stayed put. She borrowed $5,000 and founded Nocona Boot Company. Oil-field workers took a liking to Enid's lace-up boots and soon Nocona boots became known across the nation. In 1981, she merged her company with the business her brothers had founded in 1925—Justin Industries of Forth Worth. Enid died in 1990.

HIGH-TECH TEXAS

The sweet sounds of barbed wire

Barbed wire may be famous for the fencing-in of Texas, but in the early 1900s, the steely stuff also served as telephone lines between ranchers in the Panhandle. Using mail-order telephone boxes, far-flung ranchers hooked up to the top strand of wire along fences. The fences connected every ranch, and with the turn of a crank, neighbors living miles apart could suddenly share the latest gossip or commiserate about the hot, dry weather. Each telephone box along the line was assigned a specific sequence of short and long rings as its individual number. Where gates interrupted the barbed-wire fence and threatened to break the circuit, ranchers built tall fence posts and ran the wire overhead.

How Silicon Valley started in Texas

In April 1958, Jack St. Clair Kilby joined Texas Instruments in Dallas. His mission was to devise a method to fit electronic components together without wiring. Kilby didn't think the task could be done. But during July of that year, Kilby worked alone in his office while all other TI employees took their mandatory vacations. He looked at a material called silicon, and came up with the "Monolithic Idea." By making components from a single material, the components of an entire circuit could be placed in a monolithic block, or chip, of that same material. No wiring would be necessary. Kilby built a prototype of his integrated circuit, and on September 12, 1958, TI laboratories successfully tested the new device. For his work on the Monolithic Idea, Kilby received the National Medal of Science Award. He is also a member of the National Inventors Hall of Fame.

Instrumental technology

Texas Instruments started manufacturing transistors in 1952. The company made the pocket transistor possible in 1954. In the 1970s, TI developed the basic technologies for consumer products such as digital watches and home computers. Here are a few other microelectronic innovations credited to the Dallas-based high-tech firm.

Silicon transistor – 1954
Terrain-following airborne radar – 1958
Forward-looking infrared (FLIR) systems – 1964
Handheld calculators – 1967
Single-chip microcomputers – 1971
32-bit microcomputer for artificial intelligence applications – 1987

Paging Mr. Perrin

($) George M. Perrin of Plano founded Paging Network in 1981. As of 1993, the publicly held company was the largest and fastest-growing source of paging services in the nation. That same year, 47-year-old Perrin was worth about $80 million.

Tinkering into a fortune

($) Houston homeboy Michael Dell first tinkered with computers at age 13. After high school he enrolled at the University of Texas at Austin, but technology beat out schoolbooks. By spring break of his first year, Dell was working out of his dormitory room and grossing $50,000 a month working on computers. He pursued his hobby full-time during the next summer, bringing in $700,000. Finally, in 1985, he hired a few engineers and Dell Computer Corporation of Austin was born. The firm designed personal computers and sold by mail, a novel idea at the time but one that would shape the computer industry in years to come. In the first year of business, Dell sold $34 million worth of computers. In 1992, Dell Computer made the Fortune 500 list of America's largest corporations. Michael Dell, at the age of 27, was the youngest chief executive ever to make that prestigious ranking.

MOVERS AND SHAKERS

From pizza to Tex-Mex

Since 1989, *Texas Monthly* magazine has compared the wealth of the state's biggest wheeler-dealers and compiled an annual list of the 100 richest people in Texas. In 1993, Arturo Gregorio Torres of San Antonio became the first Hispanic on the magazine's rich list. Torres, a Cuban native, arrived in Amarillo in 1965 and worked as a printing-machine operator. He earned extra income by washing dishes on weekends at the city's first Pizza Hut. Torres helped his boss open new pizza outlets, moved up in the business, and in 1972, left to start his own chain. He focused on opening restaurants in small towns. The strategy worked, and by 1991, sales at his Pizza Management company had grown to $150 million. In 1992, Torres sold his business to Pizza Hut for $125 million in cash and stock. He now operates Tex-Mex restaurants in Spain through his San Antonio-based holding company TMI and boasts a personal net worth of $110 million.

The richest man in Texas

H. Ross Perot spent $60 million on his unsuccessful bid for the presidency in 1992, but he still had enough money left to be named the richest person in Texas in 1993. With an estimated net worth of $3.35 billion, Perot topped the list of *Texas Monthly* magazine's 100 wealthiest Texans. Perot amassed his megafortune through Electronic Data Systems, the company he founded in 1962. He took the firm public in 1968, then sold to General Motors in 1984 for a healthy helping of stock and cash. In 1986, GM bought Perot's shares for more than $700 million. EDS is the largest data-processing company in the United States today. But that didn't stop Perot from going head-to-head with the industry titan. In 1988, he founded Perot Systems, an EDS competitor whose revenues continue to climb.

Keep on truckin'

Although Ford Motor Company and General Motors are based in Detroit, both auto manufacturers have Texas natives in the driver's seat. Ross Roberts, general manager of Ford, hails from Gainesville. Jim Perkins, Chevrolet general manager at General Motors, comes from Waco. The Lone Star competitors have more in common than their home state. Each of their companies sells from 10 to 13 percent of their trucks in Texas, more than in any other state. In fact, Ford sells more trucks in Texas than anywhere else in the world.

It never rains on his financial parade

In 1979 the wealthy Texas Bass family hired Richard Edward Rainwater to manage the family's $50-million fortune. Rainwater parlayed the millions into more than $3 billion before striking out on his own in 1986. Since then the financier has amassed his own personal fortune of more than $700 million.

Rainwater co-founded Columbia Hospital Corporation in 1987.  Two years later he invested in the leveraged buyout of Hospital Corporation of America. When the two companies merged, they formed Columbia/HCA Healthcare Corporation, the nation's largest healthcare company with a market value of about $14 billion. Rainwater's healthy stake totals about $300 million. His other successful investments include real estate, energy, and a 9 percent share of the Texas Rangers baseball team.

End of the old boy network

The Downtown Dallas Rotary Club, which is the largest in the country, named Carol Reed its president-elect in October 1994. Reed, a public relations executive, was the first woman elected as president in the organization's 83-year history.

In memory of mom

($) Donald J. Carter of Coppell is one of the richest men in Texas and owner of the Dallas Mavericks professional basketball team. He's also a sentimental sort of guy. In June 1994, Carter announced plans to sell 51 percent of the family business—Home Interiors and Gifts—for an estimated $1 billion. But by October, the thought of severing family ties caused Carter to back out of the deal. Carter's mother, Mary Crowley, founded the company in 1957 as a direct marketer of decorative home accessories. Carter joined the business at age 24 and inherited the company when his mother died. He's now chief executive, and the firm is one of the largest private companies in Dallas-Fort Worth.

Catalog of the rich and famous

($) Neiman Marcus opened its doors in downtown Dallas in 1907 as the first specialty store in Texas. Herbert Marcus, Sr., his sister, Carrie Neiman, and her husband Al stocked the store with the highest-quality merchandise they could find. Stanley Marcus, Herbert's son, grew up amid the store's aisles, took over as president in 1952, and served until mandatory retirement forced him to step down in 1979. His merchandising magic and customer-service savvy made Marcus the most famous salesman in Texas history. Marcus created the most well-known Christmas catalog in the world. The idea stemmed from a conversation between Marcus and the late Edward R. Murrow. When Murrow requested an unusual and interesting item for a radio broadcast, Marcus suggested a live steer tied with a red ribbon. The beef-on-the-hoof would be accompanied by a silver serving cart for the barbecue—all for $5,000. Since then, annual his and her gifts have included such things as baby elephants, submarines, camels, and airplanes.

THE BEST IN THE BUSINESS

Program for success

($) CompUSA, the leading superstore computer retailer in the United States, sells more merchandise per square foot than any other major U.S. retailer. The company started as Soft Warehouse and sold directly to business customers. The first retail outlet opened in Dallas in 1985, followed three years later by the opening of the first superstore. In 1991, the name changed to CompUSA, and the company made its initial public offering. By the end of 1994, Dallas-based CompUSA operated 80 superstores. Each outlet averages 24,000 square feet and is divided into departments for hardware, software, accessories, and Apple products. Sales revenues totaled more than $2.2 billion in 1994.

Catering to a trend   💲 SYSCO Corporation of Houston sits at the top of the national food chain. The company is the largest marketer and distributor of food-service products in the United States—bigger than its five top competitors combined. In 1969, SYSCO founder John Baugh recognized the American trend for dining out. He persuaded eight other food wholesalers to join forces with his Baugh's Zero Foods to create a national distribution company. SYSCO has since swallowed up smaller competitors and grown to 70 times its original size. Sixty-nine operating companies cater to some 230,000 customers across the country and sell about 150,000 different products.

Winning the Nobel of business awards

On October 18, 1994, Mesquite-based AT&T Power Systems became the first U.S. manufacturer ever to win Japan's coveted Deming Prize for quality. The prize, considered the international Nobel of quality awards, is given by the Union of Japanese Scientists and Engineers in Tokyo. It was established in 1951 to recognize companies that achieve significant performance gains through quality control. The award is named for W. Edwards Deming, an expert on quality who helped Japan rebuild its industries after World War II.

Follow the tracks   💲 Burlington Northern, headquartered in Fort Worth, operates the longest rail system in North America. The 25,000-mile system spans 25 states and two Canadian provinces, serving regions that produce rich supplies of coal, grain, and timber. In 1993, the company made one of the biggest locomotive buys in history. Burlington Northern agreed to buy 350 locomotives between 1993 and 1997 for $675 million.

A child's best friend   💲 Texan Sheryl Leach couldn't find a good video for her 2-year-old son so she decided to make one—and Barney®, the purple dinosaur was born. Her father-in-law provided seed money for Sheryl and two friends, Kathy Parker and Dennis DeShazer. Together they produced the video

"Barney and the Backyard Gang," which debuted in 1988. By 1991 it was a best-seller. Four-year-old Leora Rifkin is responsible for Barney's PBS connection. Leora's father, a vice president for a Connecticut Public Television station, noticed how much his daughter loved the Barney video she'd checked out. That gave him an idea. He contacted Leach's company, The Lyons Group, and the rest is history. The Barney series made its PBS debut on April 6, 1992. PBS has extended broadcast rights for "Barney & Friends®"—the number-one children's television show on public television—until 1998. The 6-foot-4-inch dinosaur is the children's cultural phenomenon of the 1990s. Universal Studios Florida is building "A Day in the Park with Barney" a major attraction where children can rub shoulders with the popular purple creature. And a full-length feature film is in the works.

THE ENTREPRENEURIAL SPIRIT

Wooden nickel wealth

About 4 million wooden nickels are produced by self-proclaimed "two-bit celebrity" Louis Berkie each year. In 1950 the San Antonio businessman saw an ad in *Billboard* magazine and bought a wooden-nickel business for $50. Today, the maple "nickels" are used to commemorate special occasions, or for advertising almost anything. Apparently, wooden nickels began in the old Roman Empire when metal coins were scarce.

The pink Cadillac of Texas

After a divorce, Mary Kay Ash took $5,000, bought a cosmetics formula from a hide tanner, and started her company—Mary Kay Cosmetics. That was in 1963. Today the Dallas-based company's retail sales surpass $1 billion. About 300,000 direct-sales consultants push powder and other cosmetics in the United States and 15 other countries. Ash, now in her mid-70's, still stays up late signing birthday cards for her devoted employees. One of them, Craig Hogan of Houston, became the first man to earn a trademark pink Cadillac by selling enough products in 1993.

Mary Kay and the KGB

Dallas architect Frank L. Meier has been designing buildings for Mary Kay Cosmetics for 30 years. But in the summer of 1993, he faced one of his biggest challenges. Meier went to Moscow to renovate part of an old building near KGB headquarters for a distribution center and retail outlet for the cosmetics magnate. Since few materials were available in the Russian city, contractors in Dallas assembled plumbing fixtures, lighting, tile flooring, and other interior necessities. The materials, tools, and a construction crew of 12 were then flown to Moscow. Once the materials cleared customs, it took less than four weeks to complete the $400,000 renovation project. The retail store was the first of its kind for Mary Kay Cosmetics. And only the foyer of the upscale boutique was pink.

$ In 1945, Lonnie Alfred "Bo" Pilgrim started growing and selling chickens in the small East Texas town of Pittsburg. Pilgrim's Pride Corporation has since pecked its way to the top, becoming Texas' largest chicken producer and the fifth-largest in the United States. Sales now hit about $850 million annually.

Do chickens have lips?

Building a bigger Dallas

When Sarah Horton Cockrell's husband died, he left her with three children, a stack of debts, and a ferry business. Cockrell invested her assets wisely and thought big. She founded the Dallas Bridge Company and in 1872 built the first iron bridge over the Trinity River. She formed the S.H. Cockrell Company, which owned a flour mill, and she constructed the first three-story hotel in Dallas. Cockrell owned much of what is now Dallas' central business district. When she died in 1892 the list of her property holdings was so long it had to be published in pamphlet form.

Hispanic recognition

$ *Hispanic Business* magazine named Victor F. Ornelas National Hispanic Entrepreneur of the Year in 1994. Ornelas, president and chief executive of Dallas' Ornelas & Associates advertising agency, founded his business in 1988. By 1993, the firm boasted billings of $20 million. The agency created Pepsi-Cola's "Pepsi Man" character and Wrangler Jeans' Viva la Tradicion campaign, which featured a Mexican vaquero.

A trashy business

$ In 1967, accountant Tom Fatjo and Harvard MBA Louis Waters founded American Refuse Systems. Back then, a single truck picked up garbage for a single Houston neighborhood. The name changed in 1969 to Browning-Ferris Industries, and the business grew as America's trash piled up. But by the late 1980s, the company was down in the dumps. BFI paid millions of dollars to settle environmental-violation lawsuits. In 1988, the company cleaned up its act by recruiting William D. Ruckelshaus, a former administrator with the Environmental Protection Agency. Today, the company is North America's largest provider of medical-waste disposal services.

Cashing in

Jack R. Daugherty hocked his guitar numerous times to finance dates while a student in Texas. Finally in 1970, he quit school and opened his own pawnshop. By 1992, Daugherty and his Fort Worth company Cash America International owned more than 250 pawn shops in the United States and the United Kingdom. As chairman and CEO, Daugherty oversees the world's largest pawn company and the only one operating internationally.

Accidental fame

$ In 1899, the first gasoline-engine automobile arrived in Texas, compliments of Colonel Edward H. Robinson Green. Green purchased the vehicle and had it shipped to Terrell, about 30 miles east of Dallas. The horseless carriage arrived safely in the company of George P. Dorris, the auto manufacturer's chief designer and engineer. On October 5, 1899, Dorris and Green embarked on a historic auto trip to Dallas, traveling at about six miles per hour. In Forney, a wagon driven by a farmer forced the new auto off the road and into a ditch. It was the first automobile accident in Texas. The mishap caused damage to the auto's water tank. But a local blacksmith quickly repaired the damage— becoming the first automobile repairman in Texas.

CORPORATE CULTURE

Sell, sell, sell

$ Tandy Corporation of Fort Worth is the top retailer of consumer electronics in the United States. But the company isn't resting on its high-tech laurels. It's moving away from manufacturing and touting its talents in the retail arena through more than 6,000 Radio Shack stores. In 1993, the company unveiled a new retailing concept when it opened two superstores known as Incredible Universe. The mega-stores feature sales floors the size of three football fields and offer customers gigantic selections of electronic merchandise.

Flying whales

Southwest Airlines made its first scheduled flight, from Dallas to San Antonio, in 1971. It's been soaring ever since. Herb Kelleher, known as "Uncle Herbie" to the more than 17,000 employees, took over as chairman in 1978 and to this day insists that flying be fun. When Southwest became the official airlines for Sea World of Texas in 1988, Kelleher painted one of the Boeing 737s in the likeness of Shamu (above), the sea park's killer whale. Uncle Herbie's penchant for an uncorporate-like atmosphere paid dividends in 1992, 1993, and 1994 when Dallas-based Southwest claimed the Triple Crown in the airline industry. The high flyer won best on-time performance, best baggage-handling record, and best customer-complaint record. No other major airline had ever before been honored with the prize—even for a single month.

The best day for shopping

$ Tuesday Morning Corporation of Dallas developed a marketing strategy like no other retailer. The company stores are open only four times each year with sales that last four to eight weeks. The no-frills, low-overhead shops sell top-quality, name-brand gift merchandise—all at 50 to 80 percent off regular retail prices. Items such as gourmet housewares, luggage, linens, and toys disappear from shelves quickly, and the stores rarely feature the same merchandise twice. Founder and chairman Lloyd L. Ross started the retail business in 1974. He named the company in honor of Tuesday, the "most positive day of the week." There must be some truth to his adage. Sales at the company reached over $190 million in 1994.

Tuesday Morning

Riding the rails in style

The Katy Railroad may have been the first travel business to offer shuttle service for customers. In 1905, the company announced a new convenience for its customers in Dallas, Houston, and San Antonio. The railroad would send a wagon to the home or office of a train traveler, pick up luggage, and deliver the baggage to the terminal. Later, a carriage would be sent to collect the passenger and take the traveler to the departing train.

TEXAS-SIZE BUSINESS

Recession-proof industry

$ The world's largest undertaking business, Service Corporation International or SCI, is located in Houston. The company operates 551 funeral homes and 126 cemeteries. Annual revenues in 1989 reached $519 million.

Dubious honors

$ Irving-based Exxon Corporation takes top honors as the nation's largest oil company. The corporation conducts operations in more than 80 foreign countries as well as the United States, touts sales of about $111 billion annually, and holds $84 billion in assets. Exxon also holds several dubious honors. In September 1994, a federal jury decided that the company should pay $5 billion in punitive damages for causing the massive 1989 *Exxon Valdez* oil spill in Alaska's Prince William Sound. The assessment was the largest punitive damage award in history, a judgment the jury seemed to think matched the crime. The Exxon oil spill was the worst in U.S. history, dumping 11 million gallons of crude into the pristine waters.

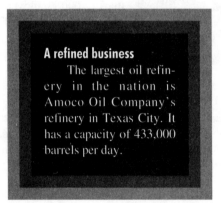

A refined business

The largest oil refinery in the nation is Amoco Oil Company's refinery in Texas City. It has a capacity of 433,000 barrels per day.

A bit of history

In 1907, Howard R. Hughes, Sr., applied for a patent on an improved oil-well drilling bit—he bought the rights for $150. The innovative bit proved invaluable in the oil field. It could chew through rock with its revolving cones and penetrate the earth 10 times faster than existing bits. Hughes and his partner, Walter B. Sharp, formed a tool company to manufacture the bit and soon established a monopoly on rock bits. When Hughes died in 1924, the Hughes Tool Company was worth $2 million and held 73 patents. The wealth passed to his reclusive son Howard R. Hughes, Jr. In 1987, Hughes Tool merged with Baker Oil Tools to become Baker Hughes Incorporated. Today the Houston company is the world's number-one manufacturer of rock-drilling bits.

Doing something right

$ J.C. Penney Company of Plano is the fourth-largest retailer in the nation, following in the footsteps of Wal-Mart, Kmart, and Sears. Look around, there's probably a Penney store nearby. The company has 1,266 stores with more than 114 million square feet of selling space.

Fashions for the masses

Dallas developer Trammel Crow opened the Dallas International Apparel Mart in 1964. Thirty years later, it has grown into the largest regional mart in the country, supplying Southwest retailers with men's, women's, and children's clothing. The massive mart encompasses 1.8 million square feet with 1,200 showrooms. Tenants represent 12,000 clothing lines that are unveiled at 25 fashion shows each year. In 1993, 27,000 retail stores shopped the Mart and ordered $2.5 billion worth of merchandise.

BUSINESS BRIEFS

⑤ The only tin smelter in the United States can be found in Texas City. It was built during World War II and later sold to a private company. Today the smelter processes tin residues, secondary tin-bearing materials, and tin concentrates from ores mined outside Texas.

The one and only

Of foam rubber and heliports

The Western Hills Hotel in Fort Worth officially opened on October 7, 1951, becoming the first hotel to use all-foam-rubber pillows, mattresses, and furniture cushions. Of the 200 rooms, no two were furnished alike at the showcase hotel that cost $2 million to build. On May 20, 1953, the Western Hills became the first hotel to establish a heliport. Surfaced with asphalt and measuring 150 by 190 feet, the heliport was constructed by the E.M. Moore Construction Company of Fort Worth.

⑤ The familiar 7-Eleven signs can be seen at more than 6,000 stores across the United States and Canada, making Southland Corporation of Dallas the owner of the world's largest convenience-store chain. The quick-shop empire began in 1927 when Claude Dawley formed Southland Ice Company. He purchased four other Texas ice plants, including Consumers Ice in Dallas. There, Dawley found an enthusiastic employee named Joe C. Thompson, Jr., selling chilled watermelons off the truck docks. Soon, Thompson stocked more groceries at the docks, and eventually all store locations adopted the practice. Thompson called the locations Tote'm Stores and erected Alaskan-made totem poles to identify the locations. By 1928, he added gas pumps at some stores, and by 1930 he was promoted to president of the company. In 1946, the name 7-Eleven was chosen in reference to the hours that the stores stayed open. Since 1991, Southland Corporation has been controlled by Japan's top retailer, Ito-Yokado, which rescued the company from bankruptcy.

It started with cold watermelons

Hand-me-down produce

$ In 1905, Florence Butt opened a quaint grocery store in the Hill Country town of Kerrville. The H.E.B. Grocery Company, as the family business is called, still prospers in the Lone Star State with sales approaching $4 billion. Today, Florence's grandson Charles Clarence Butt of San Antonio oversees the 256-store chain. He keeps a fresh eye on operations by frequently visiting stores while wearing his "Charles" name tag. He also sends handwritten congratulation notes to managers when their cash registers ring up record-breaking sales.

Did it issue life jackets?

The Flagship Hotel (left) in Galveston was the first major hotel to be built over a pier. The 240-room hotel opened June 30, 1965. The 1,500-foot-long, 340-foot-wide pier extended into the Gulf of Mexico. Guests can still hang out over the water today.

Do your own thing—but get group rates

In 1981, a group of small-business owners decided they deserved the big benefits often reserved for big business. They formed the National Association for the Self-Employed (NASE), settled the organization in Hurst, and began recruiting members. By 1993, membership had bounded to more than 300,000. Most member businesses employ five or fewer workers, and most have survived for at least five years. Through NASE, they can all do their own thing but get group rates.

Older than the state of Texas

$ A.H. Belo Corporation entered the publishing industry three years before the Republic of Texas became a state. That makes the company the oldest continuously operating business in the state. Belo began with the one-page *Galveston News* in 1842. The corporation founded the *Texas Almanac* in 1857 and started publishing the *Dallas Morning News* on October 1, 1885. In December 1991, the *News* put its only major competitor out of business by purchasing, and folding, the 112-year-old *Dallas Times Herald*.

A million-dollar haul

Standard Oil of New Jersey began doing business in Texas through a corporation known as Waters-Piece Oil Company. To avoid antitrust problems, the legal papers that were filed professed Waters-Piece to be an independent corporation. In reality, the company was a subsidiary of the national petroleum giant. When the lie came to light, the Texas attorney general sued Waters-Piece for $5 million in fines. The legal battle was waged all the way to the U.S. Supreme Court, but Waters-Piece lost in 1909. In a show of contempt for the judgment, the company delivered its $1,808,483.30 penalty by pushing a wheelbarrow full of small bills up Congress Avenue to the state Capitol.

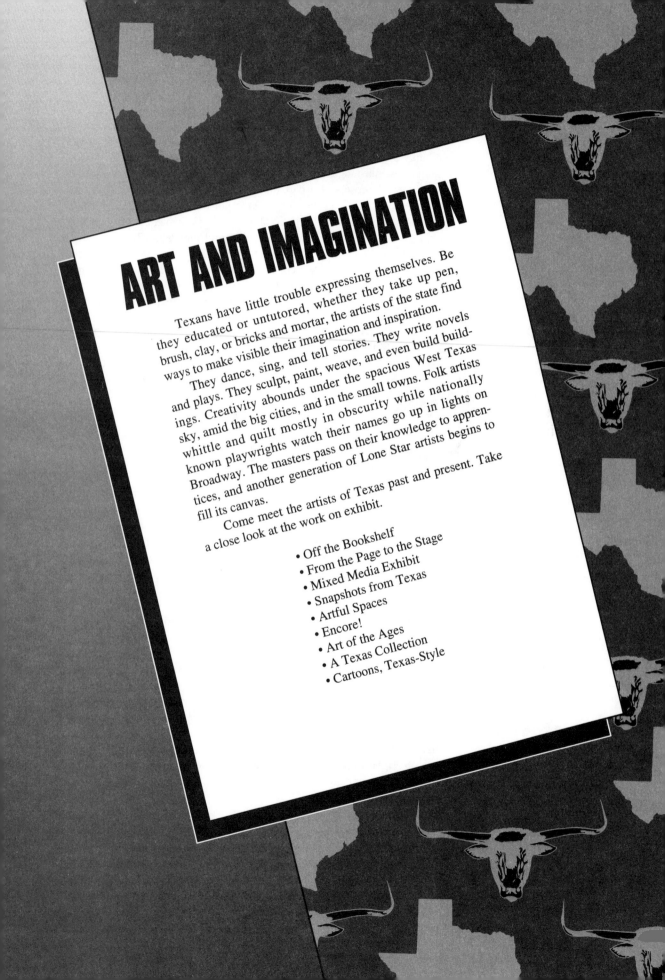

ART AND IMAGINATION

Texans have little trouble expressing themselves. Be they educated or untutored, whether they take up pen, brush, clay, or bricks and mortar, the artists of the state find ways to make visible their imagination and inspiration.

They dance, sing, and tell stories. They write novels and plays. They sculpt, paint, weave, and even build buildings. Creativity abounds under the spacious West Texas sky, amid the big cities, and in the small towns. Folk artists whittle and quilt mostly in obscurity while nationally known playwrights watch their names go up in lights on Broadway. The masters pass on their knowledge to apprentices, and another generation of Lone Star artists begins to fill its canvas.

Come meet the artists of Texas past and present. Take a close look at the work on exhibit.

- Off the Bookshelf
- From the Page to the Stage
- Mixed Media Exhibit
- Snapshots from Texas
- Artful Spaces
- Encore!
- Art of the Ages
- A Texas Collection
- Cartoons, Texas-Style

OFF THE BOOKSHELF

❧ J. Frank Dobie invented Texas literature, though some literary voices may argue the point. But Dobie's tales of roadrunners, cow camps, longhorns, mustangs, cowboys, rattlesnakes, and South Texas folklore preserved a part of Texas that might have been lost and forever forgotten if not for his words. After World War II, folklorist J. Frank Dobie, historian Walter Prescott Webb, and naturalist Roy Bedichek worked together in Austin, primarily at the University of Texas. Once a month they met at Paisano, Dobie's ranch in the Hill Country. Around campfires with invited guests, they traded stories and tales that wound their way into the books that established a tradition in Texas literature. Dobie authored 25 books, most still in print, and countless articles for magazines and newspapers. He also taught other Texas writers to find their native voices. His lively lecture course "Life and Literature of the Southwest," which began in 1930 at the University of Texas, became the most popular elective on campus. Dobie even persuaded powerful eastern publishers that Texas writings and Texas writers could attract readers outside the big state. He was right, of course. Dobie died in his sleep on September 18, 1964. The following is a list of some of Dobie's books: *The Longhorns*, *The Mustangs*, *Tales of Old-Time Texas*, *On the Open Range*, *The Voice of the Coyote*, *Coronado's Children*, *Cow People*, *A Vaquero of the Brush Country*, *Apache Gold and Yaqui Silver*, and *Tongues of the Monte*.

The father of Texas literature

A copyright for the Republic

❧ The only book copyrighted in the Republic of Texas was *Topographical Description of Texas* by George William Bonnell. It was published in 1840 in Austin by Clark, Wing, and Brown.

Arnold owes this man a thank-you

❧ All the world knows the warrior Conan the Barbarian. But his creator worked in obscurity in the small town of Cross Plains. Author Robert E. Howard wrote a series of Conan stories between 1932 and 1936 and published most of them in the magazine *Weird Tales*. He earned a sizable salary from the sales of fantasy fiction, but never married and lived most of his life with his parents. On June 11, 1936, at the age of 30, Howard committed suicide after learning that his comatose mother was near death. Conan lives on in books and movies.

Never too old to write

In a 1951 letter to J. Frank Dobie, Texas naturalist Roy Bedichek wrote, "One of the real tragedies of old age lies in its decreasing ability to squat." But Bedichek never let the years slow him down. In 1947, at the age of 71, he wrote his first full-sized book, the classic *Adventures with a Texas Naturalist*. Bedichek died in May 1959.

Verbose to say the least

Madison Cooper's two-volume work *Sironia, Texas* may very well be the longest novel ever written. It contains more than a million words, all of them based on Cooper's hometown of Waco. The writer spent 11 years of late nights in the third-floor turret room of the Cooper family mansion pouring out the words. When the novel was finally finished, it created a scandal in Waco. Too many of the town's elite society folks saw themselves and their families woven into Cooper's satire.

Examining women's lives

❦ Elizabeth Forsythe Hailey, a Dallas native, turned the life of her grandmother into a best-seller in 1978. That year she published *A Woman of Independent Means* and watched as the novel zoomed up the best-seller list. At last count in 1994, the book had sold 3 million copies. Hailey's second book, *Life Sentences*, stayed on the hit list for more than three months. She has since penned two other works, *Joanna's Husband and David's Wife* and *Home Free*.

Of Pulitzers and movies

❦ When Larry McMurtry led a modern literary movement in Texas beginning in the 1960s, he snubbed his nose at Dobie, Webb, and Bedichek, claiming that they focused too heavily on the natural setting of Texas and ignored contemporary urban themes. But McMurtry followed closer in their footsteps than he might have imagined. He attended North Texas State University, Rice University, and Stanford. He also taught at Texas Christian University and Rice. Although he wrote many books, it was the one that drew its themes from the land and the frontier that earned McMurtry his biggest award—*Lonesome Dove* won the Pulitzer Prize for fiction in 1986. He began the work as a screenplay, hoping John Wayne, Henry Fonda, and James Stewart would star in the film. All the actors turned him down. For the past 40 years, McMurtry also gave the film industry novels worthy of moviemaking every decade. Here's the list that started back in 1963.

> *Horseman, Pass* By, published in 1961, released as the movie *Hud* in 1963
>
> *Leaving Cheyenne*, published in 1962, released as the movie *Lovin' Molly* in 1974
>
> *The Last Picture Show*, published in 1966, released as the movie in 1971
>
> *Terms of Endearment*, published in 1975, released as a movie in 1983
>
> *Texasville*, published in 1987, released as a movie in 1990

Presidential plagiarism?

In 1912, Colonel Edward M. House of Austin published a novel entitled *Philip Dru: Administrator*. In the fictional account, the author espouses such innovative ideas as social security, workers' compensation insurance, and government works projects. Franklin D. Roosevelt read the story and became friends with House. That led some observers to claim that FDR's 1932 "New Deal" borrowed heavily from the imaginary policies put forth in House's book.

Top dog

In 1956, Mason-native Fred Gipson published the classic family tale of all time—*Old Yeller*.

Kindergarten knowledge

❀ Early in 1989, Robert Fulghum's book *All I Really Need to Know I Learned in Kindergarten* climbed to the number-one spot on the best-seller list. Nine months later, the sequel *It Was on Fire When I Lay Down on It* followed suit. That made Fulghum the first author to capture the number-one and number-two spots on the best-seller list. Raised with a strict Southern Baptist upbringing in Waco, Fulghum left Texas as a teenager for the University of Colorado. He returned to his native state during his junior year to finish his education at Baylor University in his hometown. After college he worked for one year as a salesman for IBM in Dallas. But Texas couldn't hold him. He struck out for California, enrolled in a Unitarian seminary, left behind his old-time religion, and went on to share with millions his own view of how to make the world a better place.

All the gore that's fit to print

❀ Worldwide fans of mystery writer David Lindsey shouldn't have any trouble finding one of his gory novels to read. Two million copies of his books had been sold in 12 languages by mid-1994, and eight of his novels were still in print. The Austin author's first book, *Black Gold, Red Death*, appeared in 1983. But that same year *A Cold Mind* hit the best-seller list and catapulted Lindsey to fame in the crime-fiction field. Other books followed, all showing Lindsey's obsession with violent death. In 1992, when *Body of Truth* was released, the publisher dropped the middle initial "L" from Lindsey's name. No matter. By any name, Lindsey still dominates the blood and guts genre of mystery. Here's a reading list for a dark and stormy night: *Heat From Another Sun* (1984), *Spiral* (1986), *In the Lake of the Moon* (1988), *Mercy* (1990), and *An Absence of Light* (1994).

Ship to fame

❀ Although born in Indian Creek near San Antonio, Katherine Anne Porter spent most of her life traveling the United States, Mexico, and Europe, contributing articles to various newspapers as she went. Her first collection of short stories, *Flowering Judas*, appeared in 1930 to critical acclaim. Other collections followed and established Porter as a leading writer of short stories. Her only novel, *Ship of Fools* in 1961, depicted a voyage on an ocean liner on the eve of World War II and was made into a motion picture in 1965. Porter's *Collected Short Stories* won the Pulitzer Prize for fiction in 1966. Her last published work was *The Never-Ending Wrong*, published in 1977. Porter died September 18, 1980.

Pulitzer Prizewinners

Katherine Anne Porter
    1966 Pulitzer Prize in fiction for
    Collected Short Stories
Larry McMurtry
    1986 Pulitzer Prize in fiction for *Lonesome Dove*
Allen Drury
    1960 Pulitzer Prize in fiction for *Advise and Consent*
Paul Horgan
    1955 Pulitzer Prize in history for *Great River: The Rio Grande in North American History*

❧ In 1994, photographer-novelist Robert James Waller decided that Iowa just wasn't big enough for him and his avid readers. Seeking more privacy, Waller took up residence in Big Bend country, just outside of Alpine. The man who authored the best-seller *The Bridges of Madison County* and later *Slow Waltz in Cedar Bend*, purchased the 971-acre Pate Altuda ranch in the foothills of the Del Norte Mountains.

The privacy of Brewster County

FROM THE PAGE TO THE STAGE

Which came first?

The novel *Urban Cowboy*, published in 1980, was based on a film that was based on a magazine article. Confused? Aaron Latham first wrote a piece for *Esquire* that showed readers life in the city-slicker cowboy bars of such cities as Houston and Pasadena. Latham and James Bridges then wrote a screenplay for the movie that booted Texas chic into the mainstream of America. Finally, Latham captured the whole scene again in a novel.

❧ Horton Foote left his home in Wharton at age 16 determined to become an actor. Early in his career, he wrote and starred in a New York stage production of *A Texas Town*. Critics panned his acting but praised his writing, and a playwright was born. In 1962, Foote won his first Academy Award for his screenplay from Harper Lee's *To Kill A Mockingbird*. In 1983, he took home his second Oscar for the screenplay *Tender Mercies*. Other memorable works from the small-town boy include *The Trip to Bountiful*, *1918*, and *On Valentine's Day*.

Tender scenes from Wharton

❧ Larry L. King didn't have a musical in mind when he wrote a non-fiction article for *Playboy* in 1974 about the closing of the famed Chicken Ranch brothel in La Grange. When approached to collaborate on a stage show based on *The Best Little Whorehouse in Texas,* King said, "Hell, no." The West Texas native had rarely seen a musical, much less written one. But King couldn't help himself. He dashed off a hilarious scene in about a week, and his first play was in the works. The hit show opened off-Broadway in 1978, moved to Broadway in 1979, and stayed on stage for almost four years.

The best little musical from Texas

Pulitzer Prize-winning dramatists
Beth Henley
    1981 for *Crimes of the Heart*
Donald Coburn
    1978 for *The Gin Game*
Joshua Logan
    1950 for *South Pacific*

MIXED MEDIA EXHIBIT

An artist at war

In 1941, nationally acclaimed El Paso muralist Tom Lea took an assignment as a war illustrator for *Life* magazine. With sketchbook in hand, Lea accompanied Allied troops to Iceland, North Africa, and China. Rough sketches became polished paintings in his studio and then illustrations on the pages of *Life*. One painting, *The Price*, depicts a fatally wounded Marine, his mangled arm dangling limp as he stumbles along. *The Price* created a controversy among *Life* readers—it was too gruesome for a family magazine. Fifty years later, in 1994, three of Lea's powerful paintings appeared in a tribute to war correspondents at the National Portrait Gallery in Washington, D.C.

The tie that binds

When the Dallas Museum of Art commissioned Swedish-born artist Claes Oldenburg and Dutch-born artist Coosje van Bruggen, the organization wanted something for the main gallery that would tie it to the rest of the museum's space. Oldenburg and van Bruggentook took the assignment literally and created the *Stake Hitch* (left). A rope 20 inches thick drapes at an angle from the 40-foot vaulted ceiling and knots around a 16-foot floor stake. The stake appears to pierce the floor, and indeed a 12-foot extension does slice into the building's basement. The massive work was installed in April 1984 by removing the large glass doors between the gallery and the sculpture garden.

Modern monuments in Marfa

The remote West Texas town of Marfa may seem an unlikely place to find some of the world's finest sculptures. Minimalist sculptor Donald Judd first saw Marfa in 1946 when he passed through on a bus trip to California. In 1971, at the peak of an internationally acclaimed career, he left New York to work under the West Texas sky. On his ranch about 50 miles south of Marfa, he continued creating freestanding metal and plexiglass sculptures of monumental size. The *New York Times* declared Judd's contemporary work "among the largest and most beautiful in the world." In February 1994, Judd died of lymphoma at the age of 65. Visitors can see his art at the converted Fort D.A. Russell, where Judd created a permanent exhibition space.

Prisoners of art

Between 1942 and 1945, 7,000 Italian prisoners of war were held in the Texas Panhandle at the Hereford Military Reservation and Reception Center. Nine of those prisoners put their artistic talents to work at St. Mary's Catholic Church in Umbarger, a town about 20 miles from the Hereford camp. Two prisoners painted eight glass windows with scenes depicting the lives of Jesus and Mary. Another created a woodcarving of the Last Supper. A 10-foot mural of the Assumption was painted in the sanctuary by prisoner and professional muralist Dino Gambetti. Throughout the church, patterns and borders provide striking remembrances of the men who continued to create their art even while captured. This religious artistry can still be seen today.

Original napkin art
In 1980, Gary Havard of Fort Worth sat in a restaurant and sketched out a drawing on a napkin. It showed only the leg of a cowboy as he sat astride his horse, complete with a portion of the saddle, a boot, a spur, chaps, and a looped rope. Havard produced the sketch as a full-color poster one year later and titled it *The Texas Drifter*. In 1986, the work became the first official Texas sesquicentennial poster. Eventually Havard sold 13,000 copies of the poster, with one going to the Metropolitan Museum of Art in New York City.

❧ The towns of Praha, Dubina, High Hill, and Ammannsville in southern Fayette County disappeared years ago, but the spectacular Art Nouveau interiors of their parish churches have survived beautifully. The turn-of-the-century art displays marbling, freehand work, and stenciling in the stylized designs of flowers, palms, and vines. Individual artists added angels, saints, cherubs, and religious symbols to each church as a distinctive touch. On the vaulted tongue-and-groove ceiling of Praha's church, the original 1895 murals have never been retouched. That church, along with those at High Hill and Ammannsville, appears in the National Register of Historic Places. Two coats of paint were splashed on the artwork of Dubina's church during a remodeling in 1952. But in 1981, a former altar boy spearheaded the campaign that restored the bold stenciled patterns in the 1912 church.

The art of angels

Technological illusions

Software designer Michael Bielinski figured out how to mass-produce holographic illusions in 1991. Holusions, as they're called, look like a canvas full of tightly packed, random-colored dots. But keep staring and suddenly the image of something more appears—an elephant or the Lone Star State. Bielinski and University of Texas at Arlington fraternity brother Paul Herber formed the company NVision Grafix in Las Colinas to make and push their new abstract art. By 1994, the high-tech artists had sold more than a million of the holusion prints.

❧ At the heart of the Las Colinas community in Irving stands a monumental sculpture known as the *Mustangs of Las Colinas* (below). The seven adult and two young mustangs gallop across an expanse of pink granite in Williams Square and plunge through a man-made stream. Internationally acclaimed wildlife artist Robert Glen of Kenya sculpted the bronze, larger-than-life mustangs. The animals surge through a 400-foot-long watercourse created by Houston designer James Reeves. The mustang grouping, dedicated in 1984, forms the largest equine sculpture in the world.

Man-made mustangs

Sculptor of Texas heroes

Elisabet Ney might have disappeared from Texas art history had it not been for the 1893 World's Columbian Exposition in Chicago. Ney was asked to sculpt statues of Sam Houston and Stephen F. Austin (left) for display at the exposition's Texas building. At age 59, Ney resumed the art career that had been laid aside since the time she arrived in Texas in 1873. Ney didn't finish the Austin work in time for the exposition. But the Houston statue created a sensation. Eventually both sculptures were purchased by the state of Texas. Ney cut each work in marble—twice. One of each graces the Texas Capitol. The duplicates stand in the Statuary Hall in Washington, D.C. Ney went on to sculpt other Texas heroes, including Governors Lubbock, Roberts, and Ross. She also completed the critically acclaimed memorial statue for Albert Sidney Johnston's grave in Austin's State Cemetery. Ney died of a heart attack in 1907 at the age of 74. She was just completing a statue of Lady Macbeth, a work that is now displayed at the Smithsonian's National Museum of American Art in Washington. In Austin, Ney's studio became a museum in 1974 and is designated as a National Historical Site.

SNAPSHOTS FROM TEXAS

Lost and found

In 1984, white folklorist Alan Govenar of Dallas began discovering the unseen work of some forgotten African-American photographers in Texas. Govenar was researching Benny Joseph's book *The Early Years of Rhythm and Blues*, a collection of photos of Texas blues musicians. After uncovering thousands of Joseph's negatives, Govenar found other images produced by African-American commercial photographers and photography teachers. By 1994, Govenar had resurrected the work of 45 men and women. With photos from those artists and others, Govenar mounted an exhibit in Dallas in 1994, "Portraits of Community: African American Photography in Texas." The images dated from the 1870s to the 1990s and conveyed the sense of stability and dignity found in everyday living.

For love of a bird

Wyman Meinzer was only 14 when he outran a young roadrunner near his North Texas home. The up-close look at the paisano inspired him later as a young man. At age 28, the nature photographer and writer started documenting roadrunner behavior. He has admired and captured the birds on film ever since. In 1994, Texas Tech University Press published Meinzer's book *The Roadrunner*, a natural history collection about the bird he loves.

❧ Amarillo-native Mark Seliger is best recognized for his quirky portraits of celebrities that bless the pages of *Rolling Stone*. Seliger fans can also catch his work in a folksy advertising campaign produced for Saturn cars. In 1994, Seliger shot five Texas ads for the automaker.

Shooting stars

ARTFUL SPACES

❧ Architect Philip Frohman, who designed the Washington National Cathedral in the nation's capital, also designed Abilene's Episcopal Church of the Heavenly Rest. The financially conservative congregation built the Gothic structure on a pay-as-you-go basis, so the project took almost 33 years to complete. The church was dedicated in 1957.

Patience is a virtue

❧ As the Lone Star State readied for its 1936 centennial, cities across the state vied for the honor of hosting the grand celebration. Austin, San Antonio, and Houston offered historical resources for the occasion. But Dallas offered money and won the prize. Work on Fair Park began in 1934, only two years before the opening of the Centennial Exposition. George Dahl served as executive architect for the project, with Paul Cret as design consultant. When the collection of buildings was complete, they stood as a monument to the art deco style of architecture. The Hall of State has been heralded as "The Cathedral of Art Deco Buildings," and the entire grouping of edifices is designated a National Historic Landmark.

Celebrating a birthday in art deco style

❧ When the main building at Texas State School of Mines and Metallurgy (now University of Texas at El Paso) was destroyed by fire in 1916, a strange thing happened. Bhutanese architecture came to the university. Mrs. Kathleen Worrell, wife of the school's dean, fell in love with the architectural style after reading a beautifully illustrated article about Bhutan and its unique buildings. She thought El Paso's Franklin Mountains even resembled the landscape of Bhutan. The dean was convinced, and by January 1918 the New Main building (Old Main today) was completed. It looked like the Paro Dzong of Thimphu—the capital of Bhutan—with its sloping walls and indented windows. Many other Bhutanese-style buildings, such as the library (right), dot the campus today. In 1967, Her Majesty Queen Ashi Kesang Wangchuk of Bhutan visited the campus and complimented the university on the beauty of its buildings. Today, the university has a Himalayan cultural center and El Paso now has a small Buddhist community.

Shangrila in El Paso

A single contribution

❧ Fort Worth's Kimball Art Museum was the last building designed by master architect Louis I. Kahn and the only building in Texas to bear his mark. The contemporary design of the $6.5-million building composed of "cycloid vaults" won the Honor Award of the American Institute of Architects.

A man of justice

❧ Some of the most picturesque courthouses in Texas owe their designs to James Riely Gordon, a Virginian who arrived in San Antonio with his parents when he was only 11. Gordon learned his craft as an apprentice under San Antonio architect W.K. Dobson before striking out on his own in 1887. He designed the Fayette County courthouse in La Grange in 1890 and the Ellis County courthouse in Waxahachie in 1894. In all, Gordon contributed his architectural imagination to 14 Texas courthouses before leaving the state in 1902. He continued the work that he started in Texas, eventually designing 72 courthouses across the nation.

The mother of all shopping centers

Highland Park Village shopping center in the exclusive Dallas enclave of Highland Park is acknowledged as the first self-contained shopping center in the United States—we call them strip malls today. Unlike other centers of the time, all the stores in the Village face inward toward the parking area rather than fronting the surrounding streets. The innovative design, conceived by developer Hugh Prather, Sr., and architect James B. Cheek, was carried out in phases between 1930 and 1947, when the center was completed. It served as a prototype for the thousands of suburban shopping centers that followed.

Making music at the Mort

❧ The Morton H. Meyerson Symphony Center opened in Dallas in September 1989 to a standing ovation and enthusiastic calls of "Bravo!" The *Wall Street Journal* proclaimed "the Meyerson may very well be the last great American piece of architecture for music for a long time to come." Known to locals simply as "the Mort," the $81-million center has drawn international rave reviews as an acoustical masterpiece and an architectural showcase joined in perfect harmony. I.M. Pei designed the contemporary glass and white-stone building. Acoustics expert Russell Johnson worked with Pei on the performance hall. The design process took almost 10 years.

ENCORE!

An operatic solo

❧ The Dallas Opera gives customers more than a song and dance. Before each performance, the company provides lectures that explain to the audience what the opera is about. Regular surveys of customers also let the organization know what audiences want to see and hear in the future. For its customer-service performance, the Dallas Opera received the first annual *Inc.* Magazine/MCI Positive Performer Customer Service Award in 1994. The company was one of only 40 businesses nationwide—and the only arts group—to win the top honor.

❦ Pianist Van Cliburn, originally named Harvey Lavan Cliburn, Jr., was born in Shreveport, Louisiana, on July 12, 1934. But by age 12 he was living with his family in the East Texas town of Kilgore and playing Tchaikovsky's "Concerto No. 1 in B-Flat Minor." The piece won him first place in a statewide Texas competition. In 1947, at age 13, Van Cliburn debuted with the Houston Symphony. A year later, he was playing in Carnegie Hall. In 1958 he became the first American to win the gold medal at the International Tchaikovsky Competition. *Time* magazine proclaimed Van Cliburn "The Texan Who Conquered Russia." The teetotaling Texan returned home a national hero, greeted with an Eisenhower White House library reception (in the picture, Van Cliburn is shown on the left, President Eisenhower on the right) and a Manhattan ticker-tape parade. Texans could not have been more proud of their adopted son. The Dallas Symphony booked Cliburn for a concert and paid him $9,000, an unprecedented fee at the time.

❦ In 1987, the Houston Ballet and the Houston Grand Opera took over their new stage in the $72-million Wortham Center. The ballet presented the world premiere of *The Hunchback of Notre Dame*. The opera offered the world premiere of *Nixon in China*.

Around the theater with Margo Jones

On June 3, 1947, Margo Jones' Theatre-in-the-Round opened in the Gulf Oil Building of the Texas State Fair. The evening's performance was William Inge's *Farther Off From Heaven*. But the big news of the night was the theater itself. It was the first professional repertory theater in the United States to use arena staging (theater-in-the-round) as its sole method of production. Born in Livingston in 1913, Margaret Virginia (Margo) Jones was a stage actor, director, and producer. In 1944, she went by invitation to New York to co-direct the original production of Tennessee Williams' *The Glass Menagerie*. After the play's success, she settled in Dallas and began work on her innovative theater. Jones produced 85 plays during her management of the theater. She died in Dallas on July 24, 1955. Her ground-breaking theater continued until 1959.

AWESOME

So long Sarah

✳ In April 1911, the great Sarah Bernhardt gave her farewell American performance at the Galveston Opera House. She starred in *Camille*.

Standing room only

✳ Alvin Ailey, founder of the Alvin Ailey American Dance Theatre in New York, gained international applause as an avante-garde dancer and choreographer. The African-American artist was born in Rogers in 1931 and moved to Los Angeles at age 12. After seeing a performance in high school of the Ballet Russe de Monte Carlo, he began formal dance training. After a few years in college, Ailey formed his dance company, which made its debut in 1958. The company wowed Australian audiences during an official State Department tour of the land down under in 1962. Three years later, Ailey's troupe made one of the most successful European tours ever by an American dance company. In Hamburg, Germany, the dancers received an unprecedented 61 curtain calls. Ticket demand in London held performances over for six weeks. The highly acclaimed Ailey died on December 1, 1989, in New York City.

A L V I N

AILEY

ART OF THE AGES

Pass it on

✳ Texas Folklife Resources, a statewide nonprofit organization in Austin, keeps the tradition of Lone Star folk arts alive by matching apprentices with the state's master artists. Awarded annually, the apprenticeships range from crafts and music to oral traditions and dance. Funding is provided to compensate master artists for their time and training or to help defray travel and supply expenses. The program gives preference to projects that help perpetuate especially endangered folk arts and to those that pass on an art in the community where it is rooted.

Artists of the forest

✳ In East Texas, the older women of the Alabama-Coushatta people practice a tradition that began when the tribe first settled in the Big Thicket just before the turn of the twentieth century. They weave the strong, supple needles of longleaf pines into practical containers and decorative animal effigies. Dyed needles, woven with those of natural color, create intricate patterns. Cones of shortleaf pines, which grow to about the size of golf balls, are attached as decoration. Scales from the cones are trimmed, rubbed to a sheen, and sewn on to baskets one at a time. Although prized by collectors, the Alabama-Coushatta pine-needle art continues perilously. Few young members of the tribe are taking an interest in learning the art from their elders.

❄ When Texans yen for a yarn, they head for gatherings of story-tellers where tall tales live forever. Storytelling, once reserved for the front porch or family dinner table, has moved into the spotlight in recent years. At the annual, three-day Texas Storytelling Festival in Denton, listeners can hear some of the state's top tale-tellers weave their words. Nationally acclaimed storyteller Gayle Ross of Fredricksburg might share Cherokee myths passed down from her Native American ancestors. Dallas storyteller Elizabeth Ellis sometimes takes the stage with tales from her Appalachian roots. In South Texas, yarn spinners gather around the 1919 courthouse square each year for the George West Storyfest. The celebration of oral tradition began in 1989 when locals swapped stories of ranch life. The community event now draws 3,000 people and features nationally known storytellers from across the country. Cowboy culture gets a tribute at the yearly National Cowboy Symposium and Celebration in Lubbock when poets, storytellers, and songsters revel in their Western heritage.

By word of mouth

❄ Chicano artists in El Paso rediscovered the age-old art of outdoor murals in the 1960s. They began by painting the bordertown barrios, then extended the colorful art to all parts of the city. Too often, the muralists watched as building owners or weather destroyed their work. Then came Los Murales in 1990, a project by the Junior League of El Paso to preserve the city's vivid murals. The successful program grew to include creating new murals. Artists conceived the mural designs, then involved young people in the actual painting process. By 1993, more than 100 murals spread boldly across El Paso, with students contributing to more than one-third of the artworks. The murals showcase the city's cultural diversity, explore its history, and depict contemporary concerns, from AIDS education to the tragedy of gang violence.

Modern-day murals

Mural on the Mall **in El Paso**

❄ Draped over front-yard fences, displayed on clotheslines, or exhibited at museums and galleries, quilts carry on a creative tradition in Texas. Each year the State Fair of Texas hands out blue ribbons to award-winning quilt makers who stitch original designs or re-create patterns such as Texas Tears and Texas Rose that have been preserved through the years. The Lone Star Quilt Conference, staged annually in Houston, pays tribute to the art and craft that still brings neighbors together for community quilting bees. In 1982, the Sam Houston Memorial Museum in Huntsville devoted two entire months to the exhibit "Patterns in Patchwork," proving that quilt making remains a valuable part of the state's artistic present as well as its past.

A colorful cover-up

A TEXAS COLLECTION

No exit

Manuel Mauricio's *Fiesta Skirt*, a large artwork that won top honors in the 1994 "Art in the Metroplex" exhibit, had to be removed from a showing because it violated fire codes. The flower and glass piece was installed, along with two other large works, in the lobby of the Moudy Building at Texas Christian University. The pieces were placed in the building lobby because the only other exhibit space, a 1,300-square-foot gallery, was too small. Mauricio's work, centrally located in the lobby, blocked the exit and posed a fire hazard, said university officials. Exhibit visitors had to settle for viewing a color photograph instead of the first-place artwork.

An everlasting gift

In 1971, transplanted French natives John and Dominique de Menil built the Rothko Chapel near Houston's University of St. Thomas. Inside, they hung 14 huge, black abstract paintings by Mark Rothko. The space and paintings were created for meditation and prayer. Outside, they installed *The Broken Obelisk*, a 26-foot-tall steel sculpture by Barnett Newman that is dedicated to Martin Luther King, Jr. When John de Menil died, great art cities such as Paris and New York tried to woo the 10,000-piece de Menil collection of modern art away from Houston. But Dominique de Menil wanted the priceless works to stay in the Bayou City. In 1987, she opened the Menil Museum one block from the Rothko Chapel. The 100,000-square-foot museum, designed by Italian architect Renzo Piano, now houses the family's collection.

Still giving to Fort Worth

Amon G. Carter wasn't born in Fort Worth, but the cowtown city captured his heart. He became a publisher, helped the city's economic development by persuading businesses to locate there, and gave his time and energy to civic projects. Even in his death, Carter's generosity continued. His will provided for a permanent home for his priceless collection of Western art.

The Amon Carter Museum, established in 1961, houses works by some of the most important American artists from the 1840s through the 1950s—Georgia O'Keeffe, Frederic Remington, Winslow Homer,

and the list goes on. Many of Charles M. Russell's paintings, including *Medicine Man* (left), are on exhibit at the museum.

Upon her death in 1979, Laura Gilpin bequeathed much of her historical work to the museum. Considered one of the foremost photographers of the American West, Gilpin's photos portray the simplicity and grace of 20th-century Native Americans. She bequeathed to the museum her library, 20,000 prints, and 27,000 negatives. Amon Carter would have been proud.

❀ In 1974, Amarillo eccentric Stanley Marsh III and a group of San Francisco designers known as the Ant Farm, created Cadillac Ranch (above). The exercise in automobile art took on national symbol status the moment the project was completed. In a Panhandle wheat field just off old Route 66 (now Interstate 40), 10 Cadillacs headed west were buried in a row grill-down, their distinctive tail fins thrust toward the Texas sky. The cars were interred in chronological order, ranging from 1949 to 1964 models. Twenty years later, Cadillac Ranch still draws tourists and the monument stands as a genuine American work of art.

❀ Modern artists in San Antonio have discovered a hip new place to create and sell their masterpieces. The area is called Blue Star, a once-bustling rail yard now converted into a contemporary inner-city village. The warehouse district dates back to the 1930s when it housed railroad-related businesses such as Blue Star Ice and Cold Storage Company. In 1986, local developers of the six-acre piece of property offered space for a contemporary art show. From that, the historic area began to draw the interest of local artists. The downtown location now boasts artists' apartments, studios, retail galleries, and alternative theaters.

A lifetime of imagination

It has horrified some art critics and been categorized as folk art by others. But the Orange Show in Houston defies classification. Created by Jeff McKissack over a 24-year period, the show opened May 9, 1979, and still entertains visitors. A labyrinth of indoor and outdoor passageways, twisting stairs, tunnels, and multi-tiered observation platforms lead around and through an improbable collection of visual attractions. Whirligigs, architectural gewgaws, small fountains, a wishing well, two steam engines, and mosaic tiles all compete for attention. There is no final destination for wanderers, no hidden treasure waiting at the end of the maze. There is simply something different and surprising to see at every turn. The complex occupies only one-tenth of an acre filled with found materials and objects that McKissack scavenged while working as a postman in Houston. The entire concoction sprang from his imagination. McKissack died of heart failure at age 78 only seven months after the opening of his unique creation. It is now operated by the Orange Foundation.

CARTOONS, TEXAS-STYLE

Cowpoke cartoonist

✣ Almost everyone west of the Mississippi River has chuckled at an Ace Reid cartoon. The native of Electra started selling "Cowpokes" cartoons in 1949. Forty years later, the weekly series was carried in more than 500 newspapers. At last estimate about 100 million Cowpoke cartoons had appeared on Ace Reid calendars that show up in small-town banks, hardware stores, and homes. Reid never had an agent or a publisher, but he and his wife managed to release 13 volumes of ranch-hand humor before Reid died in 1991 at age 66.

Animated controversy

✣ In 1989, Dallasite Mike Judge checked out a book on animation from the Richardson Public Library. Two years later, he drew his first Beavis and Butt-head sketch. Judge sent that two-minute bit, known as "Frog Baseball," to Colossal Pictures, the company behind MTV's "Liquid Television." The half-hour program that showcased offbeat animation was a perfect stage for the twisted Beavis and Butt-head. In 1992, MTV signed Judge to a 65-episode contract. The show premiered in March, became a regular in May, and immediately shot to MTV's highest-rated program. The two demented cartoon characters captured the imaginations of young and old alike. They made "ABC News" and were featured on the cover of *Rolling Stone*, even though detractors flooded MTV with hate mail for the controversial cartoon. Judge's book *Ensucklopedia* boosted Beavis and Butt-head to the paperback best-seller list in 1995.

Parenting with a sense of humor

✣ Exhausted moms and dads of the 1990s can get some daily comic relief thanks to Houston cartoonist Michael Fry. Fry draws on his own parental experience with two young daughters to create "Committed," which playfully portrays the insanity and absurdity of two-career couples raising kids in the modern age. The single-panel cartoon is distributed by United Features Syndicate and appears in more than 50 newspapers across the country.

See you in the funny papers

✣ Dallas cartoonist Buddy Hickerson got fired from his job drawing weather maps because he kept putting cities in the wrong locations. So he put his pen and ink to work on "The Quigmans," the bizarre blockhead characters who now appear daily in newspapers nationwide. The *Los Angeles Times* Syndicate snatched up the single-panel cartoon the first time Hickerson pitched his creation in the 1980s.

THAT'S ENTERTAINMENT

From make-believe movies to chart-bustin' music, Texas stakes its claim in the entertainment industry.

If you saw John Wayne's *The Alamo* or the 1950s epic film *Giant* or the box-office hit *JFK*, you got a glimpse of Texas. If you watched television's "Dallas" or "Walker, Texas Ranger," you saw a bit of it, too.

And if you turn on the radio, you're sure to hear the sounds of Texas. Country crooners George Jones and George Strait hail from the state. Tejano music sensations Selena and Emilio Navaira come from Texas. And the late blues singer Janis Joplin and guitarist Stevie Ray Vaughn were raised here.

The stars are definitely big and bright in the heart of Texas. Come meet the celebrities, the movie-makers, and the music-makers who entertain a nation. It's show time, folks.

- Texas on the Tube
- Filming In and About Texas
- Roll the Credits
- On Center Stage
- Upbeat Rhythms and Blues
- Singing Cowboys
- Entertainment Scrapbook
- Around the State Amusements

TEXAS ON THE TUBE

Texas' best-known bad guy

🖝 Fort Worth-born actor Larry Hagman (left) has played plenty of roles in his 40-year career. But as of April 1993, only once had he taken the part of a villain—J.R. Ewing on "Dallas," the first nighttime soap opera since "Peyton Place." The show debuted in 1978 on a five-week trial. By the end of the 1980-1981 season, Southfork Ranch and the Ewing family had zoomed up to first place in the ratings thanks to a season-end cliffhanger. When bad guy J.R. took a bullet at the end of the 1979-1980 season, it was a shot heard round the world. All summer, the public debated "Who Shot J.R.?" In November 1980, the episode that revealed the would-be killer rocketed the ratings of "Dallas" into the stratosphere. Unfortunately, after 13 seasons, only two of the original cast members remained—Larry Hagman and Ken Kerchival. The show finished in 43rd place at the end of the 1989-1990 season and entered re-run heaven. Dallas is remembered, however, as the show that defined Texas to the world.

Southfork sold

The ranch that was known as Southfork to millions of "Dallas" viewers was sold at auction to Arizonan Rex Maughan for $2.6 million in May 1992. Up to 100,000 tourists a year still visit the home of the famed Ewing family. Southfork is now a popular museum and convention center.

The familiar funny face

🖝 Carol Burnett, born in San Antonio on April 26, 1934, started her career as a singer but switched to comedy in the mid-1950s. She first gained national attention through the television program "The Garry Moore Show" in 1956. As host of "The Carol Burnett Show" on CBS, she became a fixture in comedy television. The highly popular show ran for 11 years, from 1967 until 1978. Burnett's film performances include a dramatic role in *The Four Seasons* (1981) and a comedic role in *Annie* (1982). In 1981, she became the first person to win a libel suit against the gossip tabloid *National Enquirer*. More recently, she's been seen in a guest role on daytime TV's soap opera "All My Children."

Kicking up their heels

🖝 In the fall of 1993, the television series "Walker, Texas Ranger" began getting viewer attention and winning its Saturday-night time slot. With pickup truck chases, spinning heel kicks from karate star Chuck Norris, and plenty of violence where the good guys always win, the show established a following in 68 countries. In early 1994, CBS ordered another 22 episodes of the program, which is shot in and around Dallas. The show's success has led some couch potato critics to claim that Norris could become the J.R. Ewing of the 1990s.

Bandstand on the border

In 1988, the most successful syndicated television show produced outside of Hollywood or New York came from an unlikely location. "The Johnny Canales Show" was taped at TV station KVEO in Brownsville. Each week Canales, the show's host, featured three tejano music bands, and the program attracted more than 100,000 fans in seven states and Mexico. It was the only U.S.-produced Hispanic program aired in Mexico. As producer, talent coordinator, distributor, and star, the bilingual Canales did for Tex-Mex music what Dick Clark did for rock and roll. *Billboard* magazine ranked the hour-long show as one of the most popular non-network variety shows in America. It was the only Spanish-language show to make the list.

AWESOME

In 1994, three of the original stars of "The Mighty Morphin Power Rangers" moved on to other roles. Two of their replacements came from Texas. Arlington's Karan Ashley became Aisha, the Yellow Ranger, and Johnny Yong Bosch morphed into Adam, the Black Ranger. The two auditioned for the parts in July 1994 at KD Studios in Dallas and won the jobs after a nationwide search.

More power to them

FILMING IN AND ABOUT TEXAS

Remember the Alamo

Before filmmakers discovered the rest of Texas, they were drawn to the Alamo. In 1911, French filmmaker Gaston Méliès cast himself as William B. Travis in the first movie ever made about the legendary battle. He shot *The Immortal Alamo* in San Antonio using extras from the Peacock Military Academy. *The Last Command*, 1955, was shot in Bracketville and starred Sterling Hayden as Jim Bowie. That same year, Fess Parker took the lead role in *Davy Crockett* and fought off Mexicans in the Texas shrine. In 1960, John Wayne's picture *The Alamo* was released. Wayne produced and directed the $12-million film that was also shot in Bracketville. He starred as Colonel Davy Crockett.

Governor Preston Smith was an admitted movie buff and even owned a chain of theaters at one time. In 1971, he created the Texas Film Commission, which markets the Lone Star State as a moviemaking mecca. The commission also helps filmmakers scout possible locations, stocking a library with more than 25,000 photographs of cities, landscapes, architecture, and towns. When local talent is needed, the commission can provide contact names for anyone from animal trainers to costume designers.

Selling Texas to the moviemakers

Flying high in San Antonio

San Antonio played a major part in the first Oscar winner. William Wellman's silent film *Wings* was shot in and around the city using pilots from Kelly Field and soldiers from Fort Sam Houston. The movie depicted aviation battles during World War I and premiered in 1927 at San Antonio's Texas Theater. That same year, the film won the first Academy Award for best picture.

Hollywood comes to Texas

In 1923, Hollywood made its first official big-budget film in Texas—the Civil War drama *The Warrens of Virginia*. Director Elmer Clifton focused his camera on San Antonio's Brackenridge Park and the antebellum homes of the King William District. Tragedy occurred on the set when star Martha Mansfield's Victorian costume caught fire. She died the next day.

A hands-on script writer

When the film *Jason's Lyric* opened in theaters in 1994, it grossed $6.3 million in its first five days. Corpus Christi native Bobby Smith, Jr., wrote the script about heartbreak and love in Houston's Fifth Ward. He also showed up every day on the set during the filming in Houston.

No commuters invited

Director Oliver Stone and the city of Dallas struck a blockbuster deal in 1991 during the filming of *JFK*. The city closed off 16 downtown blocks near Dealey Plaza, which forced more than 21,000 commuters to find other routes to work for two weeks. In return for the inconvenience, production of the movie pumped almost $10 million into the Dallas economy.

Stars in Marfa

The three-hour epic *Giant*, released in 1956, brought Elizabeth Taylor, Rock Hudson, and James Dean to Texas for the filming of the classic cattle-empire story. Director George Stevens shot the film in Marfa and garnered an Oscar for his West Texas work that defined the state for moviegoers across the country. Dean's role as young oil wildcatter Jett Rink turned out to be his last.

Touring Texas

When native Texan Dennis Quaid teamed up with real-life wife Meg Ryan to make the 1993 film *Flesh and Bone* in Texas, Quaid called the work "the Motel 6 tour of West Texas." The cast took over motels as sets in nine small towns: Alpine, Big Lake, Cuero, Luling, Marfa, Monahans, Pecos, Valley Springs, and Stanton. Mark Rosenberg, the film's producer, died of a heart attack while supervising one of the scenes in Stanton.

From gore to ghosts

In 1974, University of Texas film student Tobe Hooper took $160,000, rented a few cameras and shot the gory movie *The Texas Chainsaw Massacre* in the Austin area. Since then the low-budget film has grossed more than $25 million. Hooper didn't do too bad himself. He later directed *Poltergeist*.

Other films made in Texas

Places in the Heart – Waxahachie

Born on the Fourth of July – Oak Cliff neighborhood of Dallas

The Great Waldo Pepper – Elgin, Lockhart, Floresville, and Kerrville

Benji – McKinney

Leap of Faith – Plainview

Pure Country – Fort Worth and Terrell

Terms of Endearment – Houston and Galveston

RoboCop – Dallas

What's Eating Gilbert Grape? – Austin, Manor, and Pflugerville

Raggedy Man – Maxwell

Sugarland Express – San Antonio, Floresville, and Del Rio

Urban Cowboy – Houston

The Big Parade – Fort Sam Houston

True Stories – Dallas

Tender Mercies – Waxahachie

D.O.A. – Austin

Logan's Run – Dallas, Houston, and Fort Worth

State Fair – Dallas

Bonnie and Clyde – Dallas and Denton

Hellfighters – Houston

The Andromeda Strain – Shafter

Semi-Tough – Dallas

Honeysuckle Rose – Austin

The Long Riders – Palestine

Resurrection – Shiner and El Paso

Viva, Zapata – Rio Grande City

Tilt – Corpus Christi

Middle Age Crazy – Houston and Dallas

The Oldest Living Graduate – Dallas

Bad Girls – Del Rio and Bracketville

The Border – El Paso

The Last Picture Show – Archer City

Lovin' Molly – Bastrop

Outlaw Blues – Austin

FM - Houston

Eyewitness – Dallas

Brewster McCloud – Houston

For the Love of Benji – Houston

The Getaway – El Paso, Huntsville, San Marcos, and San Antonio

Necessary Roughness – Denton

The Thief Who Came to Dinner – Houston

Not slacking off

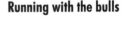 Richard T. Linklater of Austin debuted his 1990 film *Slacker* to local art audiences and University of Texas students. But the movie gained national attention when complimentary reviews appeared in *The New York Times*. In 1992, Hollywood producers offered Linklater a $5-million budget to produce another Austin movie, *Dazed and Confused*. He accepted.

Running with the bulls

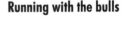 Television teen idol Luke Perry seemed to be tempting fate when he opted to do his own bull-riding stunts for the role of Lane Frost in the film *Eight Seconds*. Frost, who earned a reputation as a star bull rider at Texas rodeos, was fatally gored in July 1989 at the age of 25. Parts of the movie were shot at Guadalupe and Val Verde County fairgrounds and HemisFair Arena in San Antonio.

From the White House to *Wayne's World*

When directors and actors tire of dusty on-location shoots in West Texas, they can travel to The Studios at Las Colinas in Irving for more comfortable surroundings. Since 1992, The Studios has offered tours of the soundstages that hosted interior shoots for *Silkwood*, *Talk Radio*, *Problem Child*, and other films, as well as

television commercials, music videos, and TV productions. Visitors can get an up-close look at two very different scenes from two very different movies—the Oval Office set from Oliver Stone's film *JFK* and the set used in *Wayne's World* (above). Along with sets from movies made in Texas, The Studios maintains a display of costumes and props from other major films. The headpiece worn by Darth Vader and the costume donned by Robin Williams in television's "Mork and Mindy" are on display. At The Studios, visitors see that the airplane used in the film *Airplane* always moved across the screen from right to left because only one side of the plane was painted.

Saturday matinee shoot-em-ups

Hollywood cashed in on desperadoes and cowboys by producing more than 20,000 Western films. Blazing guns, saloon brawls, horseback chases, and fistfights filled Technicolor movie screens from the late 1930s to the 1950s. The Texas mystique was a box-office draw for young and old alike, and Tinseltown used the state's name to grab viewer attention. Here are 10 of the many Texas-named movies that entertained audiences during Saturday matinees.

The Texans, 1938, starring Joan Bennett and Randolph Scott
Texas Wildcatters, 1939, starring Joan Barclay and Ben Corbett
Texas Stampede, 1939, with Charles Starrett
Men of Texas, 1942, starring Robert Stack and Jackie Cooper
Deep in the Heart of Texas, 1942, with Tex Ritter and Johnny Mack Brown
Texas Masquerade, 1944, with William Boyd
Outlaws of Texas, 1950, with Whip Wilson
The Tall Texans, 1953, starring Lloyd Bridges and Lee J. Cobb
Texas Lady, 1955, with Claudette Colbert
From Hell to Texas, 1958, with Don Murray and Diane Varsi

ROLL THE CREDITS

A Texas-grown talent

✈ Born in the small East Texas town of Quitman on Christmas Day 1949, Mary Elizabeth "Sissy" Spacek was a majorette at the local high school before achieving stardom on the silver screen. Spacek captured an Academy Award as best actress for her role in the 1980 film *Coal Miner's Daughter*. In 1981, she returned to her native state to film *Raggedy Man* in Maxwell. Other film credits include *Missing* (1982), *The River* (1984), *Marie* (1958), *Crimes of the Heart* (1986), and *The Long Walk Home* (1990).

An athlete and an actor

Most fans know Patrick Swayze as the sexy leading man in blockbuster films such as *Dirty Dancing*, *Ghost*, or TV's "North and South." But before he found fame, the Houston-born actor plied his talents as a high-school gymnast and football star in Texas. He attended San Jacinto College in Houston and then started in show business as Prince Charming in "Disney on Parade." After moving to New York, Swayze studied dance with the Joffrey Ballet Company and performed with the Buffalo Ballet Company. When an old football injury came back to haunt him, Swayze added acting lessons to his dancing expertise and landed a lead in the Broadway show *Grease*. After that it was on to Hollywood for a film career that included *City of Joy*, *Fatherhood*, and *Point Break*.

From Chireno to Broadway

✈ Lucille Ann Collier was born in Chireno on April 12, 1923, but the world came to know her as Ann Miller. She suffered from rickets as a child and turned to dancing to help rehabilitate her legs. She broke into films in 1937, stringing together a number of low-budget movies during World War II. She even danced with Fred Astaire in *Easter Parade*. But most male dancers of the day fell short of Miller's five-feet, six-inch height. When the era of the Hollywood musicals faded, Miller found the lights brighter on Broadway. She's known as the star of such hits as *Mame* and *Sugar Babies*.

The reel thing

The Harry Ransom Humanities Research Center of the University of Texas protects one of the preeminent film collections in the world. More than 800 reels of priceless films, 30 tons of manuscript papers, and thousands of movie mementos make up the 16 major collections housed in the archives. The David O. Selznick collection includes home movies and a negative of *Gone With the Wind*, as well as footage of the Lana Turner and Tallulah Bankhead screen tests for the role of Scarlett. Most of the movies kept in the center were made before 1952 and produced on highly combustible nitrate film. To protect the valuables, many are stored in a former Nike missile bunker near Austin.

Bitten by the movie bug

Three Texans got extra helpings for their careers with the 1994 film *Reality Bites*. Houston's Helen Childress wrote the script and set the story in her hometown, where it was filmed. A demo recording, "Stay," by Dallas native Lisa Loeb, made it to the movie's soundtrack. And Austin-born actor Ethan Hawke starred in the movie with Winona Ryder.

The singing cowboy

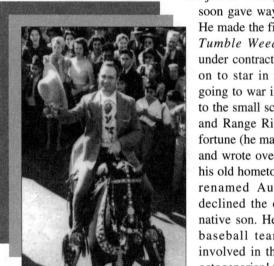

Gene Autry, the original singing cowboy, moved to Hollywood in 1934 and became the top Western box office draw for seven years. Autry was born on September 29, 1907, in the Grayson County town of Tioga. He moved to Oklahoma after graduating from high school, but his job as a telegraph operator for the railroad soon gave way to more entertaining pursuits. He made the first singing Western—*Tumbling Tumble Weeds*—released in 1935, while under contract to Republic Studios, and went on to star in more than 100 movies. After going to war in 1941, he returned and moved to the small screen, starring in Melody Ranch and Range Rider. After achieving fame and fortune (he made 82 films between 1934-1954 and wrote over 250 songs), he offered to buy his old hometown—on the condition that it be renamed Autry Springs. The residents declined the offer from their most notable native son. He bought the California Angels baseball team instead, where he's still involved in the day-to-day operations as an octogenarian! Old cowboys never die!

He's still right here

Henry Thomas, the 10-year-old who starred as Elliot in the 1982 film *E.T.: The Extraterrestrial*, never landed far from home. Born September 8, 1971, in San Antonio, Thomas now lives on a ranch and raises quarter horses just outside the city. He also plays guitar, writes songs, and sings for a San Antonio band called the Rain Dogs. And, of course, he still makes a movie now and then, such as the 1994 film *Legends of the Fall*.

Out on the town and into the movies

University of Texas film student Matthew McConaughey happened into the right place at the right time. While sipping a few drinks in an Austin bar with his girlfriend, McConaughey met Don Phillips, producer of *Fast Times at Ridgemont High*. By the time the evening was over, Phillips had cast the Uvalde-born McConaughey in the Austin film *Dazed and Confused*. That role led to another part, and by the time McConaughey graduated from college he was headed for a movie career in Los Angeles. In 1993, he played a center fielder in *Angels in the Outfield*. The next year he landed his first starring role in *Boys on the Side*, sharing the screen with Whoopi Goldberg and Drew Barrymore.

The Oscar went to mommie dearest

Joan Crawford was born Lucille Le Sueur in San Antonio, on March 23, 1908, but she traded Texas for Tinseltown. Crawford began her career as a dancer, first on the stage and later in silent films. Her first starring role came in *Our Modern Maidens* in 1929. She went on to become one of Hollywood's most glamorous actresses, starring in more than 70 films, such as *Grand Hotel* (1932), *The Women* (1939), and *What Ever Happened to Baby Jane?* (1962). In 1945 she won an Academy Award for her performance in the title role of *Mildred Pierce*. Crawford died on May 10, 1977. Two years later her adopted daughter Christina Crawford published *Mommie Dearest*, an unsympathetic biography about the actress.

 In 1979, University of Texas graduate Robert Benton walked away with an Academy Award for directing the film *Kramer vs. Kramer*, starring Meryl Streep and Dustin Hoffman. The movie captured five other Oscars. Benton's film was ranked the number-two grossing movie in Texas in 1980, behind *The Empire Strikes Back*.

A famous ex-Longhorn

Jumping his way to stardom

Actor Woody Harrelson, born in Midland July 23, 1961, grew up with the nickname Woody Boyd and then played a charming, if dim-witted, character by the same name on the NBC sitcom "Cheers." He won an Emmy for his performance before moving on to more serious roles. His career took a major leap with his first leading role in 1992 in the feature film *White Men Can't Jump*. Since then he's also starred in *Natural Born Killers* and *The Cowboy Way*. When he's not making movies, Harrelson's been known to moonlight as the lead singer of a 10-piece "blues-a-billy" band—Manly Moondog and the Three Kool Kats.

CHEERS

An uncanny likeness

Oscar, the coveted Academy Award statuette, was presumably named for Texan Oscar Pierce. Pierce's niece worked in Hollywood for the Academy of Motion Pictures Arts and Sciences. When she saw the gold statuette, she supposedly exclaimed, "Why that looks just like my Uncle Oscar!"

The winding road of Tommy Lee Jones

🔫 Tommy Lee Jones' high-school teachers once described him as "sullen, morose and belligerent," but he was intelligent. When he attended Harvard on a scholarship, he roomed with Vice President Al Gore. In the early 1970s, he performed on the soap opera "One Life to Live." He moved from New York to Los Angeles in 1976 and rented the home where Marilyn Monroe committed suicide. Finally, Jones settled back home in 1981. An eighth-generation Texan, Jones has no desire to leave the Lone Star State. He owns San Saba ranch were he ropes calves and plays polo between making movies. (His polo team won the U.S. Polo Association's Western Challenge Cup in 1993.) He won an Emmy for his work in *The Executioner's Song* and more recently an Oscar for best supporting actor in *The Fugitive*. His big-screen film credits read like a list of blockbusters: *JFK*, *The Client*, *Under Siege*, and *Natural Born Killers*, just to name a few.

ON CENTER STAGE

Dancing away with Tony awards

Long tall Texan Tommy Tune may very well be Broadway's most recognizable man. Audiences know him as the star of acclaimed shows such as *My One and Only* and *Bye Bye Birdie*. He directed the likes of *Nine*, *Grand Hotel*, and *The Will Rogers Follies*. By 1994, his credits added up to nine Tony awards, making him the most successful choreographer-director in American musical theater. And to think it all started with his first formal tap lesson at the age of 5.

All things Texan on Broadway

🔫 The hit musical *The Best Little Whorehouse* in Texas stayed on Broadway for nearly four years, making it the seventeenth-longest-running show in Broadway history. Not bad for four Texans who weathered a stormy collaboration to get the show to the stage. Author Larry L. King of Putnam wrote the script. Actor-director Peter Masterson of Angleton co-wrote the story and co-directed the musical. Carol Hall of Dallas composed the songs and lyrics. None had ever written a musical before. Tommy Tune of Wichita Falls co-directed and choreographed the show, something he had never done before on Broadway.

Fifteen years after that smashing success, the foursome reunited for a Broadway sequel, *The Best Little Whorehouse Goes Public*. Whatever magic had waved its wand over the first work disappeared in 1993. The sequel was panned by critics and closed within a few days.

UPBEAT RHYTHMS AND BLUES

Penning a song in Pampa

On April 14, 1935, as dust swirled into the Texas Panhandle, Woody Guthrie sat down inside a house in Pampa, looked out the window at the darkening day, and wrote the classic song, "So Long, It's Been Good to Know You."

From a Waco choir to Broadway

Jules Bledsoe, born in Waco in 1898, developed his young baritone voice by singing in the Baptist church choir. In 1924, he made his New York concert debut. Four years later he delighted audiences by singing the venerable "Ol' Man River" in the Broadway musical *Show Boat*. Bledsoe died in 1943.

From opera to hillbilly twang

Marion T. Slaughter, born in Jefferson in 1883, successfully sang light opera until 1916 when hillbilly music became the rage. Slaughter gave his voice a more rural accent to accommodate the new musical style and changed his name to Vernon Dalhart, borrowing from two Texas towns. Dalhart's first recording, "The Prisoner's Song" and its flip side "The Wreck of the Old 97," sold 25 million copies. He went on to produce hundreds of records under as many as 50 different names. Unfortunately, he didn't copyright his work and died broke.

The king lived here
In 1958, Elvis Presley was stationed at Fort Hood while doing duty in the army. The King of Rock 'n' Roll rented a house in the city of Killeen in Bell County.

Rhythmic mix of cultures

When the Tejano Music Awards premiered in San Antonio in 1980, only about 1,300 people witnessed the presentations. Fourteen years later, the 1994 show attracted an audience of 32,500. The awards presentation, known as the Grammy awards of Tejano music, was telecast on all major English-language networks, as well as Spanish-language Telemundo and Univisión.

Tejano music—named because Texans of Mexican descent are called *tejanos* in Mexico—fuses country, pop, and rock with fast-paced cumbia (a mixture of Mexican, Caribbean, and Jamaican) rhythms. And the very danceable beat is as hot as a Texas summer. The state boasts more than 20 tejano radio stations and has given the musical genre some of its top stars: La Mafia of Houston, Grupo Mazz from Brownsville, San Antonio's Emilio Navaira, David Lee Garza of Poteet, and Laura Canales (above) of Kingsville.

Ruling over tejano music

⭐ Tejano music fans know Selena Quintanilla Perez simply as Selena. Born in 1971 in Lake Jackson, Selena was only 23 when she took home a 1994 Grammy for Best Mexican-American Album with *Selena Live!* Her album *Amor Prohibido* went quadruple platinum in the United States. Sales exceeded 400,000 and were expected to do just as well in Mexico by the end of 1994. The "queen of Tejano music" was working on her first English-language album when she was allegedly shot and killed by Yolanda Saldivar—an employee suspected of embezzlement—on March 31, 1995, in Corpus Christi.

Collecting tejano treasures

⭐ The Little Joe Museum in Temple pays tribute to the tejano music group Little Joe y Familia that has performed for more than 30 years. The museum showcases the musicians' 1992 Grammy Award along with stage costumes and musical instruments. It also houses the Ramón Hernández Hispanic Entertainment Archives, a collection of 30,000 tejano albums and information about the recording artists.

Still goin' strong

✈ The Texas Tornados, formed in 1989 by old-timers Doug Sahm and Freddie Fender, can still sell 22,000 tickets at San Antonio's Sea World for a performance of authentic Tex-Mex music.

Catalyst for trouble

✈ Symbol of the 1960s hippie movement, raspy-voiced singer Janis Joplin was born in Port Arthur in 1943. She showed her intelligence and artistic talent early by writing plays in the first grade. But she was not a particularly attractive child, and in a world obsessed with appearance, that proved difficult. During high school, she began singing with records and displayed an obvious gift for mimicking others' voices. She also gained weight and developed a bad skin condition. Not feeling accepted she started drinking heavily, dressing sloppily, speaking crudely, and hanging with the wrong crowd. Joplin graduated from Thomas Jefferson High in 1960 with excellent grades and moved on to college attending Lamar and the University of Texas. But she suffered a crushing blow when she was nominated as a contestant in the "Ugliest Man on Campus" contest at UT. She headed for San Francisco, tormented by her lack of acceptance. There, she ultimately got her big break as a singer with Big Brother and the Holding Company. Living in Haight-Ashbury, Joplin became heavily involved in heroin and alcohol. Several weeks before she died, the lonely rock star lamented that she was working on a new song entitled "I Just Made Love to 25,000 People But I'm Going Home Alone." She died of an apparent heroin overdose at age 27.

Smart star

Most music enthusiasts know that Brownsville-native Kris Kristofferson wrote such classic songs as "Help Me Make It Through the Night" and "Me and Bobby McGee" before pursuing his own successful recording career. Film buffs know him as an actor in numerous movies, including *Alice Doesn't Live Here Anymore*. But the fact that Kristofferson was a Rhodes scholar may come as a surprise.

Yea, Yea, Yea

On September 18, 1964, the world's most recognizable rock and roll band played a concert at Dallas Memorial Auditorium. It was one of 32 performances given during a 25-city tour by the Fab Four rock group that defined the 1960s. A ticket to see and hear the Beatles that evening cost $5.50.

Meat Loaf, without potatoes

✈ Meat Loaf, the bulky musician and actor from Dallas, was born in 1948 as Marvin Lee Aday. Coming from a family of large people—his father weighed 350 pounds and his uncle 700—Meat weighed 240 pounds in the seventh grade. His high-school football coach gave him his now-famous nickname. The singer became a mega-success in 1977 with the release of the album *Bat Out of Hell*. But in the 1980s, he was burned with 22 lawsuits totaling $85 million and bankruptcy. In 1993

Meat Loaf served up his classic style again with *Bat Out of Hell II*. It debuted at the number-three spot on the *Billboard* pop chart and has since sold more than 2 million copies.

At the top

An El Paso band, ZZ Top (right), has rocked the charts for more than 20 years with albums such as *La Grange* and *Tres Hombres*. The band's original 1969 members included Dan Mitchell as drummer, Lanier Greig on bass, and guitarist Billy Gibbons. Greig was replaced by Frank Beard and Mitchell by Dusty Hill in late 1969. The band chose "Z.Z." after Texas bluesman Z.Z. Hill—adding the "Top" was a little different. One day while driving past an old barn with the hayloft doors open, a friend of Billy

Gibbons pointed to the old Z-shaped beams on the hayloft doors and said, "Look, Z.Z. Top!" That was it—the band had a name.

Singin' and playin' the blues

Over the years, blues musicians in Texas have wailed their way to popularity with audiences and in the process have taken on some unique monikers. John T. Smith assumed such names as "Howling Wolf" and "Funny Paper" Smith. Aaron "T-Bone" Walker went from singing on the streets of Dallas' Oak Cliff neighborhood to touring foreign capitals. Henry "Ragtime Texas" Thomas, from East Texas, rode the rails as a hobo in addition to tapping the roots of blues music. Clarence "Gatemouth" Brown made the crossover to country music. Johnny "Guitar" Watson and Sam "Lightnin" Hopkins also left their marks on generations of blues lovers.

Other native Texas rockers

- Stephen Stills of Dallas added his voice to the Buffalo Springfield, then Crosby, Stills, Nash, and Young before going solo.
- Sly Stone, also of Dallas, formed the band Family Stone in 1967 and produced hits including "Dance to the Music" and "Everybody Is a Star."
- East Texan Don Henley co-founded The Eagles before going solo.
- Jimmy Gilmer, raised in Amarillo, had his biggest hit in 1963 with the number-one song "Sugar Shack."
- One of the pioneers of psychedelic rock, the 13th Floor Elevators, began in Austin in 1965.

A premature death ⚡ Dallas-native Stevie Ray Vaughn died in a helicopter crash in August 1990, just as his contemporary rhythm-and-blues music was gaining full force. Considered one of the most gifted guitar players in the state, he won Grammies in 1984 for *Texas Flood* and in 1989 for *In Step*. Some blues enthusiasts claim Vaughn's brother Jimmy, formerly a guitarist with the Fabulous Thunderbirds, is one of the most authentic white blues guitarists of modern times. Stevie Ray and Jimmy recorded an album together in 1990 entitled *Family Style*.

Singing the blues ⚡ Blind Lemon Jefferson could sing the country blues like none before. He was born blind on a farm near Wortham on July 3, 1897, and spent his childhood singing on streets and in churches. He took his talent to the dive bars of Dallas and eventually to audiences in Chicago. Jefferson started recording at the age of 28 and was one of the first country blues singers in the nation to gain wide acceptance. The records he made are still prized today. But his musical contributions were cut short. At 32, he froze to death in a Chicago snowbank.

SINGING COWBOYS

The life and hard times of Willie ⚡ If Texas designated an official country musician for the state, Willie Nelson would most likely be chosen. He left his home state in 1960 to pursue songwriting in Nashville. Composing classics such as

"Crazy," "Night Life," and "Funny How Time Slips Away" earned him a place in the Nashville Songwriters Hall of Fame. But "Willie," as Texans call him, thumbed his nose at the Nashville scene and headed for home in 1972. He took his braided hair, bandana, and beat-up guitar and began performing his own brand of outlaw country music. He also began hosting his annual Fourth of July picnic in Dripping Springs, a mecca for younger listeners of the new Texas-style country music. With hit albums such as *Red-Headed Stranger* (1975) and gold records such as "Blue Eyes Cryin' in the Rain," Willie's voice became the sound of the state. Million-dollar tax problems with the IRS and turning the big six-o in 1993, didn't stop his music. Today, Willie is still singing and Texans still embrace their native son.

Straight from Pearsall to fame

George Strait, born in Pearsall on May 18, 1952, didn't learn to play a guitar until he served a stint in the army. Since then, he's put more number-one songs on the charts than any other solo country performer. His clean-cut image, boot-tapping swing music, and crooning ballads have earned him Entertainer of the Year status five times.

⭐ Clint Black, born in the Houston suburb of Katy in 1962, played plenty of Texas honky-tonks before the Country Music Association named him the promising newcomer in 1989. Black, a former steelworker, took only one formal guitar lesson and played bass in his brother's band. The family hosted backyard barbecues where the Black brothers entertained guests. Through the *Urban Cowboy* craze of the early 1980s, Black made a name for himself playing the C &W circuit in Houston. When he finally released his debut single, "A Better Man," the song topped the charts.

Suburban cowboy

More twang from Texas

Vidor-native Tracy Byrd can trace his country music twang straight through the heart of Texas. His dad introduced him to Western Swing music through a massive collection of old 78's. But Byrd's hankering for country music took hold in 1985 when he discovered the music of George Strait while attending classes at Southwest Texas State University in San Marcos. His college days ended when he won a talent contest at Cutters, Beaumont's famous honky-tonk. Byrd led the house band at Cutters for three years before signing a record deal and releasing his debut album, *Tracy Byrd*, in 1993. The record produced a list of Top 20 singles and turned the young Texan into a star. He's best known for "Holdin' Heaven."

A Capitol first

Tex Ritter, long known as "America's Most Beloved Cowboy," hailed from Murvaul in Panola County. He made his first recording, "Rye Whiskey," in 1931 then went on to star on eight radio shows during the 1930s. He also starred in more than 80 films, starting with *Song of the Gringo* in 1936. Ritter was the first artist to be signed by Capitol Records, and in 1964 he became only the second living person ever inducted into the Country Music Hall of Fame. Ritter died in 1974.

⭐ In 1960, Texan Jim Reeves was known as the number-one male singer in country and western music. But before he hit the top of the charts, Reeves had tried to get his mitts on a professional baseball career. He signed with the St. Louis Cardinals after he graduated from the University of Texas. An injured nerve sent him back to his music after only two years of hardball. Reeves died in 1964 in an airplane crash outside of Nashville. Three years later he was elected into the Country Music Hall of Fame.

Hitting home runs in country music

⭐ *Time* magazine once described Lyle Lovett's hairdo as "resembling a road-kill toupee." Lovett, a native of Klein, may not look the part of the typical country music crooner, but his slightly bizarre appearance hasn't hampered his success. He shocked celebrity watchers when he married Hollywood star Julia Roberts. His bluesy music in the song "Here I Am" garnered a Grammy in 1989. The Texan even took a role as a detective in Robert Altman's movie *The Player*.

What's with the hair?

Traveling troubadour

★ Grand Ol' Opry star Ernest Tubb and his band the Texas Troubadours traveled some 100,000 miles each year performing such classic country and western tunes as "I'm Walking the Floor Over You." The grueling pace paid off for the native Texan. He was elected to the Country Music Hall of Fame in 1965, and his record sales surpassed 20 million.

AWESOME

What's in a name?
When country and western music star Harold Lloyd Jenkins changed his name, he took Conway from Conway, Arkansas, and Twitty from Twitty, Texas.

The king of swing

★ In 1940, one of the greatest country classics of all time, "San Antonio Rose," sold more than a million copies. It was only one of the 500 songs penned by Texas' own Bob Wills. In 1933, Wills formed his legendary band—the Texas Playboys—in Waco. He introduced horns and reed instruments into country music and created a new sound known as Western Swing. The band included vocalist Tommy Duncan and steel guitarist Leon McAuliffe. Wills' famous "Ahhh-Ha" and "Take it Away, Leon" still echo today in the music that demands boot-scootin'. The great bandleader was elected to the Country Music Hall of Fame in 1968 and died in 1975.

East Texas escape artist

★ When country music artist Mark Chesnutt isn't stringing together hits, he tries to hide out from the bright lights on his 60-acre spread in the Big Thicket near Jasper. But with 11 consecutive Top 10 singles, including "Blame it on Texas" and "Old Flames Have New Names," the East Texas singer is finding privacy harder to come by. And he can't escape the fact that his 3 albums have sold more than 2 million copies.

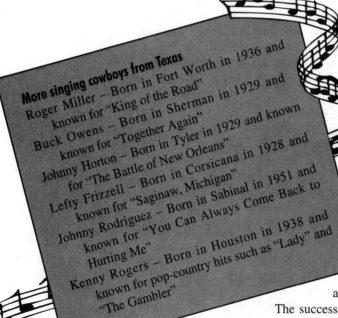

More singing cowboys from Texas
Roger Miller – Born in Fort Worth in 1936 and known for "King of the Road"
Buck Owens – Born in Sherman in 1929 and known for "Together Again"
Johnny Horton – Born in Tyler in 1929 and known for "The Battle of New Orleans"
Lefty Frizzell – Born in Corsicana in 1928 and known for "Saginaw, Michigan"
Johnny Rodriguez – Born in Sabinal in 1951 and known for "You Can Always Come Back to Hurting Me"
Kenny Rogers – Born in Houston in 1938 and known for pop-country hits such as "Lady" and "The Gambler"

Performance premonition
Clay Walker's singles "What's it to You?" and "Live Until I Die" went to number-one on the country music charts in 1993, only one year after he was discovered playing at Beaumont's Neon Armadillo. The success came as no surprise to Walker. He knew he was destined for show business when he received a standing ovation after a performance at his high-school talent show.

➤ The National Academy of Recording Arts and Sciences established the Grammy Awards in 1958 to honor achievements in 28 categories of recording. In 1960, "El Paso" by singer Marty Robbins was the first country song to win a Grammy.

A first for El Paso

George Jones' favorite song

Nearly 40 years ago, Saratoga-native George Jones put $50 in his pocket for four hours on the stage. These days, he banks $20,000 to $50,000 per show and performs about 120 times each year. But after all the performances and all the memorable country hits, Jones' favorite song remains "Window Up Above," written in 1960 when he lived in Vidor. He composed the song in about 20 minutes while sitting in his den waiting for his breakfast.

Some singing cowgirls from Texas

Dale Evans – Born in Uvalde in 1912
Tanya Tucker (right) – Born in
    Seminole in 1958
Barbara Mandrell – Born in Houston
    in 1948
Jeannie C. Riley – Born in Anson in
    1945

ENTERTAINMENT SCRAPBOOK

➤ Electric-guitar maker Mark Erlewine of Austin designed an original yellow "Chiquita" guitar with a smaller-than-usual body so it could be conveniently carried aboard an airplane. The odd-shaped instrument was featured in the film *Back to the Future*.

Instrumental design

Captain of the airwaves

Most radio listeners don't know the name Gordon McClendon, but they've benefited from his pioneering work. McClendon helped create the Top 40 format and helped found what was once the most popular radio station in the nation, Dallas' KLIF. A master at promotion, he touted DJ personalities until they became household names and devised publicity stunts that made listeners remember the station's call letters. McClendon once tossed balloons with money attached out of a downtown Dallas hotel, a stunt that tied up rush-hour traffic. His innovations included bumper stickers to promote his stations and billboard advertising for hot disk jockeys. He's credited with creating the first all-news and easy-listening formats, as well as putting the first mobile news unit to use. McClendon died in 1986 at the age of 65. In November 1994, creative McClendon was inducted into Chicago's Museum of Broadcast Communications' Radio Hall of Fame.

The music man

John A. Lomax grew up on a farm in Bosque County listening to cowboys croon. Even though he wasn't a musician, the folk songs spoke to him, and he began capturing the voices and the music. In 1908, Lomax recorded "Home on the Range" as it was sung by an elderly African-American man in San Antonio. By 1910, he had recorded enough material to publish the first-ever collection of folk songs, *Cowboy Songs and Other Frontier Ballads*. For the next 30 years, Lomax, later joined by his son Alan, traveled and listened and gathered more than 10,000 folk songs for the Library of Congress. In 1933, they went into a prison and discovered Huddie "Leadbelly" Ledbetter. With his 12-string guitar and powerful voice, Leadbelly took Texas blues to the world with such songs as "Rock Island Line," "Midnight Special," and "Goodnight Irene." Without the pioneering work of Lomax, countless voices would have undoubtedly gone unheard.

Tickling the ivories in Texas

David Guion grew up in the West Texas town of Ballinger listening to cowboys of the late 1800s fiddle, strum, and whistle their folk songs. Although Guion picked the piano as his instrument, he never strayed far from his musical roots. At age 15, he put "Home on the Range" in manuscript form, composing the melody and writing down the lyrics he had heard so often. In 1919, he turned his attention to "Turkey in the Straw," a favorite tune of cowboy fiddlers. Guion was the first composer to arrange an old fiddle tune for the piano. Both of those compositions were performed at the Roxy Theater in New York in 1924 during a cowboy production initiated by Guion, and the Big Apple got its first slice of Texas music.

Gathering at the 'Dillo

In the summer of 1970, the Armadillo World Headquarters (left) opened its doors in Austin and spent the next decade becoming the musical heart of the city. It was a National Guard Armory converted into a concert hall with a beer-joint atmosphere. And it attracted an eclectic mix of legendary performers. Count Basie packed the house. For a $1 cover charge, folks could hear a youthful Bruce Springsteen play. The audience could munch on nachos while watching the Austin Ballet Theater dance. Willie Nelson and Waylon Jennings brought their new brand of Texas outlaw music to the stage. But the lights dimmed as the 1970s faded. In 1980, the great Armadillo experiment ended. The building was razed and replaced by a high-rise office. Austin's musical heart and its culture were changed forever.

A brazen style from a Texas gal

In the early 1900s, a flashy former cowgirl from Waco found success on the Hollywood screen. Mary Louise Cecilia Guinan left her family ranch in 1898 at the age of 14 and went to work as a circus trick rider in Chicago. She adopted the nickname "Texas" and rode her success all the way to Hollywood. There she appeared in more than 200 two-reelers, including *The Gun Woman* (1918) and *Little Miss Deputy* (1919). Unsatisfied, the brassy Texas Guinan moved to New York and took roles in Broadway musicals. But her sassy style was more suited to the high-class night-clubs of the prohibition times than to theater. Her speakeasy shows won adoring fans as she perched atop a piano and greeted customers with "Hello, suckers!" She ended every show with the line that has endured as a Broadway classic, "Give the little ladies a great big hand!" Texas returned to Hollywood in 1929 to make the film *Queen of the Night Clubs*. She died in 1933 while on tour with a revue.

The circus comes to town

For nearly 40 years around the turn of the 20th century, "The Mollie A. Bailey Show" toured Texas. Stopping in about 100 small Texas towns each year, the circus show featured 21 trained ponies, elephants, and camels at its height, as well as an entourage of clowns, dancers, and acrobats. More than 30 wagons and 170 head of stock moved with the show. Based in Dallas, Mollie usually left the city in early spring and headed the circus for the sawmill towns of East Texas. From there, the route went to South Texas, through the blackland cotton region, on to the Panhandle, and then to West Texas. By December the show returned to Dallas. Traveling through unsettled Texas had its dangers back then, but Mollie wouldn't be stopped. As one story goes, she single-handedly chased off a band of Indians one night. When the Indians began circling the circus wagons, Mollie supposedly fired her pistol into the air, then beat the brass circus drum. The Indians, thinking the drum was a cannon, quickly dispersed.

Names in the news

From network anchors to columnists and critics, native Texans have a nose for news. These few can sniff out a good story or spot a hot celebrity in a crowd.

TV journalist Sam Donaldson, born March 11, 1934, in El Paso
TV journalist Linda Ellerbee, born August 15, 1944, in Bryan
TV journalist/news anchor Dan Rather, born October 31, 1931, in Wharton
TV journalist Bob Schieffer, born February 25, 1937, in Austin
Columnist Liz Smith, born February 2, 1923, in Fort Worth
Movie critic Rex Reed, born October 2, 1939, in Fort Worth
Journalist and White House watchdog Sarah McClendon, born July 8, 1910, in Tyler

AROUND THE STATE AMUSEMENTS

Grab your partner

After falling out of favor around 1900, square dancing, the official folk dance of Texas, regained popularity in the early 1930s thanks to Herb Greggerson of El Paso and Jimmy Clossin of Abilene. The two conducted clinics and taught classes across northwest Texas and led a revival in the do-si-do dance. Today, the Texas State Federation of Square and Round Dancers hosts an annual festival in Amarillo that draws more than 3,000 twirling dancers.

Just fiddlin' around

Texas fiddlers rosin up their bows every June for the World Championship Fiddlers' Festival in Crockett. Originated in 1936 by master fiddler Barker Tunstall, the event requires contestants to play three tunes; a breakdown, a waltz, and a song of their own picking. Fiddle greats James "Texas Shorty" Chancellor (left) and Louis Franklin have played their way to the top of the competition multiple times. Homegrown players who fiddle the best are honored at the Texas Fiddlers' Hall of Fame in Hallettsville.

Hill Country hoe-down

The granddaddy of all Lone Star music festivals, the Kerrville Folk Festival, started in 1971 and remains one of the most successful gathering of musicians in the country. The eclectic mix of singers and songwriters fans out over multiple days and numerous events. At the Ballad Tree, songsters share original tunes and swap turns strumming the guitar. Along with watching evening performances in the amphitheater, audience members can participate in songwriting and guitar-picking classes. Plenty of toe-tappin' rhythms for the music-meister in every Texan.

Honky-tonk heaven

First it was Gilley's in Pasadena in the 1970s. Then Billy Bob's Texas reigned in Fort Worth during the 1980s. For the 1990s, the hot country and western music spot is Beaumont's Cutters, a 10,000-square-foot honky-tonk that has been heralded as the launching pad for the new Texas stars of the country charts. Young hunks like Mark Chesnutt and Tracy Byrd led house bands at the club before rocketing to stardom. In fact, the Cutters table where the two signed their recording deals with MCA Records is now the property of the Country Music Hall of Fame in Nashville.

The granddaddy of all Texas parties

Texans hold bragging rights to the largest state fair in North America. The State Fair of Texas was chartered in 1886 in Dallas. Attendance topped the 1 million mark in 1914 with the appearance of the first auto show. The big celebration of all things Texan generally runs for 24 days, but the 1986 Sesquicentennial event lasted 52 days. A performance by country music superstar Garth Brooks on October 13, 1990, contributed to the highest single day attendance—193,184 visitors. In 1993, more than 3 million fair lovers entertained themselves at the statewide party.

THE SPORTS ARENA

In 1994, another Texan made the sports record books. Kenny Rogers of the Texas Rangers pitched a perfect game—no hits, no walks, no errors—against the California Angels.

From the Friday-night heroics of high-school football to Olympic gold medal glory, Texas athletics span all sports. The achievements of great Texas athletes endure in Halls of Fame and the records of winning teams can be seen on tall trophies. Whether on a thoroughbred horse-racing track or a golf course, a basketball court or a motor speedway, the competitive spirit prevails in the Lone Star State.

Come meet the individuals and the teams who made the great moments in Texas sports.

RIDIN', ROPIN', AND SHOOTIN'

Doing the suicide drag and other stunts

Tad Lucas moved to Fort Worth in 1920 as a teenager and lived there for 70 years while she established herself as one of the greatest trick riders of all time. During the 1920s and 1930s, Lucas won the all-around and trick-riding championships eight times. She pioneered the dangerous stunt of passing under the belly of a galloping horse and coming up on the other side. In 1967, Lucas was the first woman inducted into the Cowboy Hall of Fame in Oklahoma City. She was also inducted into the Cowgirl Hall of Fame in Hereford, Texas, in 1978. Lucas died in 1990.

Ride 'em cowboy

Some say that native Texan Bill Pickett invented the rodeo sport of bulldogging in 1903. His daredevil style paid off when he became the first African American inducted into the National Cowboy Hall of Fame in Oklahoma City in 1972. Pickett, all 5 feet 9 inches tall and 165 pounds, bulldogged steers like no other cowboy. Leaping from his horse, Pickett would grab hold of a steer's horns and then twist the head until he could sink his teeth into the animal's upper lip and sling the mad steer to the ground. One of his assistants was a boy named Tom Mix, later a cowboy star of the silent movies. Pickett's bulldogging days came to a tragic end on April 2, 1932, when a horse trampled him to death.

Bull-riding's best ◀ Donnie Gay of Mesquite rode his first bull at the age of 3. He moved on to the professional scene in 1970 and stayed on bulls long enough to win eight bull-riding championships. He remains the all-time leader of that event. In 1988, Kermit-native Jim Sharp won the first of two bull-riding titles at the National Finals Rodeo in Las Vegas. He cleanly rode all 10 of his bulls, a feat that had never before been accomplished.

Tough enough

Tuff Hedeman, pictured at far left with Lane Frost, lives up to his name. The El Paso native rode his first calf at age 4, then straddled the big bulls as a professional rodeo star. In 1986, at age 23, Hedeman won his first world title riding bulls. He also set a new income record for the premier rodeo event—$137,061. He added two more world titles to his name in 1989 and 1991. By 1993, the three-time world champion was the event's all-time leading money winner. In July 1993, Hedeman became the first rodeo cowboy to hit $1 million in lifetime earnings as a bull rider.

A bovine bull's-eye

Stock contractor Sammy Andrews of Addielou knows bulls. At the 1993 National Finals Rodeo in Las Vegas, 12 of his bulls were featured, the most of any contractor. Riders seem to like Andrews' animals, even though they make for a rough outing. In 1991, the top 30 bull riders in the Professional Rodeo Cowboys Association selected Andrews' bull Outlaw Willie as the Bull of the Year. Andrews had a repeat performance in 1993 when his 2,000-pound bull Bodacious was named the favorite of all cowboy bull riders.

Riding to the top

◄In 1989, Ty Murray of Stephenville became the youngest cowboy to win the Professional Rodeo Cowboy Association's All-Around Champion title. He was only 20 at the time. Four years later, Murray set another world record by earning the most prize money in a single season—$297,896 in 1993.

Paying tribute to cowgirls

The Cowgirl Hall of Fame and Western Heritage Center in Hereford honors more than 100 women who rode, roped, yodeled, and rodeoed their way into the history books. Established in 1975, the Hall of Fame honors such greats as trick rider Tad Lucas of Fort Worth and cowgirl singer Patsy Montana, whose 1936 album *I Want to Be a Cowboy's Sweetheart* sold more than a million copies. Inductee Dixie Reger Mosley (right) of Amarillo was one of the first female rodeo clowns and one of the founders of the Women's Professional Rodeo Association. Two prized items on display are the red, white, and blue shirt and scarf that inductee Martha Josey wore at the 1988 Winter Olympics in Calgary. That year the U.S. team won the gold medal in barrel racing.

Down the stretch they ran

◄Max Justice Hirsch wanted to be a jockey when he ran away from his Fredericksburg home at the age of 12. Instead, he became one of the foremost trainers of winning racehorses. In all, his four-legged pupils finished first in 1,933 races. Bold Venture won the Kentucky Derby and the Preakness in 1936. In 1950, Middleground won the Derby and the Belmont Stakes. But none matched Hirsch's champion Assault, who won the Triple Crown in 1946. Hirsch died on April 3, 1969, one day after watching his horse Heartland win at Aqueduct. In 1970, he was elected into the Texas Sports Hall of Fame.

The stats on "The Shoe"

◄Willie "The Shoe" Shoemaker, born in Fabens, rode in and won more Thoroughbred horse races than anyone else in history. Here's how he did it until he retired in 1990.

Height: 4 feet 11 inches	Total races: 40,350
Racing weight: 97 pounds	First-place finishes: 8,833
First race: March 19, 1949	Second-place finishes: 6,136
First win: April 20, 1949	Third-place finishes: 4,987

FRIDAY–NIGHT FOOTBALL

State champions

◀ In 1913, Houston's Sam Houston football team blanked Comanche 20-0 in the state finals. But the University Interscholastic League never recognized the championship because of ineligible rulings. Instead, the first "official" state high school championship went down in the record books as a scoreless tie between Cleburne and Houston Heights in 1921.

Corsicana and Masonic Home played to a scoreless tie in the 1932 state football championship. But officials awarded the win to Corsicana because the team beat Masonic Home 5 to 1 in 20-yard line penetrations. It was the only state championship ever decided on statistics.

In 1982, the Daingerfield Tigers became the first team to win 16 games in a single season. The perfect 16-0 streak included 14 shutouts and led Daingerfield to the Class 3A championship, where the team aced Sweeney 42-0.

Never missing a beat

During the 1993 season, the Bulldog varsity football team of North Dallas High School fielded some quick-change artists. Four players would suit up for the game, play the first half, then shed their pads in the locker room. They reappeared on the turf at half-time as members of the marching band. Two played trumpets, one pounded the drum, and another was a drum major. After their musical contributions, the boys suited up for the second half of the game.

How Hutto became the Hippos

Back in 1915, a hippopotamus somehow freed itself from a traveling carnival that had stopped in the small, central Texas community of Hutto. The giant beast settled in the water and mud of a creek and became belligerent when folks tried to lure it out. The hippo's determination and fighting spirit impressed the people of Hutto, who decided that the school football team should adopt the name "Hippos."

Name that team

◀ The Amarillo Sandies took their name from a sandstorm that blew into town in 1922. The Nazareth Swifts named themselves after the swift foxes found in the Panhandle region. The Polar Bears hail from Frost, and the Bisons hail from Buffalo. The Gobblers come from Cuero, the turkey capital of Texas. Other curious high-school team names include:

Knippa Purple Rock Crushers
Hamlin Pied Pipers
Itasca Wampus Cats
Sommerville Yeguas
El Campo Ricebirds
Killeen Kangaroos
Fredericksburg Battlin' Billies
Rotan Yellowhammers
Rocksprings Angoras

Forget the record, please

In 1993, Houston's Jeff Davis High School set a national record in football. The team posted 80 straight losses.

Why Frankie couldn't play

In 1948, the high-school coach at Stinnett recruited Frankie Groves for the football team. The 16-year-old, 105-pound tackler played in that year's homecoming game. Unfortunately, the University Interscholastic League ruled Frankie ineligible because she was a female. The school fired the coach.

◀ Professional football linebacker and one-time Houston Oiler coach Jack Pardee got his start on the gridiron by playing on the six-man team from Christoval. He led the team to a 1952 regional championship by scoring 57 touchdowns during the season. Pardee, a senior, was one of 16 young men attending Christoval High School at the time. Of those, 15 played football. Other professional stars who got their start in Texas high-school football are listed below.

They started in Texas high-school football

Offensive guard Gene Upshaw of Robstown
Defensive lineman Joe Greene (top right) of Temple
Offensive tackle and coach Forrest Gregg of
    Sulphur Springs
Running back Duane Thomas of Dallas
Running back Walt Garrison of Lewisville
Defensive lineman Bob Lilly of Throckmorton
Running back Robert Newhouse of Hallsville
Defensive lineman Harvey Martin of Dallas
Kicker Mark Moseley of Livingston
Defensive lineman Dexter Manley of Houston
Running back Eric Dickerson (right) of Sealy
Quarterback Don Meredith of Mt. Vernon
Defensive back and coach Tom Landry
    of Mission

THE COLLEGE RANKS

The rise and fall of the Southwest Conference

The Southwest Conference became official on December 8, 1914, thanks to the efforts of L. Theo Bellmont, the athletic director at the University of Texas. Bellmont lined up Arkansas, Baylor, Oklahoma, Southwestern, Texas A&M, Oklahoma A&M, and Rice as members. Over the years, the makeup of the conference changed, finally settling on the University of Texas, Arkansas, Southern Methodist University, Baylor, Texas Tech, Rice, the University of Houston, Texas Christian University, and Texas A&M. There were some great football games over the years, such as 1935, when SMU beat TCU 20-14 for the national championship—a first for the Southwest Conference. In 1938, TCU reigned as the undefeated national champ. Darrell Royal's Texas Longhorns whipped Notre Dame for the 1969 national championship. But in 1988, SMU got the death penalty from the NCAA, and it wasn't the only school flagged for recruiting violations. In 1991, Arkansas left the Conference. Baylor, Texas A&M, and Texas Tech followed by joining the Big Eight. Eighty years and many glories after Bellmont's idea took shape, the dream had faded.

The end of a 28-year losing streak

In 1994, the Rice University football team decided enough was enough. The rival University of Texas Longhorns had won every meeting on the gridiron since 1965, a total of 28 straight games. Finally, on October 16, 1994, the Rice Owls snapped the Longhorns' winning streak. The Owls won 19-17 in the first Sunday game ever played in Southwest Conference history.

Giving a hoot for a mascot

◀ Rice University's owl mascot came by his name in a rather unusual way. In 1917, students from the rival Agricultural and Mechanical College bird-napped the canvas owl and carted him to their campus. Rice students hired a private detective to find the bird. He succeeded and sent a telegraph message that read, "Sammy is fairly well and would like to see his parents at 11 o'clock." Rice retrieved the owl, and he's been known as Sammy ever since.

RICE

Some Aggie history

◀ In 1897, Texas A&M University was known as the Agricultural and Mechanical College of Texas. It was also a school with no money to hire a football coach. So the players hired C.W. Taylor. At each game, they passed a hat to pay the coach's salary. In a 1915 game against the University of Texas, Texas A&M kicker Warren "Rip" Collins punted 23 times with an amazing 55-yard average. Two years later, he helped lead the team to an undefeated season.

Music to march by

The first Fightin' Texas Aggie Band marched into Texas A&M University history in 1894 when 12 men assembled the group. To celebrate its 100th anniversary in 1994, more than 900 former band members returned for a reunion. They joined the 350 members of the 1994-1995 band for a performance during a September football game between A&M and the University of Southern Mississippi. Together, the marchers took to the field and formed a 120-yard letter "T," the band's signature formation since 1929.

The Heisman Trophy

In 1977 and 1978, two East Texans scored back-to-back Heisman Trophies. Tyler's Earl Campbell, a running back at the University of Texas, took the honor in 1977. In Campbell's four seasons at Texas he rushed for 4,444 yards and was named to the All-Conference team four times. The Texas legislature officially designated Campbell a state "legend." Billy Sims, a running back from the small town of Hooks, went on to Oklahoma and won the Heisman in 1978. Both runners wore the number 20 on their college jerseys. Other Lone Star Heisman winners include:

David O'Brien, 1938, quarterback at Texas Christian University
Doak Walker, 1948, halfback at Southern Methodist University
John David Crow, 1957, halfback at Texas A&M University
Andre Ware, 1989, quarterback at University of Houston

The only hoopster champs from Texas

Back in 1966, when the University of Texas at El Paso was known as Texas Western College, the school won the NCAA championship in basketball. As of the end of 1994, it was still the only university in Texas ever to have won bragging rights as NCAA roundball champs.

A long shot

Randy Matson, a Pampa native who attended Texas A&M, set a pair of shot-put records back in the 1960s. On May 8, 1965, he was the first to toss a shot more than 70 feet when he covered a distance of 70 feet 7 inches at the Southwest Conference track meet in College Station. Two years later he beat that record by hefting the 16-pound shot 71 feet 5-1/2 inches. The throw, made on April 22, 1967, was the first shot-put toss over 71 feet.

Soaring to new heights

Track and field star Billy Olson of Abilene set seven pole-vaulting records in only 13 months during 1982 and 1983 while attending Abilene Christian University. He topped the achievement on February 4, 1983, in Toronto, Canada, by becoming the first person ever to clear 19 feet indoors. Olson vaulted 19 feet, 1/4 inch.

Aerial attack

Sammy Baugh of Temple got his nickname "Slinging Sammy" during the 1930s when he turned Texas Christian University football into a passing attack. Once, during a game against the University of Texas, the TCU center announced to the Texas players, "Gentlemen, Mr. Baugh is going to pass again. I don't know just where it'll go, but it'll be good. Ready?" The completed pass went for a 25-yard gain, and Baugh went on to play 16 seasons of professional football with the Washington Redskins. He switched from tailback to quarterback halfway through his professional career and set many NFL passing records. His completion percentage of 70.33 in 1945 still stands as a record.

PROFESSIONAL FOOTBALL FACTS

◄ Lamar Hunt, a Dallas businessman, formed the new American Football League in 1959. Regular-season games began in 1960, and on January 1, 1961, the first AFL championship was played in Houston. The Houston Oilers walloped the Los Angeles Chargers 24-16 in front of about 32,200 fans. Each Oilers player was paid $1,025 for the game. By 1970, the AFL had merged with the National Football League and became today's American Football Conference.

A league of its own

Professional football teams

•The Dallas Cowboys were a National Football League expansion team in 1960. Clint Murchison, Jr., and Bedford Wynne paid $5,000 for the franchise. In 1984, they sold the team for $80 million. The team boasts an NFL record of 20 consecutive winning seasons, 1966 to 1985. During the streak, the Cowboys won 13 division titles and went to the playoffs 18 times. Team colors are royal blue, metallic silver blue, and white. Jerry Jones is the owner.

•The Houston Oilers became one of the original teams in the American Football League in 1960. They won the first two AFL Championships in 1960 and 1961, but have never played in the Super Bowl. Team colors are Columbia blue, scarlet, and white. Bud Adams, Jr., owns the team.

Coach of "America's Team"

◀ The Dallas Cowboys have had their share of fantastic football players, but longtime Cowboys coach Tom Landry was the real architect of "America's Team." Born in Mission in 1924, Landry played fullback at Mission High. He was a defensive back and fullback on UT teams that won the Sugar Bowl and the Orange Bowl in 1948 and 1949. Moving on to professional ball, Landry played in the All-America Football Conference for the New York Yankees in 1949. He moved across town in 1950 to the New York Giants of the National Football League. Times were different then and players were more versatile. Landry played four positions as a Giant—punter, kick returner, defensive back, and quarterback a couple of times.

When the Dallas coaching offer came up, Landry wasn't looking for a job. But, he couldn't say no to Dallas. The first three years produced dismal results—the Cowboys posted a 13-38-3 record. Instead of firing Landry, Murchison extended his contract for 10 years and the Cowboys signed talented athletes. But Murchison was not around in February 1989 when the new Cowboys owner—Jerry Jones—fired Landry. That same year the 'Boys won only 1 game and lost 15 under new head coach Jimmy Johnson. Admired by players and the public, Landry became a "martyred hero." Several weeks after his dismissal, a Tom Landry Appreciation Day parade brought out thousands of cheering fans. Remembered for his 20 winning seasons, Landry was inducted into the Football Hall of Fame in 1990.

They keep going and going and going and ...

As of the end of the 1993 National Football League season, the Dallas Cowboys had appeared in seven Super Bowl games, more than any other team. The team played in Super Bowls V, VI, X, XII, XIII, XXVII, and XXVIII with a record of four wins and three losses.

The elliptical Texas Stadium was completed in 1971 in Irving. The hole in the roof measures 2-1/4 acres. The roof's major axis stretches 787 feet and 4 inches—the world's largest roof span.

Two miracle catches

On December 28, 1975, the Dallas Cowboys fell behind the Minnesota Vikings 14-10. With little more than a minute to go in the game, the Cowboys got the ball for a final drive that began 91 yards away from their end zone. Less than a minute remained on the clock when quarterback Roger Staubach dropped back and launched a long pass to Drew Pearson. The ball dropped into Pearson's hands as he backed into the end zone for the game-winning touchdown with 24 seconds left. It was a miracle catch forever known as the "Hail Mary" and it set in motion the Cowboys' climb to become America's Team.

And then there's Percy Howard. He made only one pass reception in the National Football League when he caught one for a Cowboys touchdown in Super Bowl X. Dallas lost to Pittsburgh 17-21.

Leading the cheers in Dallas

In the fall of 1972, seven halter-topped beauties in white go-go boots strutted into Texas Stadium and the Dallas Cowboy Cheerleaders became the first professional cheerleading squad. Four years later in 1976, they became the first women ever to participate in a Super Bowl—Super Bowl X at Miami. Cowboys general manager Tex Schramm conceived the idea for pro-cheerleaders. But when Jerry Jones bought the team in 1989, he thought he could improve on the idea by changing the cheerleading outfits to spandex biker shorts. Fans' fury convinced Jones to save the shorts and halters. While the costumes may appear provocative, the image of the Dallas Cowboys Cheerleaders remains squeaky clean. Uniforms can be worn only to approved events. No gum, alcohol, tobacco, or hair-curlers are allowed while in uniform. And fraternizing with Cowboys football heroes is cause for immediate dismissal.

The big choke

The Houston Oilers traveled to New York on January 3, 1993, for the 1993 AFC Wild Card game against the Buffalo Bills. During the first half, the Oilers ran up an impressive 35-3 score against Buffalo. But the Bills rallied with only 28 minutes to go in the game. Buffalo scored 35 unanswered points and took the lead with a little more than three minutes remaining on the clock. Houston tied with a field goal, sending the game into overtime. But the Bills eventually won the game and became known as the team that overcame the largest deficit in NFL history—32 points. Houston became known as the team with the biggest choke in football history.

Home-state hero ◀Born in Tyler in 1955, Earl Campbell was reared by his mother in a family of 11 children. His father died when he was in sixth grade, leaving his mom to raise the family by working as a maid and selling flowers from her rose field. Campbell was the first player taken in the 1978 football draft, signing with the Oilers for $1.4 million. That same year he was named Rookie of the Year and the NFL's Most Outstanding Offensive player. For six and a half years Campbell kept the Oiler offense moving. After Campbell suffered a serious knee injury, he was traded to the New Orleans Saints in 1985. He always said he only wanted to play in the league seven years, but he played an eighth mediocre year because his good friend, Bum Phillips, was coaching the Saints. Campbell gave up football after two pre-season games in 1986. Today, he's a counselor at the University of Texas and runs a football camp for young aspiring football heroes.

Mr. Mom ◀In 1993, Houston Oiler offensive tackle David Williams missed a game because he wanted to be with his wife during the birth of their child. The action caused a media firestorm that came to be known as "Babygate." Williams was fined by the team but offered no regrets for his parental decision.

The fans made history

On August 15, 1994, the largest crowd in National Football League history gathered in Mexico City's Azteca Stadium for a preseason game between the Dallas Cowboys and the Houston Oilers. Although the spectators clearly favored Dallas, the Oilers won 6-0. The final attendance for the Monday-night game was 112,376, more fans than had ever watched a preseason, regular season, or Super Bowl game.

Professional Football Hall of Fame
(Birthplace and year inducted)

Lance Alworth, Houston, 1978
Sammy Baugh, Temple, 1963
Raymond Berry, Corpus Christi, 1973
Earl Campbell, Tyler, 1991
Joe Greene, Temple, 1987
Forrest Gregg, Birthright, 1977
Jimmy Johnson, Dallas, 1994
Ken Houston, Lufkin, 1986
Tom Landry, Mission, 1990
Yale Lary, Fort Worth, 1979

Dick "Night Train" Lane, Austin, 1974
Bob Lilly, Olney, 1980
Ollie Matson, Trinity, 1972
Don Maynard, Crosbyton, 1987
Charley Taylor, Grand Prairie, 1984
Y.A. Tittle, Marshall, 1971
Clyde "Bulldog" Turner, Sweetwater, 1966
Gene Upshaw, Robstown, 1987
Doak Walker, Dallas, 1986

PLAYING HARDBALL

◀ When Tristram E. "Tris" Speaker started playing baseball for the old North Texas League in 1906, he earned $50 a month. But during his 22-year career in major league baseball, the Hubbard native played for the love of the game—not for money. Fans called him the "Gray Eagle," and he wowed them with flawless fielding. Speaker still holds baseball's record for most double plays by an outfielder, with a total of 139. In 1912, he led the Boston Red Sox to a World Series win and was named the American League's Most Valuable Player. Speaker and the Sox played to another Series victory in 1915. In 1919, while still an active player, Speaker took over as manager of the Cleveland Indians. The next year he guided the team to a World Series win over the Brooklyn Dodgers. In 1937, Speaker was elected to the Baseball Hall of Fame, the seventh player installed.

An eagle in the outfield

Fly balls from the Lone Star State

In baseball, the term "Texas leaguer" refers to a fly ball that sails just over the reach of an infielder but too close in to be caught by an outfielder. The term is named after the state's minor league, although no one seems to know for sure how the description originated.

AWESOME

Missing in action

Andrew "Rube" Foster, a pitcher from Calvert, won 51 of 55 games in 1905. In the 1920s he formed the Negro National League. But not until 1981 was the "father of Black Baseball," inducted into the Baseball Hall of Fame. Many other African-American baseball stars were still conspicuously missing from Cooperstown as of the end of 1994. "Biz" Mackey, a defensive catcher from Seguin who played during the 1920s and is still considered one of the best players ever, hadn't received the honor. And Willie "Devil" Wells of Austin, the best all-around short stop of his day, was still not inducted.

Beaumont's biggest baseball contribution

Baseball Hall of Fame outfielder Frank Robinson (below), a native of Beaumont, hit the professional diamond in 1956 when he joined the National League's Cincinnati Reds. He made his mark on the game immediately by being named Rookie of the Year, then followed that achievement five years later as the National League's Most Valuable Player. Robinson moved to the American League when he was traded to the Baltimore Orioles. He didn't miss a step when he made the change. That year Robinson won the Triple Crown in baseball. He led the American League in batting with a .316 average; in home runs, with a total of 49; and with runs-batted-in, 122 in all. He was also voted the league's MVP, making him the only man ever to be MVP in both leagues. Robinson's contribution to baseball didn't stop when his playing career ended. He became the first African-American manager in the major leagues when he took the job with the Cleveland Indians in 1975. Today Frank Robinson is the assistant general manager for the Baltimore

Hardball hero

On May 1, 1991, during a game between the Texas Rangers and the Toronto Blue Jays, right-handed, blazing fast-ball pitcher Nolan Ryan (left) tossed his seventh career no-hitter, the most in baseball history. The native Texan also holds the world's record for most strike-outs with an amazing 5,714. But Ryan wasn't perfect during his career. He walked more batters than any other pitcher, giving away a total of 2,795 between 1968 and 1993. Drafted by the Mets in 1965, he was inconsistent. If he hadn't been traded to the California Angels in 1971 and finally realized some success, he probably would have gone back to Texas and raised cattle. But in 1973 he pitched two no-hitters and posted 383 strikeouts. The rest is history. Most folks don't know about Ryan's remedy for the bothersome calluses on his right hand—he soaked his hand in pickle juice.

Swinging to a season record

Rogers Hornsby played his best major league baseball in 1924 when he smashed 227 hits at 536 at-bats. The .424 batting streak still stands as a season record in modern baseball history. Hornsby, nicknamed the "Magnificent Rajah" by sportswriters, played shortstop and second base for five different teams during his career. In 1942, the Winters native was elected into the Baseball Hall of Fame.

Professional baseball teams

- The Houston Astros were founded in 1962 as the Houston Colt .45s. The name was changed in 1965. Team colors are orange and blue and the owner is Dr. John McMullen.
- The Texas Rangers began in 1960 in Washington, D.C., as the Senators. They moved to Arlington in 1972. Texas Governor George W. Bush is part-owner of the team. Royal blue and red are the team's colors.

Professional Baseball Hall of Fame

As of 1994, only 8 of 220 Hall of Fame inductees were born in Texas.

The players' birthplaces and the years they were inducted include:

Ernie Banks, Dallas, 1977
Rube Foster, Calvert, 1981
Rogers Hornsby, Winters, 1942
Eddie Mathews, Texarkana, 1978
Joe Morgan, Bonham, 1990
Frank Robinson, Beaumont, 1982
Tris Speaker, Hubbard, 1937
Ross Youngs, Shiner, 1972

ROUNDBALL HIGHLIGHTS

Driving a big deal

Billy Joe "Red" McCombs dropped out of law school in 1953 and steered his ambitions toward automobiles. With a $25,000 loan he opened a used-car lot. Eventually, the high-powered salesman expanded his business into a fleet of more than 30 auto dealerships. McCombs invested his car allowance into assets such as ranchland and the San Antonio Spurs professional basketball team. In 1993, the 65-year-old drove his biggest deal ever. He sold the Spurs for $89 million.

Professional basketball teams

•The Houston Rockets began in 1967 as the San Diego Rockets and moved to Houston in 1971. In 1981, the Boston Celtics beat the Houston Rockets in the NBA championship. In 1986, it was a rematch with the same outcome. Finally, in 1994, the Rockets outscored the New York Knicks and brought home Houston's first major sports championship. Team colors are red and gold. The owner is Charlie Thomas.

•The San Antonio Spurs began in 1967 as the Dallas Chaparrals of the American Basketball Association. The team moved to San Antonio in 1973 and joined the National Basketball Association in 1976. Team colors are metallic silver and black. The San Athletic Club, Inc. owns the team.

•The Dallas Mavericks began playing in 1980 as an NBA expansion team. Team colors are blue and green. The owner is Donald Carter.

The rocket from Nigeria

Before 1980, Hakeem Olajuwon starred as a high-school soccer goalie in Lagos, Nigeria. Then a State Department official, who had connections at the University of Houston, spotted the 7-foot-tall young man. When Olajuwon stepped into the gym at the University of Houston in the summer of 1980, he knew little about big-time U.S. basketball. But it took him only 14 years to move from a red-shirted college freshman to Most Valuable Player in the NBA. Moments after Abdul Hakeem Ajibola Olajuwon led the Houston Rockets to the 1994 NBA championship, he simply walked over to the player's bench and sat quietly as if to ponder the short course of his journey.

◄The Dallas Mavericks drafted Kentucky forward Jamal Mashburn as their number-one pick in 1993. Before he even took his first shot on the court, he had his own line of "The Monster Mash" basketball shoes, compliments of a $7-million contract with the Italian company Fila. When he did start shooting baskets with the Mavs in the 1993-94 season, Mashburn became the top scoring rookie in the NBA.

Monster mash

Professional Basketball Hall of Fame
(Birthplace and year inducted)

Bruce Drake, Gentry, 1972
Slater Martin, Elmira, 1981
Bill Sharman, Abilene, 1975

A basketball triple crown

Bill Sharman's jersey hangs atop the Boston Garden, a tribute to the Abilene native's ten outstanding seasons with the Celtics between 1951-1961. Sharman ranks as one of the top all-time foul shooters with an 89 percent lifetime mark. And his incredible career didn't end when he stepped off the court as a player. He's the only coach to have won championships in three professional leagues—taking the ABL title with the Cleveland Pipers in 1962, the ABA title with Utah in 1971, and the NBA championship with Los Angeles in 1972. In 1975, he was elected as a player to the NBA Hall of Fame.

ON THE LINKS

He came back swinging

Ben Hogan of Dublin, Texas, learned the golf game by becoming a caddie at the age of 12. By the time he was 19, he had turned pro, but it took eight years for him to finally win a championship. Once he started winning, Hogan was hard to stop. He won the Professional Golfers Association (PGA) title in 1946 and 1948 and was named PGA Player of the Year in 1948. Then in 1949, his career almost ended in a tragic automobile accident. Hogan fought his way back during months of recuperation. The courageous comeback made him a national hero and inspired the movie *Follow the Sun*. When he hit the links again, he dominated golf courses and swung his way to these impressive achievements:

Won the U.S. Open in 1950, 1951, and 1953
Won the Masters in 1951 and 1953
Won the British Open in 1953
Named PGA Player of the Year in 1950, 1951, and 1952

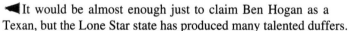

Other great Texas golfers

It would be almost enough just to claim Ben Hogan as a Texan, but the Lone Star state has produced many talented duffers.

•Ralph Guldahl of Dallas won U.S Opens in 1937 and 1938.
•Houston's Jimmy Demaret was a three-time Masters champion.
•Lloyd Mangrum of Dallas swung his way to first-place finishes in 11 major golf tournaments in 1948.
•Byron Nelson of Longbranch, who caddied with Ben Hogan in the 1930s, scored 19 victories in 1945, including a world-record 11 consecutive tournaments between March 8 and August 4, 1945.
•Tom Kite (left) of Austin, winner of the 1992 U.S. Open, was the all-time leading money winner on the PGA circuit as of June 1994 with $8,963,804 in earnings.
•Sandra Palmer of Fort Worth won the U.S. Women's Open, was voted LPGA Player of the Year, and led the LPGA in prize money in 1975. She joined the LPGA just one year earlier.

The most wins for a woman

Hall of Fame golfer Kathy Whitworth of Monahans won the Ladies Professional Golf Association (LPGA) championship tournament three times (1967, 1971, and 1975) and was voted LPGA Player of the Year an astounding seven times. The Associated Press named her Woman Athlete of the Year in 1965 and 1966. Her overall record of 88 LPGA career wins between 1962 and 1985 still stands as the best in women's golf.

◀ Born in Houston, relaxed golfer Lee Trevino had to quit school to help the family when he was 14. His job as a part-time groundskeeper and caddie introduced him to golf. He sharpened his skills while serving in the Marines as a member of the corps golf team. Before hitting the big time, Trevino worked as a part-time pro in El Paso. For the ever-popular and always entertaining Trevino, 1971 was a very good year. He won the U.S. Open, the British Open, and the Canadian Open. After these feats, the citizens of Juarez, Mexico, and El Paso sponsored a Lee Trevino Day. In 1975 his career was threatened when he was struck by lightning, which injured his back severely. But he fought back and at age 44, won the PGA Tournament, one of the oldest golfers ever to win such a prestigious event.

The easygoing golfer

The shot of a short lifetime

Coby Orr, a 5-year-old from Littleton, Colorado, was the youngest golfer ever to hit a hole-in-one. He made the historic shot on the 103-yard fifth hole at San Antonio's Riverside Golf Course in 1975.

Best-selling golf lessons

Harvey Penick coached golf at the University of Texas for 30 years. He was an instructor at PGA schools, and gave lessons to 7 of the 13 members in the Ladies Professional Golf Association Hall of Fame. During more than 60 years of golfing, Penick jotted down his observations and tips and kept them in a small red notebook. Then in May 1992, with co-author Bud Shrake, Penick, age 88, published his personal insights in the *Little Red Book*. It stayed on the best-seller list for 54 weeks. Excluding encyclopedias and record books, Penick's *Little Red Book* is the best-selling sports book of all time.

◀ Robert Landers doesn't look like a professional golfer. At the 1994 Senior PGA Tour qualifying tournament, he played the course in muddy sneakers and used clubs he bought from his cousin for $70. But Landers took sixth place, earned $4,270, and qualified for the Senior PGA Tour in 1995. Back in 1980, Landers qualified for the U.S. Open and the U.S. Amateur, but he missed the cut in both tournaments. In 1981, he gave up pro golf. Then in 1992, the Azle clothing store that Landers managed went out of business. He eked out a living chopping wood and farming. In his spare time, he practiced his golf game by hitting balls in the cow pasture. His stroke improved. So in 1994, he cashed in an IRA and paid the $2,000 entrance fee for the Senior Tour qualifying tournament. It paid off. At age 50, Landers was back on the links, still looking like a Texas farmer.

Practice in a cow pasture pays off

OLYMPIC STARS

A leap into history ◀ Four months before the 1968 Olympic Games, University of Texas at El Paso student Bob Beamon was suspended from the track team. He refused to compete against Brigham Young University because he thought the school supported racist policies. Without a coach, Beamon continued preparing for the Olympics. In Mexico City, Beamon's long jump outdistanced the state-of-the-art electronic measuring device. Using an old-fashioned tape measure, officials recorded the jump at 8.9 meters. Beamon knew he had made a record jump, but he didn't know the metric system. He waited for the conversion to feet before realizing his world-record jump of 29 feet 2 inches surpassed the world record by almost two feet. His gold medal distance stood until 1991.

The greatest athlete of all

Without question, the greatest athlete to come out of Texas was Mildred "Babe" Didrikson Zaharias of Port Arthur. She honed her competitive spirit and physical prowess in Beaumont where she jumped hedges between her house and the corner grocery. She hit so many home runs while playing sandlot baseball that friends nicknamed her "Babe" after Babe Ruth. At age 16, the all-around athlete was an All-American in high-school basketball.

At the 1932 Los Angeles Games she proved her incredible athletic versatility. Only five events were open to women at the time, and competitors could enter no more than three. Babe participated in the javelin, the 80-meter hurdles, and the high jump. On her first javelin throw, she broke the world record by more than 11 feet. Her throw flew 143 feet and 4 inches to win the gold medal. She also won a gold in the 80-meter hurdles and took a silver medal in the high jump. That year, the Associated Press named Babe the Woman Athlete of the Year. She captured the honor a record five more times in 1945, 1946, 1947, 1950, and 1954.

After the Olympics, Babe turned her attention to golf. Between 1940 and 1950, she won every major golf title. In the mid-1940s, she strung together an unprecedented 17 wins. She finished first in 82 tournaments, including the 1948 and 1950 U.S. Women's Open. In 1947, Babe became the first American to win the British Women's Amateur. The Associated Press named Babe the Greatest Woman Athlete of the Half Century in 1950. Then three years later, doctors discovered cancer in her lower intestine. She had a colostomy, but three months later returned to the golf course to play in the 1953 Tam O'Shanter All-American Championship. She played so poorly that on the third day of the tournament, she broke down and cried. Friends encouraged her to quit and rest, but Babe replied, "I don't pick up the ball." By 1954, Babe was winning again. She took the U.S. Women's Open by 12 strokes and won the Vare Trophy for the LPGA's lowest stroke average with a 75.48. In 1955, the cancer returned. She kept her golf clubs in her room at Galveston's John Sealy Hospital and died September 27, 1956.

They got the gold

• At the 1956 Olympic Games in Melbourne, Australia, Bobby Morrow of San Benito ran away with three gold medals in track and field—more than anyone since Jesse Owens won four in 1936.

• David "Skippy" Browning won a gold medal in diving at the 1952 Olympic Games in Helsinki, Finland. Four years later, while training for the 1956 games, Browning was killed in a plane crash in Kansas.

• Rafer Lewis Johnson of Hillsboro set a world record in the decathlon at the 1960 Rome Olympics. He retired that same year.

Going for the golden ring

Pugilist George Foreman, a 20-year-old from Marshall, punched his way to a heavyweight boxing gold medal at the 1968 Olympic Games in Mexico City. Five years later, on January 22, 1973, he took boxing's world heavyweight title from Joe Frazier with a second-round knockout. He reigned as undisputed champ from 1973 until October 30, 1974, when Muhammad Ali took the title. Twenty-six years after winning his gold medal, Foreman was still stepping into the ring—and winning. When he knocked out Michael Moorer on November 5, 1994, Foreman became the oldest man ever to win boxing's heavyweight championship title—he was just two months shy of his 46th birthday. The winning punch to Moorer improved Foreman's boxing record to 73 wins and 4 losses. With 68 knockouts to his name, the big man from Marshall owned the best KO ratio in heavyweight history.

SPEED DEMONS

◀ Most Texans don't even know Kevin Schwantz. But in the Netherlands once, a fan wheeled his motorcycle into a restaurant, walked it up to Schwantz, and asked the champion to autograph the gas tank. In 1993, only five years after joining the Grand Prix motorcycle circuit, Schwantz rode to glory as the world champion. The 29-year-old competitor, known for his fearless approach to race-track curves, earned almost $6 million in 1993 from winnings, incentives, and sponsorships. Yet he practically goes unnoticed in Texas, where he lives on a ranch near Wimberly. The story is very different in Europe. He can barely pass through an airport without being mobbed by fans who recognize the international motorcycle champion on sight.

An anonymous champion

◀ In 1949, Jim Roper drove a new Lincoln automobile to a win at the first ever NASCAR Grand National race. The hot, dusty competition took place in Charlotte, North Carolina, and Roper sped away with first-prize earnings of $2,000. These days, the retired racing pioneer is involved with a different type of horsepower. He raises thoroughbred horses on his farm in the rural town of Kaufman.

A lifetime of horsepower

On land and sea

In 1987, Eddie "The Thrill" Hill of Wichita Falls held the speed records on land and in the water. He gave up drag boating after he was thrown through the hull of his boat as it traveled 217 miles per hour. When he returned to four-wheel dragsters, he became the first man to break the famous five-second barrier for the quarter-mile.

Many a checkered flag for Foyt

◀Houston-native A.J. Foyt—the most successful Indy car driver in racing history—posted 67 wins and a record-setting seven national championships (1960, 1961, 1963, 1964, 1967, 1975, and 1979) in his career. Between 1958 and 1992, Foyt started a record 35 Indianapolis 500 races, winning four—in 1961, 1964, 1967, and 1977. Cars and engines came naturally to Foyt. His dad owned a garage and had been a race driver, too. Dropping out of school at 17, Foyt dedicated himself to learning everything about racing and building cars. It paid off—when he was just 23, he qualified for the Indy 500. A year later, in 1958, he placed 10th.

IN THE RING OR ON THE MAT

Lightweight history in Laredo

◀On October 15, 1994, Laredo-native Orlando Canizales won his 16th straight International Boxing Federation bantam-weight title, surpassing the previous record of 15 set by Manual Ortiz between 1943 and 1946. The 12-round bout was fought outdoors in front of a home-town crowd of 5,000. Canizales didn't wilt under the 90-degree heat while making boxing history. He defeated Fort Worth's Sergio Reyes with a unanimous decision.

A boxing first

◀John Arthur "Jack" Johnson of Galveston was boxing's first African-American heavyweight champion. He won the title by defeating Tommy Burns in Australia in 1908 and remained champion for seven years. In 1915, Jess Willard knocked out Johnson in the 26th round of a bout in Havana. Johnson's career included 80 victories, 7 losses, 14 draws, and 13 no-decisions in 114 fights.

A champion of community spirit

Cal Farley (left) was a world welterweight wrestling champion during the 1920s. But he's remembered more for his sense of community service than for his ahtleticism. After retiring from sports, he settled in Amarillo and in 1939, founded the Boy's Ranch in Tascosa. Today, the facilities cover 10,600 acres where more than 400 boys and girls receive guidance, help operate the ranch, and attend school.

WHERE THE GAMES ARE PLAYED

Cotton Bowl memories

In May 1930, construction began on Fair Park Stadium in Dallas. The stadium seated 46,200 spectators, making it the largest stadium in the South. In 1936, it was renamed the Cotton Bowl. The annual New Year's Day Cotton Bowl Classic began the same year. Oilman J. Curtis Stanford paid the expenses for the first four games out of his own pocket. Since then the Cotton Bowl has hosted high-school and college football games as well as professional teams. The stadium served as one of nine national venues for soccer's World Cup in 1994. Three Super Bowl-winning National Football League teams have called the turf home field: the Dallas Texans (became the Kansas City Chiefs), the 1952 Dallas Texans (became the Baltimore Colts), and the Dallas Cowboys.

Through all the years and all the games, one single play stands out in Cotton Bowl history. In 1954, Rice University player Dick Maegle streaked down the field with the football as Alabama players gave chase. Maegle's route took him close to the sideline, in front of the Alabama team's bench. Suddenly, Alabama player Tommy Lewis jumped off the bench, darted onto the field, and tackled Maegle. The play shocked spectators, surprised both teams, and made history. Maegle was awarded the 95-yard touchdown run, and Rice beat Alabama 28-6 in spite of Lewis' enthusiastic effort.

The dome of domes

When Judge Roy Hofheinz opened the Harris County Domed Stadium on April 9, 1965, he named it the Astrodome, calling it the "eighth wonder of the world." The Astrodome was the first fully enclosed sports arena, measuring 710 feet in diameter and 218 feet high. On opening day, President Lyndon Johnson watched as one of baseball's favorite sons, Mickey Mantle, belted a towering home run to right center field. But Mantle's New York Yankees lost to the Houston Astros. Final score: Astros 2, Yanks 1.

Hooping it up on the hockey rink

When the Dallas Stars came to town from Minneapolis in 1993, Reunion Arena began hosting professional hockey as well as professional basketball games. The ice for the rink is made in September at the beginning of the season and is kept frozen by a series of 298 pipes. But about 50 to 60 times each season, the arena is converted to a basketball court. About 560 pieces of fiberboard, measuring 4 by 8 feet each, cover the ice. Then the basketball flooring is laid down like a puzzle, piece by piece. The process takes a crew of 30 about 12 hours to complete.

◄ When the Texas Rangers baseball team got a new home stadium in 1994, its name caused quite a controversy. The Ballpark in Arlington, as it is officially known, has old-fashioned style and high-tech conveniences. Here are a few of the stats about the Ballpark:

- There are 48,100 dark-green seats in the stadium.
- The field is Bermuda Tifway 419 and rye grass.
- Besides the Jumbo Tron scoreboard and electronic sports ticker, there's a manually operated scoreboard in left field.
- The 118 luxury boxes are priced from $48,000 to $200,000.
- On opening day, piano virtuoso Van Cliburn played the national anthem.

A diamond of a stadium

THE SPORTS PAGE

Doing the Herkie

◀ Every time Texas cheerleaders vault into a "Herkie" jump, they pay tribute to the granddaddy of cheerleading. Dallas-native Lawrence "Herkie" Herkimer led yells as a head cheerleader at Southern Methodist University and invented the free-form jump that now bears his name. He went on to found the Dallas-based National Cheerleaders Association in 1948. Today, the organization sponsors the largest cheerleading camp in the country where high-school squads train for the national championships. Herkimer organized history's first cheerleading camp in the late 1940s at Huntsville's Sam Houston State University. He also introduced gymnastic stunts into the act of leading cheers. In the early 1950s, Herkimer invented the pom-pon by attaching streamers of colored crepe paper to short sticks—all in an effort to attract the attention of TV cameras. Every cheerleader since then has waved a pom-pon and learned to do the "Herkie."

Striking out

On June 12, 1994, Brian and Denise Welker of Sugar Land made *The Guinness Book of Records 1995* when they rolled the highest bowling score of any couple ever. The big event took place at the Texas State Bowling Association Tournament. Denise scored a perfect 300; Brian came in with a score of 299.

Holding court in Houston

In 1970, nine professional women tennis players, including Billy Jean King, founded the first-ever women's tennis tour. Gladys Heldman, Houstonite and longtime publisher of *World Tennis* magazine, signed the founders to $1 contracts and organized a $5,000 tennis tournament at the Houston Racquet Club. Heldman also persuaded Virginia Slims to sponsor the women's tour. In 1994, the Virginia Slims of Houston awarded prize money totaling $400,000.

Heaving and hurling

◀ If you like throwing things, you should join the International Hurling Society of Fort Worth. Engineer Richard Clifford and his friend dentist John Quincy got the idea from the Monty Python movie *The Holy Grail*, in which a cow was hurled by a *trebuchet* (medieval siege weapon or catapult). Deciding how to build one of the contraptions wasn't easy—they haven't been made since 1350. But with the help of a group of University of Texas engineers, Quincy and Clifford built their first catapult and hurled a bowling ball 75 feet. They plan to build a 100-foot-tall trebuchet by 1996 that can hurl a Buick 600 feet. Clifford and Quincy intend to use their catapults to raise money for charity by putting on events such as "Hurling for Hospice." Only in Texas …

When Vivian Villarreal started playing pool at age 8, she stood on a chair to shoot the balls on a coin-operated table in her grandma's restaurant. Twenty years later, in 1993, the San Antonio native was ranked the best woman pool player in the world.

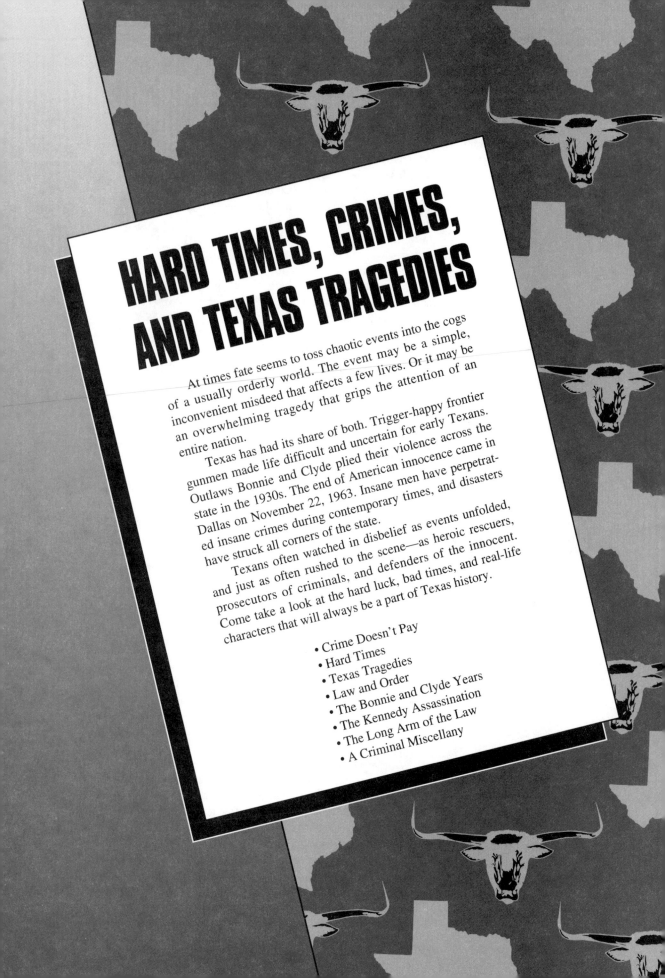

HARD TIMES, CRIMES, AND TEXAS TRAGEDIES

At times fate seems to toss chaotic events into the cogs of a usually orderly world. The event may be a simple, inconvenient misdeed that affects a few lives. Or it may be an overwhelming tragedy that grips the attention of an entire nation.

Texas has had its share of both. Trigger-happy frontier gunmen made life difficult and uncertain for early Texans. Outlaws Bonnie and Clyde plied their violence across the state in the 1930s. The end of American innocence came in Dallas on November 22, 1963. Insane men have perpetrated insane crimes during contemporary times, and disasters have struck all corners of the state.

Texans often watched in disbelief as events unfolded, and just as often rushed to the scene—as heroic rescuers, prosecutors of criminals, and defenders of the innocent. Come take a look at the hard luck, bad times, and real-life characters that will always be a part of Texas history.

- Crime Doesn't Pay
- Hard Times
- Texas Tragedies
- Law and Order
- The Bonnie and Clyde Years
- The Kennedy Assassination
- The Long Arm of the Law
- A Criminal Miscellany

CRIME DOESN'T PAY

Yo-ho-ho on the Texas coast

Jean Laffite (right) came from New Orleans to Galveston Island in 1817. With his brother Pierre, the French-born pirate settled about 1,000 people on Snake Island and called the pirate colony Campeachy. From there, the outlaws of the sea raided ships, hanged sea captains, and smuggled stolen goods overland to the black market in New Orleans. Finally, in May 1821, the U.S. Navy forced Laffite to leave. He sailed off into the Caribbean aboard his ship *Pride*. No one knows for sure what happened to the famed pirate who became a folk hero.

Hang 'em high

The last public hanging in the Lone Star State happened on a hot summer day in Waco. Roy Mitchell, who had confessed to killing eight people, was hanged on July 30, 1923. More than 5,000 people witnessed his hanging.

The first female hanging

A slave named Jane was the first woman legally hanged in Texas. Although some sources claim her last name was Elkins, official court records identify her only as Jane. The records also show that on May 16, 1853, Jane was convicted of first-degree murder. The next day, she was condemned to be hanged. On May 27, the sentence was carried out in Dallas County.

The last roll of the dice

John Wesley Hardin had killed almost 40 men, served prison time, and been pardoned by the governor by the time he died. But the greatest six-gun shooter of all the outlaws didn't go down fighting. On the hot night of August 19, 1895, he stood at the bar of the Acme Saloon in El Paso rolling cupped dice. El Paso constable John Selman walked up and shot Hardin in the head before the bad guy had a chance to go for his guns. Hardin's last words were, "Four sixes to beat."

A skeptical jury

William H. Irvin III believed in miracles, or so he told a Dallas jury. Irvin mistakenly received a government check for $836,939.19 and cashed it in June 1992. He told a federal jury that the money was a gift from God and that it appeared after he prayed for self-sufficiency one night along a lonely road. Irvin, a Persian Gulf War veteran, earned about $12,000 a year as an airport security officer and he was actually entitled to only $183.69 from the government. The Dallas jury didn't believe in his miracle. Irvin was found guilty of filing a false tax return, knowingly spending government money, and laundering some of that money through cashier's checks. He faced up to 43 years in prison and a $1.25-million fine.

A spy in Texas

Lothar Witzke was the first German spy to receive a death sentence from American forces during World War I. Witzke, alias Pablo Waberski, arrived at Fort Sam Houston on Friday, August 16, 1918. A court-martial found him guilty and sentenced him to hang. But the signing of the armistice saved Witzke's neck from the noose, and in May 1920, President Wilson commuted the sentence to life with hard labor. Three years later, on November 22, 1923, President Coolidge pardoned Witzke on condition that the German leave the United States and never return. The spy sailed for Berlin on November 29, 1923.

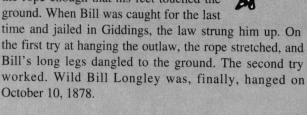

Third time's the charm

Legends claim that William P. "Wild Bill" Longley was hanged three times for his murderous ways. The first time he was suspected of stealing horses and was noosed by vigilantes. As the mob rode away, one member turned and fired at Bill's body as it hung from the end of the rope. The shot missed Bill, but cut the rope enough that his feet touched the ground. When Bill was caught for the last time and jailed in Giddings, the law strung him up. On the first try at hanging the outlaw, the rope stretched, and Bill's long legs dangled to the ground. The second try worked. Wild Bill Longley was, finally, hanged on October 10, 1878.

HARD TIMES

🔫 Georgetown buzzed with bad news over the Labor Day weekend in 1994. On Saturday, September 3, J.C. Johnson, 86, disturbed a hive of African bees while mowing his lawn. The bees, known as "killer bees," stung Johnson more than 1,000 times. When Johnson's 59-year-old son tried to rescue him, the bees stung him 500 times. A police officer and an emergency rescue worker who responded to the call for help received more than 20 stings each. Firefighters finally used water to wash the bees off all the victims. Beekeepers later destroyed a 10-foot-tall hive—and everyone except the bees survived.

Bombarded by bees

Yield to oncoming cows

In 1959, Texas finally made it unlawful to graze livestock on state and federal rights of way. Owners of stock became liable for damages caused by animal accidents. The 1959 law meant little to the more than 100 steers running loose along Dallas freeways on September 23, 1994. The cattle escaped when a tractor-trailer rig hauling the bovines overturned on R.L. Thornton Expressway. Nearly 20 head were killed in the crash, but others ran off into East Dallas. A beige and white steer jumped through a plate-glass window at Fair Park Music Hall. Many more stopped traffic on Interstate 30 for six hours while city slickers tried to round up the steers. Mounted Dallas County sheriffs, firefighters, city police, and volunteers all tested their roping skills. At last count, 14 steers were still missing from the wreck.

Losing a landmark

The end of an era came in Sunnyvale on October 4, 1994, when a 105-year-old local landmark burned to a pile of ashes and rubble. The Lander's Mercantile-E.E. Kearney, Dealers in Everything was one of the oldest stores in eastern Dallas County. Lander's, as the locals called it, opened in 1899 and had been a sort of social gathering spot for those who patronized the general store. The crowded shelves and narrow, wooden-floored aisles stocked everything from horse feed and hardware to saddles, shoes, and candlewicks.

The Dust Bowl days

As early as 1897, the federal government warned cattle raisers about the risks of overgrazing the range. But no one paid attention. Overgrazing was followed by sodbusters who plowed millions of acres of Texas into bare dirt by the 1930s. The drought came and then a

plague of grasshoppers that ate any surviving crops. Finally the winds arrived, churning the barren ground into dust storms that blackened the sky for miles. John Fischer drove his Model T through one of the storms in 1932. While traveling from Oklahoma City to Amarillo, Fischer encountered 50 miles-per-hour north winds that stirred up the gritty dirt. He reached his destination only to find that the right side of his automobile, the one facing north, had been naturally sand-blasted to bare, shiny metal.

Fiery spring storms

The spring of 1993 sparked the worst fires in recent memory for residents of Fort Davis and Marathon in far southwestern Texas. On Monday, March 29, a high-voltage wire packing 2,000 degrees of heat blew to the ground between Alpine and Marathon. The hot wire ignited ranchland south of U.S. Highway 90. Wind gusts up to 60 miles per hour stoked the blaze. Shifting winds blew the blaze first in one direction, then another. The fire crept within four miles of Marathon, but the town was spared when the wind shifted again. By Friday, the blaze was officially extinguished, but not before it had charred more than 38,000 acres.

Just as the Marathon blaze was being brought under control, another flared up 27 miles northwest of Fort Davis. On Thursday, April 1, heat lightning struck in Locke's Gap. The fiery frenzy that followed lasted 13 days. Flames inched their way into cracks in the towering ponderosa pines, and entire trees exploded, hurling cinders hundreds of feet. On Wednesday, April 7, Texas Forest Service firefighters arrived. Their traditional equipment proved useless in the rough terrain. The most effective weapon against the raging fire became wet tow sacks, or gunnysacks. Along with Forest Service personnel, cowboys, ranchers, laborers, and business people took turns toting the sacks for nearly two weeks until the blaze was brought under control.

Too close for comfort

On June 8, 1990, a fire and explosion broke open the Norwegian supertanker *Mega Borg*, sending 4.3 million gallons of oil splashing into the Gulf of Mexico. It could have been much worse. Some say the Texas spill could have been three times worse than the Alaskan spill of the *Exxon Valdez*. But in the Gulf, the *Mega Borg* held together. Cleanup methods recovered only about a tenth of the spilled oil. On top of that, a dispersant frequently used to battle oil spills actually drove much of the oil deeper into the water until it reached the floor of the Gulf of Mexico.

Finally, a happy ending in Midland

On Wednesday, October 14, 1987, Jessica McClure slipped into a well in her aunt's backyard in Midland. The 18-month-old remained desperately trapped underground for 58 hours. As a nation watched, workers clawed their way to Jessica's rescue. Somehow little Jessica had managed to tumble into an 8-inch opening and become wedged in a narrow shaft 22 feet below the surface. While the girl hummed a Winnie-the-Pooh song, Midland volunteers did what they've done best since the oil boom days—drill. The drillers tunneled until they hit hard limestone that snapped off drill bits. They took up jackhammers and chewed through rock around the clock, inching their way toward the tiring child. On Friday, they opened a 2-inch hole that finally allowed a shimmer of light into Jessica's dark hole. That evening, high-pressure water drills cut through the last rock. At 8 P.M., the three major television networks went on the air live from Midland. As the nation held its breath, a dusty, dirty paramedic emerged from the rescue tunnel. In his arms was Jessica—bandaged, bruised, and frightened, but alive.

TEXAS TRAGEDIES

How important is cheerleading?

Even people outside the Lone Star State know Texans take their football and cheerleading seriously. Before many Friday-night games a typical prayer might be, "God protect our players and the cheerleaders." But Wanda Holloway, a church organist in Channelview, took cheerleading a little *too* seriously. Holloway had never had the social status she wanted as a teenager. But her second and third marriages had been to successful businessmen much older than herself and she was able to brag about how much money she spent. Only one thing was missing. Her daughter Shanna failed to garner a coveted position on the high-school cheerleading squad. Holloway didn't think the process was fair. Somehow Shanna's friend, Amber Heath, always made the squad while Shanna sat on the sidelines. Obsessed with her daughter's unfair fate, Holloway allegedly hired a hit man to wipe out Shanna's snooty rival, Amber Heath, and mother Verna. But Holloway was discovered and arrested before the deed was done. At the trial, her lawyers asserted that Holloway "… was just curious about this stuff, wondering if there was such a thing as hit men." She hadn't meant anyone any harm, they argued. The jury didn't buy it. Holloway was found guilty and sentenced to 15 years. The case is on appeal.

The Texas City inferno

On April 16, 1947, a fire broke out in the hold of the S.S. *Grandcamp* as it was taking on cargo at a dock in Texas City. Loaded with more than 1,000 tons of ammonium nitrate, a substance used in explosives, and 16 cases of ammunition, the French ship exploded. The blast threw the vessel's anchor a mile and a half from the dock and ignited oil tanks on the land nearby. A seismograph in Denver, Colorado, recorded the shock, and towns 200 miles away felt the blast. Buildings vanished. A towering tidal wave rushed through the harbor. The American-owned *High Flyer*, also carrying ammonium nitrate, caught fire and exploded 16 hours later.

The series of blasts claimed almost 600 lives. In a town of only 18,000, 3,000 were injured. Medical personnel administered so much penicillin that the nation's supply of the new drug was threatened. Some 2,500 were left homeless. Power, water, and telephone service was severed for days. Property damage totaled nearly $70 million. The explosions came to be known as the Texas City disaster, one of the nation's worst man-made disasters. More than $1 million in relief donations flooded in from all over the world.

The Texas tower sniper

On the morning of August 1, 1966, ex-Marine Charles Whitman, 25, killed his wife and mother and then lugged a footlocker full of guns to the 29th-floor observation deck at Austin's University of Texas tower. He barricaded himself there with three rifles, two pistols, and a shotgun. Whitman then began shooting at people on the campus below. One by one, the sniper picked off and killed 13 people as they scurried for shelter in the panic or stopped to help those already shot. Another 31 were wounded before police reached Whitman and shot him dead. The UT campus was the scene of the biggest mass murder in the 20th century up to that time.

🔫 The Texas summer sky darkened on August 2, 1985, as Delta Air Lines Flight 191 from Fort Lauderdale approached Dallas/Fort Worth International Airport. A thunderstorm suddenly let loose a torrential rain, and lightning bolts streaked through the clouds. A downdraft estimated at 80 miles per hour rushed through the storm as the wide-bodied Lockheed L-1011 descended for landing. Without warning, the plane plunged belly first toward the ground. It hit one mile north of Runway 17 and bounced. A quarter-mile away, it crashed to the ground again, demolishing an automobile on Highway 114 and killing its driver. The huge plane careened across a grassy field, clipped a water tower, and burst into a wall of flames as it skidded across the tarmac. The only recognizable part of the scattered wreckage was the tail section with one of the plane's three engines and the last 10 rows of passenger seats. Of the 160 people aboard the flight, 31 somehow survived the disaster. Most had been seated in the rear of the plane. Two dogs in the rear cargo section also miraculously lived.

Tragic landing

The New London School disaster

On Monday, March 18, 1937, about 2,000 students arrived for classes as usual at the New London Consolidated School in Rusk County. Built with East Texas oil boom money, the showcase school had seven oil wells pumping on the campus grounds. Intermediate grades dismissed at 2:30 P.M. that day, leaving 1,500 students and their teachers who were scheduled to end classes at 3:30. But at 3:20, an explosion lifted the school's massive tile roof into the air. When the roof crashed down, it smashed into rubble and crushed automobiles parked round the school.

Only a single classroom and a second-story study hall remained standing. About 75 students saved themselves by jumping from the study hall windows. Rescuers soon jammed the area and began digging through the debris. The death count eventually totaled 293, one of the worst school disasters in the nation's history. Dr. E.P. Schoch, an explosives expert from the University of Texas, determined the cause of the blast. Of the 72 radiators that operated independently, most were vented directly into the walls. But the walls had no flues to the outside. Leaking gas accumulated in the walls and in the crawl space until it finally exploded. The horrendous disaster spurred the Texas Legislature to action. In July, it passed a law requiring the odorization of natural gas. Texas was the first state to enact such a law.

Mass murder in Killeen

George Jo Hennard rammed his pickup truck into a crowded Luby's cafeteria in Killeen on October 16, 1991, jumped out of his vehicle, and began firing two semi-automatic pistols in every direction. The massacre continued for 10 minutes as Hennard picked and chose who to kill and who to let live. When police finally wounded him, he stumbled into the rear of the cafeteria and shot himself in the head. Hennard took the lives of 23 people that awful autumn day in Killeen. At the time, it was the worst mass murder in U.S. history.

A national tragedy

John Warnock Hinckley, Jr., the man behind the gun that shot President Ronald Reagan on March 30, 1981, grew up in a ritzy home in Highland Park, an affluent enclave of Dallas. The son of an influential oilman, Hinckley attended Highland Park High School and enrolled at Texas Tech University. He never graduated, despite making the dean's honor list in 1977 and attending the college on and off for seven years. Described as a loner and a drifter, Hinckley developed a twisted obsession with actress Jodie Foster. Authorities speculated Hinckley hoped to gain Foster's attention by assassinating President Reagan.

At 2:30 on a rainy Monday afternoon, the president left the Washington Hilton Hotel and walked to his waiting limousine. Hinckley approached and fired six shots. White House Press Secretary James Brady, Secret Service Agent Timothy J. McCarthy, and Washington police officer Thomas K. Delahanty were all seriously injured. The president suffered a wound to his left chest and a collapsed lung. Hinckley, 25, was taken into custody at the scene. In May 1982, a jury declared him not guilty by reason of insanity. The loner from Texas was committed to a federal mental institution.

Officers push John Hinckley, Jr., into a police car after his attempt on President Ronald Reagan's life in 1981.

David Koresh and his Branch Davidian followers killed four agents from the Bureau of Alcohol, Tobacco and Firearms and wounded 16 in a barrage of gunfire that erupted from the cult compound in Waco on February 28, 1993. It was the worst loss of federal law-enforcement personnel in this century. It also began a 51-day siege that would end with the largest death count of any federal law-enforcement action in memory.

Ranch Apocalypse

After the botched raid in February, federal officials successfully negotiated with Koresh to release 37 cult members, including 21 children, from the compound. But as the standoff wore on and no other hostages were released, and law-enforcement authorities began to tighten the noose around the cult compound. Tanks moved in closer. The FBI removed a fence encircling the area. Koresh and his followers stood firm, stockpiled with guns, ammunition, hand grenades, and enough food to last for months. Finally on April 19, federal officials made their move. Tanks rammed the compound and released clouds of non-lethal tear gas. The hope was that the adults and children still inside would succumb to the gas and surrender peacefully. Instead, cult members donned gas masks and opened fire on the agents. The ramming and gassing continued from 6 A.M. until about noon. Then the first wisps of smoke floated from the compound. The fire rushed through the long corridors of the building, fueled by arms and ammunition. A huge fireball engulfed the structure. Within 45 minutes, all that remained were ashes. Some of the cultists survived the inferno. But officials found about 40 bodies in the debris and estimated that the dead included 25 children.

LAW AND ORDER

The hanging judge

The only case on Texas record of a justice of the peace handing down a death sentence occurred in the Navarro County town of Dresden. A man was tried and found guilty of robbing and murdering a peddler. The death sentence was carried out in a nearby cemetery where the man was hanged from a tree. Folks still talk about the Justice Tree, even though the man's name, the actual date of the hanging, and even the town of Dresden have been lost in history.

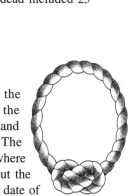

Lived to tell about it

In 1904, a man was discovered hanging by his neck in a San Antonio saloon. Fortunately, good Samaritans cut him down and revived him. Unfortunately, he was arrested and charged for being disorderly in public. The fine cost him $5.

Bean's brand of justice 🔫 Judge Roy Bean, the self-proclaimed "Law West of the Pecos," displayed a peculiar sense of right and wrong in his town of Langtry. The Texas Rangers appointed him justice of the peace in 1882 to help bring law and order to the railroad towns in the southwestern part of Texas. The judge once found a pistol and some cash on a dead man who had fallen from a bridge. Judge Bean confiscated the weapon and the money. He made his action "legal" by charging the poor dead soul with carrying a concealed weapon. Judge Bean fined the dead man the exact amount of money removed from his pockets.

A killer lawyer 🔫 Infamous gunman and murderer John Wesley Hardin was sent to prison in 1878 where he became superintendent of the Sunday School. He also studied law during his confinement. Hardin was admitted to the bar when he was pardoned in 1894. Between drinking and gambling, he practiced as an attorney in El Paso before being shot to death in 1895.

High-flying honesty 🔫 David Sisson, president of Superior Air Parts in Dallas, proved himself an honest man in the summer of 1994. Two men tried to sell Sisson stolen blueprints of a competitor's aircraft parts. Sisson cleverly expressed interest in the plans, then contacted the FBI and the competitor. Working with the FBI, Sisson even went so far as to make a $5,000 down payment on the purchase of the blueprints. In return he received diagrams of rocker arms and camshaft engine parts valued at $5 million. The blueprint thieves, Michael Hammond and Michael Peter Elcott, were arrested by the FBI and faced prison sentences of up to 10 years.

Buggy whips for police
Austin motorcycle police carry guns to fend off the bad guys. But they once also toted buggy whips to beat off dogs that chased their two-wheel vehicles.

Serving on both sides of the courtroom

Wes Hocker of Houston served as the foreman of a 1989 jury that found John Charles Zimmerman guilty of capital murder. When an appeal overturned the conviction, Hocker agreed to become Zimmerman's new lawyer.

In October 1994, the entire Texas Supreme Court was asked to disqualify itself on a case that centered around a plastics research laboratory. Because of safety violations, the lab could allegedly release hazardous chemicals. An accidental release of volatile chemicals reputedly could cause death and injury to anyone within a 10-mile radius of the Austin lab. The Supreme Court building sat within that radius. Lawyers argued that because of the mere threat of a toxic release, the Court could not remain neutral in the case.

Hazardous to the court's health

City officials in San Antonio proclaimed in 1993 that people who ignore warnings and unsuccessfully attempt to drive through flooded streets will have to pay to be rescued.

Testing the waters

THE BONNIE AND CLYDE YEARS

Bonnie Parker and Clyde Barrow robbed banks, stole automobiles, killed lawmen, and generally terrorized people from Iowa to Louisiana between 1932 and their demise in 1934. The outlaw pair garnered front-page publicity across the nation for their escapades and captured the public's imagination. Each time law officers appeared to have the criminals cornered, the elusive pair leveled their guns and shot their way out of the situation. Constantly on the run and careful not to reveal their whereabouts, Bonnie and Clyde developed an elaborate scheme for making contact with their families. The strategy centered around Bonnie's favorite food—red beans.

The red bean connection

When the two wanted to see their families, they arranged for a friend to drive by the Parker family home and toss a soda bottle into the yard. Mrs. Parker would retrieve the bottle, feigning displeasure at the apparent litter as nosy neighbors watched. But inside the bottle, a message stated a time and place for a meeting. Mrs. Parker would then telephone the Barrow family and invite them over for red beans. The signal, sounding innocent enough to anyone monitoring the phone call, alerted the Barrows to a planned meeting. The families then gathered on the appointed evening and together ventured to the place designated by Bonnie and Clyde.

An unlikely pair

Clyde Barrow, born in Teleco in 1910, dropped out of school in the fifth grade. Bonnie Parker was born October 1, 1910, in Rowena. Her family moved to Cement City West Dallas in about 1914. Bonnie later attended Bryan Adams High School and became a city-wide spelling champion.

The man who finally put Bonnie and Clyde to rest

Frank Hamer (below) had been retired from the Texas Rangers for nearly two years when duty called again. On February 10, 1934, he was commissioned as a state highway patrolman with a single order—get Clyde Barrow and Bonnie Parker. Frank Hamer had never laid eyes on the notorious outlaws. But during the 102 days that he pursued Bonnie and Clyde, he came to know the pair rather well.

"Before the chase ended," Hamer said, "I not only knew the general appearance and mental habits of the pair, but I learned the kind of whiskey they drank, what they ate, and the color, size, and texture of their clothes." Hamer also learned that the two criminals kept a secret "post office" for communicating with other people while they were on the lam. It was located on a side road about eight miles from Plain Dealing, Louisiana. Just off the road near a large pine tree stump, mail was stashed beneath a board on the ground.

In the pre-dawn hours of May 23, 1934, Hamer and five other lawmen staked out their positions along the "post office" road and began a seven-hour wait for Bonnie and Clyde. At 9:10 A.M., the gray Ford sedan came speeding into view. The outlaws slowed to a stop at the exact spot Hamer had expected. At the command "Stick 'em up," the criminals went for their guns and the firing began. Clyde's foot released the car's clutch, and the idling auto rolled forward and slid into a ditch. Hamer looked at his watch. It was 9:20 A.M. The blast of bullets came so furiously that no one ever knew who fired the fatal shots.

For his success in finally stopping the reign of Bonnie and Clyde, Hamer received payment of $180 a month and the promise of paid expenses. But the state refused to make good on about $14 worth of Hamer's telephone bills because he couldn't produce receipts.

A less cordial meeting Ted Hinton, a Dallas County deputy sheriff, was among the lawmen who fired on Bonnie and Clyde the day they were ambushed in 1934. Hinton had known Bonnie several years before when she was a waitress at the American Cafe in Dallas. Then a postal worker, Hinton often lunched at the cafe and visited with the soon-to-be criminal.

Fact and fiction

An autopsy proved that Bonnie was not pregnant when she was killed, although the romantic rumor persists to this day.

Tattooed on Bonnie's right thigh were the words "Bonnie and Roy." She married Roy Thornton sometime in the mid-1920s and left him in 1930. Bonnie (right) went on to infamy alongside her new love Clyde. Roy wound up with a 50-year prison sentence for robbery. On the day Bonnie Parker died, she was still legally Mrs. Roy Thornton.

The man before Clyde

No smoking

The famous photo of Bonnie seemingly smoking a cigar was found when a roll of film was confiscated after a shoot-out in Joplin, Missouri. It came to the public's attention when newspapers nationwide gave it front-page placement. The snapshot shows Bonnie leaning on the headlamp of a Ford, one foot propped on the bumper. Her right hand holds a large pistol, and a big, black cigar dangles from her mouth. Bonnie claimed that she posed for the photo as a personal joke, and adamantly denied ever actually smoking cigars. But the image of the petite outlaw smoking a fat stogie added to the public's fascination with the elusive criminal.

THE KENNEDY ASSASSINATION

The last words Nellie Connally spoke to President Kennedy were "You can't say now that Dallas doesn't love you, Mr. President." With that sentence, the motorcade turned off Houston Street and passed in front of the Texas School Book Depository Building. At approximately 12:30 P.M. on November 22, 1963, the shots that killed President John F. Kennedy and wounded Governor Connally rang out.

Final words

How Nellie Connally saved her husband's life

John Connally, a native of Floresville, was governor for less than 11 months when he and his wife, Nellie, joined Mr. and Mrs. Kennedy in the 1961 Lincoln limousine for the motorcade through Dallas. The Connallys sat in the front seat, with the governor riding next to the door. When the shots were fired, Connally felt a sharp thud in his back and doubled over in pain. Mrs. Connally pulled the collapsed governor into her lap. That instinctive act saved his life. The pressure of the governor's arm against the bullet's exit wound closed the hole in his chest as he huddled in his wife's lap. The three-time governor died in June 1993 at age 76. He was buried in Austin's State Cemetery.

President John F. Kennedy (left) and John Connally at the White House

Thirty years of skepticism

The Warren Commission Report, which laid the blame of assassination solely at the feet of Lee Harvey Oswald, never washed with many Americans. Over the years, books, magazine articles, and even feature films have debated who killed John F. Kennedy on that day in Dallas—and why. Names such as Fidel Castro and even John Connally have been mentioned in some theories. Other conspiracy theorists claim the Mafia, the CIA, the Soviets, or the oil cartel sponsored the assassination. The public may never know the truth. But a Cable News Network poll conducted in 1993 showed that 80 percent of the American people thought the assassination was indeed a conspiracy.

Shooting with a camera

Tom Alyea was a cameraman for WFAA-TV on the day of the assassination. He was also the first person to film Oswald's L-shaped sniper nest amid boxes at the sixth-floor window in the Texas School Book Depository Building.

The first televised murder

At 12:20 P.M. on November 24, 1963, millions of viewers witnessed the first actual murder ever shown on television. As Lee Harvey Oswald was being led through police headquarters in Dallas, Jacob L. Rubenstein, better known as Jack Ruby, pulled out a concealed pistol and shot Oswald to death.

Watching Ruby get the death penalty

On March 4, 1964, the trial of Jack Ruby began for his murder of Oswald. It lasted only 10 days, presided over by Judge Joseph Brantley Brown. On March 14, the verdict came in from the Third Criminal District Court of Dallas County. CBS was in the courtroom with its cameras rolling. Between 12:37 P.M. and 2:00 P.M., the network sent the broadcast live to New York and shared it with ABC and NBC. It was the first courtroom verdict ever telecast live. The nation watched as Ruby was sentenced to death in the electric chair for "murder with malice."

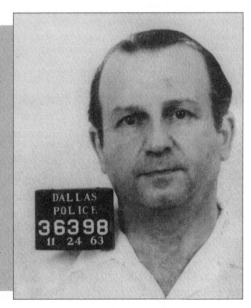

Surviving through history

The Texas School Book Depository Building seemed destined to survive its place in history. After the assassination, two arsonists tried but failed to burn down the structure. A demolition attempt was thwarted when the city of Dallas refused to issue a permit. A promoter purchased the old textbook warehouse in 1977 and sought funding for a museum. That failed, too. Finally, in 1977, Dallas County bought the building for $400,000. The county converted the space into a commissioner's court and offices, but left the sixth floor empty. Today the building is known as the Dallas County Administration Building.

Opening the sixth floor

🔫 Since November 22, 1963, people from across the globe have trekked to Dallas to see the spot where the president was slain. For most of those years, visitors could only stand on the streets of Dealey Plaza and look up at the window on the sixth floor of the Texas School Book Depository (right). Finally, on President's Day, February 20, 1989, the Dallas County Historical Foundation formally opened The Sixth Floor Museum.

Inside, visitors can now tour the infamous site. Photographs, videos, interpretive exhibits, films, and texts examine the life, death, and legacy of John F. Kennedy. The south windows look down to Elm Street and the grassy knoll, the spot where some witnesses say a second gunman fired. But most intriguing are two sixth-floor areas now enclosed by glass. Around the window where Oswald reportedly took aim, three spent shells can be seen amid the boxes. The corner staircase that Oswald allegedly took to make his escape and the freight elevator are also enclosed in glass. Here visitors find the mail-order, $12.78, bolt-action Mannlicher rifle that the assassin supposedly used to kill the president. There is also the clipboard, with textbook orders that Oswald never filled. All the settings and items used in the displays were reconstructed from police photographs. The actual evidence is stored in the National Archives. But the mood and atmosphere are real, even for those who were not yet born on the day President Kennedy died. "The Book of Memories" is the last step visitors take through the museum. It provides the opportunity to express feelings and thoughts about the historical event.

A final farewell

🔫 Thirty years to the day, Nellie Connally returned to the exact site of President's Kennedy's assassination. The occasion was the dedication of Dealey Plaza as a National Historic Landmark on November 22, 1993. For more than a quarter of a century, Dallas residents and visitors to the site had placed flowers, wreaths, candles, and cards along Elm Street on each anniversary of the president's death. But no official marker had ever been erected until that day in 1993.

During a solemn ceremony that lasted only one hour, Mrs. Connally made the landmark dedication address. At 12:30 P.M., almost the exact time that President Kennedy was shot 30 years earlier, jets roared overhead and 30 white doves were released. Although the wonder and theories and questions about the assassination may persist forever, the city of Dallas, at least, had made its final farewell.

THE LONG ARM OF THE LAW

**The greatest lawyer
who ever lived**

Percy Foreman stood six feet five inches tall, weighed nearly 300 pounds, and his booming voice reverberated in courtrooms. He was morally opposed to capital punishment and defended thousands of accused murderers for more than 60 years. Only one was ever executed by the state.

Born in the obscure East Texas town of Bold Spring near Livingston, Foreman began practicing law in 1927 in Houston. He was already a Texas legend when he rose to national prominence defending James Earl Ray, the assassin of Martin Luther King, Jr. Later, he took the appeal of Jack Ruby for his murder of Lee Harvey Oswald, although Foreman later left the case because of differences with the Ruby family. Foreman had no equal in the courtroom. He would scream, sob, or perform any other theatric he thought might sway a jury. He personally investigated most of the cases he took. He charged high fees and made millions of dollars. But Foreman also defended many clients for free.

In the summer of 1988, the big man's heart failed. He was 86 years old, but continued to consult on a case from his hospital room. On the morning of August 29, the Harris County Courthouse closed for Percy Foreman's funeral.

Bloodhound

Crime investigators in Texas know Sergeant Dusty Hesskew of the Austin Police Department as the state's leading blood detective. Hesskew can tell from a spot or splat of blood what type of violent action caused the stain. He can tell from a bloodstain what type of weapon was used in a crime, and whether the perpetrator was left-handed or right-handed. A police officer for 22 years, Hesskew attended the exclusive Corning Forensic Institute in New York in 1985. The subject of bloodstain analysis grabbed his attention. Hesskew has examined more than 1,000 crime scenes that involved violent deaths, and he often testifies in murder trials as a state's witness. During a trial in the late 1980s, Hesskew set up a victim's bedroom in front of a courtroom jury. He then crouched beside the bed with gun in hand and showed how the killer had attempted to make the murder look like suicide. The demonstration proved more effective than he could have imagined. The defendant jumped up and ran out of the courtroom as if she'd seen a ghost. She was sentenced to life in prison.

Murder, he wrote

Thomas Thompson's book *Blood and Money* immortalized the high-profile trial of Lilla Paulus who was accused of conspiring to murder Dr. John Hill after his wife died under strange circumstances. Houston trial lawyer Dick DeGuerin defended Paulus under the glare of media lights—and lost. Paulus was sentenced to 35 years in prison. DeGuerin, however, later won a reversal. In 1993, DeGuerin became the lawyer for David Koresh, the Branch Davidian cult leader who died in the fiery end of a 51-day siege in Waco.

Video verdicts

Windle Turley holds the record for the heftiest personal injury verdicts in Dallas County. The Dallas lawyer, owner of a 20-attorney firm, specializes in wrongful death suits, personal injury cases, and video reenactments.

Video dramas that play out life and death moments of cases being tried were considered unconventional when Turley began producing them and bringing them into courtrooms in the early 1990s. Since then they've become commonplace for large law firms. But the few minutes of realistic accident footage created by Turley for his cases have helped him win suits for his clients. In one, he hired a stunt man to play the role of a young man who burned to death. The case never went to trial. Upon seeing the fiery image on video, the defendant immediately settled out of court.

Prosecuting a president

As Watergate special prosecutor, Houston attorney Leon Jaworski's pursuit of the White House tape recordings paved the way for President Richard Nixon's resignation on August 9, 1974. The Watergate scandal elevated Jaworski to the pedestal of national hero and was the pinnacle of a distinguished legal career.

In 1924, when he was only 19, Jaworski became the youngest lawyer in Texas history. He defended bootleggers in Waco before moving on to Houston and eventually becoming the senior partner in the firm that is known today as Fulbright and Jaworski. After World War II, he prosecuted Nazi war criminals at Dachau and Darmstadt. Jaworski voted for Nixon in 1968 and 1972, only to chase the president out of office in 1974. The lawyer spent 11 months in Washington, but many criticized him publicly for walking away from his job as special prosecutor before all the scoundrels had been rounded up and branded. Others were outraged when he refused to challenge President Ford's pardon of Nixon. When Jaworski left Washington, he headed back to Houston. He continued trying cases, and on December 9, 1982, he died of a heart attack while chopping wood at his ranch in Wimberly.

> #### Musical chairs
> Dallas District Court Judge Catherine Crier traded her seat on the bench for a chair at the anchor desk of the Cable News Network in 1989. She's since moved to the ABC network.

Setting the record straight

Moman Pruiett arrived in Texas with a criminal record. In Arkansas, he was wrongly convicted of forgery and served six months in the Little Rock penitentiary. After coming to Texas, he was sent to Huntsville penitentiary for a robbery he didn't commit. Pruiett was released from prison in 1894, finally found his way to the right side of the law, and proceeded to become one of the country's most successful criminal attorneys. He won acquittals for 304 of the 342 murder defendants he represented.

A CRIMINAL MISCELLANY

The joint ☛ The Texas State Penitentiary at Huntsville received its first prisoner on October 1, 1849, when a cattle thief named William Samson arrived. Samson was sentenced to a three-year term, but was paroled less than a year after being incarcerated.

Time will tell ☛ Albert Howard professed his innocence of any crime right up until the day he was hanged in Gonzales. As Howard waited for the fateful hour to arrive, he watched one of the clock towers in the Gonzales County Courthouse. The clock, he warned, would forever testify to his innocence by never again keeping the correct time. Howard was hanged on March 21, 1921. Since that day, the four clock faces have not kept the same time, although many attempts have been made to fix the old tickers.

G.I. Joe's greatest heist

Joe Thomas Meador of Whitewright may have pulled off the heist of the century while serving as an army lieutenant during World War II. When Allied forces converged on the medieval town of Quedlinburg in East Germany, priceless treasures collected over centuries by the church were hidden in a mine shaft. Meador somehow laid his hands on a few of the ancient artworks, sneaked them out of East Germany, and got them to his home town of Whitewright. One of the pieces in Meador's possession was the Four Gospels, a magnificent manuscript bound in gold and silver with a bas-relief of Christ. Precious stones studded each corner, and inside was a hand-gilded illustrated version of the Gospels. Meador also made off with an ornate crown, a breviary in a finely wrought silver binding, an ivory comb, a bird-shaped rock-crystal flask, and much, much more.

Meador died on February 1, 1980, bequeathing his estate to his sister Jane and his brother Jack. Although no mention was made in his will about the Quedlinburg treasures, the siblings did indeed come to own them. For 45 years, no one knew what became of the valuable works. Then in April 1990, the Meador heirs sold the Four Gospels for $3 million to a West German foundation that recovers artwork for museums. The breviary bound in silver was purchased by a West German art dealer. Finally, 45 years after the ancient works were stolen, a court ordered an inventory of the Meador family's safe-deposit box. Some, but not nearly all, of the missing pieces were found. The German government, however, agreed to pay the Meador heirs $1 million to recoup the missing treasures.

Just trying for a raise

In 1993, outgoing Nueces County Sheriff James Hickey was indicted by a federal grand jury for writing himself a $48,000 check. Hickey took the money from a federal drug-forfeiture fund and called the loot a "salary adjustment."

A TEXAS TREASURY

The spirit of early Texas is alive and well in modern-day pioneers. While colonists explored the land, today's frontier seekers push the limits of science and technology, education, and medicine. The first U.S. heart transplant took place at Houston's Texas Medical Center, the largest facility of its kind in the world. An astronaut from San Antonio was the first man to walk in space. A Texas school produced the first university showing of the play *Long Day's Journey Into Night*. And computerized "Smart Houses" got their very first showcase in a small Texas community.

The list of the best and the brightest goes on, and the stories are all here. Come meet the people and relive the moments that make Texas a new frontier.

- Getting an Education
- At the Front of the Class
- Up, Up, and Away
- Medicinal Purposes
- Medical Histories
- Checking Out Lone Star Libraries
- Awards and Honors
- Science and Technology
- The Bold and the Beautiful
- Etcetera

GETTING AN EDUCATION

Kohlberg's kindergartens

❖ When Olga Bernstein Kohlberg arrived in El Paso from her native Germany, she brought with her the concept of pre-school training. In 1892, she led the El Paso Women's Club to open the first private kindergarten in Texas. A year later, Kohlberg and the club persuaded the local school board to start the first public kindergarten in the state. She followed those achievements by becoming a founder of the El Paso Public Library. She was also instrumental in establishing the community's first public hospital. Kohlberg died in 1944, but her public service work will be forever remembered.

TV journalist Walter Cronkite is one of the most famous graduates of Houston's Sam Jacinto High School. He anchored "CBS Evening News" from 1962 to 1981.

Universities founded during the Republic

Rutersville College was established by Methodists near La Grange in 1840 and began to decline in 1850. The University of San Augustine opened in 1842 and McKenzie College was founded in 1841 near Clarksville. Baylor University was chartered at Independence in 1845. In 1866, it was consolidated with Waco University and located in Waco.

Setting a precedent

In the 1950 case of *Sweatt v. Painter*, the U.S. Supreme Court found it was unconstitutional for the University of Texas to maintain racial segregation by establishing a separate law school for black applicant Herman Sweatt. The high court ordered Sweatt admitted to the UT law school. That decision ended legal racial segregation in Texas institutions of higher education. Four years later, the Sweatt case surfaced again as a precedent in the historic *Brown v. Board of Education of Topeka* school-desegregation case.

Contemplating the navel

The first belly-dancing course ever offered at a college was "Body Conditioning Through the Art of Oriental Belly Dance" at the University of Texas at Arlington. Sixty students paid $25 for the six-lesson noncredit course in August 1973.

Aggies and Maggies

❖ The Agricultural and Mechanical College of Texas, now Texas A&M University, opened its doors in 1876, becoming the state's first publicly supported institution of higher education. The student body consisted of about 40 men. Not until 1963 were women permitted to enroll as students.

A Lone Star link with Notre Dame

❖ Edward Sorin, the Superior General of the Congregation of Holy Cross who founded Notre Dame University, also established St. Edward's University in Austin. The school enrolled its first three students in 1881 and was chartered in 1885 as St. Edward's College. In 1925, a new charter renamed the college St. Edward's University.

❖ The Universidad Nacional Autónoma de México, founded in 1551, is Mexico's national university and the oldest institution of higher education in the Americas. A campus of the university was established in San Antonio in 1972, the only branch outside of Mexico.

An international university

Santa Claus in a business suit

John Jay Moores of Sugar Land is one of the richest men in Texas. For 12 years he made millions selling software through BMC, the company he founded in 1980. He also gave away millions—about $25 million over the years—to businesses and charitable causes that were close to his heart. In 1991, Moores donated $51.4 million to the University of Houston with the money tagged for creative writing programs, athletics, and the music department. At the time, Moores' generous donation was the largest private gift ever bestowed on a public university.

❖ When the Rice School/La Escuela Rice opened in the Houston Independent School District in September 1994, 7,000 students applied for 1,275 openings in kindergarten through eighth grade. A lottery determined who would be admitted. About 700 teachers vied for the 70 available jobs. So why was everyone making such a fuss about attending the new educational institution?

Tomorrow's education today

The Rice School combined the best of basics—such as uniforms and real homework—with a contemporary approach to learning. Teachers do not work alone but with counselors, parents, and professors at Rice University who help develop the curriculum. Bright kids advance based on their abilities, not on their ages. The small, bilingual classes are economically as well as racially mixed. Houston-based Compaq donated 1,100 computers to the school. That's almost one computer for each student and each teacher.

New twists on an old tradition

The Ranch Management Program at Fort Worth's Texas Christian University began in 1956 as a way to teach new tricks in an old trade. Since then, about 1,000 men and women from 34 states and 21 countries have graduated from the classroom to home on the range. The TCU program isn't for city slickers aspiring to be cowboys. Enrollment is limited to 35 students a year, and each applicant must show previous ranching experience. During the intensive two-semester program, students focus only on the ranch-management curriculum and must complete 12 required courses before earning a ranch-management certificate. About one-third of the graduates find management positions at corporate-owned ranches. The other two-thirds get back in the saddle and return to family ranching operations.

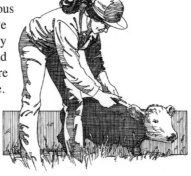

An educational drill

When the University of Texas opened in 1883, it owned plenty of land in West Texas. The legislature had given some 2 million acres of arid country to the school as

an endowment. Although the land was of dubious agricultural value, some money was earned from grazing leases. Then on May 28, 1923, Rupert Ricker's Santa Rita No. 1 oil well (left) blew in. The Reagan County well was the first—but not the last—well drilled on the dusty plains owned by the University of Texas. Over the years, income derived from oil on university land has surpassed $1 trillion, making the school one of the richest universities in the world.

A study in university history

❖ In 1869, three Cumberland Presbyterian synods established Trinity University, a four-year, coeducational, liberal arts institution in Tehuacana, about 40 miles northeast of Waco. Construction of the main building, known as Texas Hall, began in 1873. Trinity moved to Waco in 1902 and eventually settled in San Antonio. The Presbyterians gave the campus in Tehuacana to the Methodist Protestant Church, which opened it in the fall of 1902 as Westminster College. Westminster continued as a four-year university until 1916, when it became one of the first two-year colleges in the nation. The buildings and grounds were sold several times until they were finally purchased by Trinity Institute, an educational foundation, in 1991.

AT THE FRONT OF THE CLASS

A first in education

❖ Dr. Mary Elizabeth Blanton, an African-American educator, became the first woman to head a Texas college when she was named president of Tillotson College in Austin in 1930. She held the position until 1944.

Play rights

❖ Paul Baker, chairman of Baylor University's drama department in 1962, secured the rights to the first university production of Eugene O'Neill's *Long Day's Journey into Night*. During the play's run, a Baptist minister visiting Waco took a bunch of 9-year-old boys to see the show. The play offended the minister, who lodged a complaint with Baylor's president, Abner McCall. McCall asked Baker to edit out the offensive language. When Baker refused, McCall closed the curtain on the play. Three months later, Baker and his entire staff resigned. They took their talents to Trinity University in San Antonio. There, the Dallas Theater Center-affiliated graduate program, which had been at Baylor, played on successfully for more than 20 years.

❖ Charles Alan Wright (below) began teaching at the University of Texas School of Law in Austin in 1955. In addition to striking fear into freshmen, he has garnered an international reputation as an expert on the U.S. Constitution and the federal courts. He has won groundbreaking cases and scored victories in the presence of the U.S. Supreme Court. He has also been a lifelong lover of good murder mystery books. Since the early 1980s, Wright has combined his legal knowledge with his penchant for fiction by writing book reviews for *The Practical Lawyer*, a publication of the American Law Institute. In his review column, "The Fictional Lawyer," Wright sticks as close to the letter of the law as do his legal briefs. No goof, however small, goes unnoticed. Take, for instance, his eye for detail in the book *The Twelfth Juror*. In one scene, author B.M. Gill mentions the sunlight illuminating a judge's crimson robes in England's Old Bailey Number One Court. Wright had visited the court, but could not remember any windows in the location where the scene took place. To check the fact for his review, Wright enlisted the help of a London judge, who confirmed that the legendary courtroom had a single skylight, but no windows. No wonder freshman law schoolers quake under Wright's tutelage.

Reviewing the mysteries of law

❖ After 40 years of teaching social sciences at predominantly African-American colleges in the South, Henry A. Bullock arrived at the University of Texas in 1970. He taught a course entitled "The Negro in America" and became the first African-American faculty member of the university's Arts and Sciences department. Dr. Bullock later established the first ethnic studies program at the school.

A first for the faculty

UP, UP, AND AWAY

First flight

Frenchman Louis Paulhan performed the first public demonstration of an airplane flight in Texas on February 18, 1910. Paulhan took off from a field just outside Houston in his fabric-and-wood Farman biplane. He made at least two flights to fulfill a $20,000 contract.

❖ Edward Higgins White II, a San Antonio native, blasted off with Jim McDivitt in *Gemini 4* on June 3, 1965. During the third revolution around the Earth, White stepped out of the craft and became America's first man to walk in space. He worked at the end of a 21-foot tether as he maneuvered with thrusts from a twin-barreled gas gun. After that mission, White was selected as the command-module pilot for the first manned *Apollo 1* flight. But on January 27, 1967, he was killed with crewmates Virgil Grissom and Roger Chaffee when a fire broke out in the spacecraft at Cape Kennedy, Florida, during a preflight ground test. They were the only U.S. astronauts killed in space tests.

The first space walker

Did he say Houston?

♦ On Sunday, July 20, 1969, Neil Armstrong took man's first steps on the moon, as he uttered the now-famous words, "That's one small step for man, one giant leap for mankind." Actually the first word ever spoken from the moon was the name of a Texas city. Armstrong said, "Houston, Tranquility Base here. The Eagle has landed."

To the moon and back

Alan L. Bean (left), a native of Wheeler, made the second landing on the moon in November 1969 aboard *Apollo-Saturn 12*. Bean and Conrad collected 74.7 pounds of moon samples during a lunar stay that lasted 13 hours and 44 minutes. In 1973, Bean returned to space aboard the *Skylab 3* mission, which included 13 hours and 44 minutes of walking in space.

A few advances, compliments of NASA

Research by scientists at the National Aeronautics and Space Administration in Houston have led to dozens of advances that proved useful back on Earth. For instance, NASA developed dry, spray-on electrode techniques that allow accurate electrocardiograms to be taken on bumpy ambulance rides. The agency also pioneered more reliable batteries that last longer. Here are a few other ideas and items developed by NASA.

- Ballpoint pens that write in any position
- Wheelchairs that can be operated by voice command
- Procedures to control contamination in operating and recovery rooms
- Fire-retardant paint and flameproof materials
- Pressure-sensitive fasteners and closures
- Transducers first used to measure the splashdown impact of a spacecraft were incorporated into a device for precision fitting of artificial limbs
- Cookware that goes from freezer to oven without cracking and can be easily cleaned
- Miniature tape recorders

More astronauts from Texas and their space shuttle missions

William F. Fisher of Dallas – *Discovery*, June 1985

John M. Fabian of Goosecreek – *Challenger*, June 1983

Robert L. Crippen of Beaumont – *Columbia*, November 1981; *Challenger*, June 1983, April 1984, and October 1984

John O. Creighton of Orange – *Atlantis*, February and March 1990; *Discovery*, June 1985 and September 1991

Kenneth D. Cockrell of Austin – *Discovery*, April 1993

John E. Blaha of San Antonio – *Discovery*, March 1989 and November 1989; *Atlantis*, August 1991

❖ At Space Center Houston, visitors can get an up-close look at five samples from the largest collection of moon rocks on Earth. They can even touch a small slice of the cosmos that's estimated to be 3.8 billion years old. Bringing the space experience down to earth is the whole idea behind Space Center Houston, a $70-million educational and entertainment complex that serves as the visitor center for the Lyndon B. Johnson Space Center. The nonprofit, 183,000-square-foot center offers hands-on exhibits. Actual space vehicles—from Project Mercury in the 1960s to present-day shuttles—are on display. Visitors can even walk through the Skylab Trainer, the training module for America's first space station. The huge trainer was moved to the site of the center before construction began so that the entire facility could be built around the module.

Down to Earth

Stargazing

When William Johnson McDonald, a banker and amateur astronomer in Paris, Texas, died in 1926, the terms of his will shocked his heirs. McDonald left most of his worldly fortune—more than $1 million—to the University of Texas to build an observatory for the study of astronomical science. His heirs contested the will, claiming the old banker was insane for giving so much money to the study of stars. It took four trials and a hung jury to finally end the argument over his money. The university settled out of court for $840,000 and agreed to build an observatory, even though the school had no astronomers at the time. On May 5, 1939, McDonald Observatory inaugurated its first telescope atop Mount Locke in the Davis Mountains. Today, McDonald is one of about a dozen major observatories in the world.

MEDICINAL PURPOSES

❖ Monroe D. Anderson, a Houston philanthropist, had a vision of advancing medical knowledge and relieving human suffering. He conceived the idea of the phenomenal Texas Medical Center (right) and made it possible by providing $20 million upon his death in 1939. In 1942, the M.D. Anderson Hospital for Cancer Re-search was built near the existing Hermann Hospital. In 1943, the Baylor College of Medicine and the University of Texas School of Dentistry were located nearby. The vision was coming into focus, and in 1945, the M.D. Anderson Foundation donated 134 acres for the incorporation of the Texas Medical Center. M.D. Anderson made possible the world's largest medical facility of its kind.

The making of Texas Medical Center

The vital statistics on Texas Medical Center

- The complex occupies 650 acres.
- The center incorporates 41 institutions—including the LifeGift Organ Donation Center, Gulf Coast Regional Blood Center, Institute for Rehabilitation and Research, M.D. Anderson Cancer Center, and Ronald McDonald House. All function under different policies and pursue independent directions; and all operate on a nonprofit basis.
- Fourteen hospitals provide more than 6,600 licensed patient beds.
- The center spends approximately $3 billion a year on thousands of operations.
- More than 1,500 medical research projects are conducted daily.
- Inpatient and outpatient visits total more than 2.5 million annually.
- The Lyndon B. Johnson General Hospital delivers more than 15,000 babies each year.
- Texas Children's Hospital is the nation's largest pediatric medical complex.
- Hermann Hospital was the first in the country to use Life Flight helicopters as air ambulances.
- America's first and only Children's Nutrition Research Center is located in the complex.
- Six universities conduct major programs at the center: Baylor University, Prairie View A&M, Texas A&M, Texas Woman's University, University of Houston, and University of Texas.
- Each day, 10,000 students study and train at the complex.
- The center employs more than 50,000 workers.
- About 8,000 volunteers assist at the center.

A man with many hearts

❖ Houston cardiovascular surgeon Dr. Denton Arthur Cooley (left) performed the first successful U.S. heart transplant on May 2, 1968, at the Texas Heart Institute in Houston. Cooley removed the damaged heart of a 47-year-old male patient and replaced it with the heart of a 15-year-old female who had died of a brain injury. Less than a year later, on April 4, 1969, Cooley implanted the world's first entirely artificial heart, made of Dacron and plastic, into a human. By the early 1990s, Cooley, surgeon-in-chief at the Texas Heart Institute, and his team of trained surgeons had performed more than 75,000 heart surgical procedures.

Healing the heart

In 1948, a young Louisiana doctor named Michael DeBakey became the head of surgery at the Baylor College of Medicine in Houston. The heart surgeon shocked the world and made medical history only six years later. In 1954, he performed heart surgery on public television as surgeons on six continents watched simultaneously via a global cable network. The operation took place at the Methodist Hospital of Texas Medical Center in Houston. DeBakey's pioneering work in the treatment of cardiovascular disease led him to become the first surgeon to perform numerous operations that are now standard procedures. In 1964, he performed the first aortocoronary artery bypass using part of a vein from the patient's leg.

A not-so-mad scientist

❖ Dr. James Robinson Bailey, a chemist and professor at the University of Texas, decoded secret German formulas during World War I. He introduced novocaine and synthetic adrenalin into the United States and developed more than 20 new drugs.

❖ The Human Genome Project was established in 1989 to determine the location of all the genes in the human body. The goal of the project was to identify defective genes that might cause inherited diseases such as cancer and diabetes. The task sounded inconceivable. At least 100,000 genes pack themselves along the body's 23 pairs of chromosomes. But Dr. Tom Caskey took up the hunt. His lab at Baylor Medical Center in Houston, one of nine designated Genome Centers, was given the job of finding disease-causing genes on the X chromosome and the chromosomes 6 and 17. At last count toward the end of 1994, Caskey and his colleagues had found about 20 such genes and were still searching for more.

Genetic detective

❖ Eight-month-old Sara Remington made history in 1984 when she became the youngest heart-transplant recipient in the world. In 1994, she made medical history again. At the age of 10, Sara was the world's longest-surviving pediatric transplant recipient. To celebrate the 10-year anniversary, Sara turned cartwheels for her Houston surgeons, whom she referred to as "the old geezers." The doctors didn't seem to mind. Between Sara's surgery and 1994, there were 60 pediatric transplant recipients at Texas Children's Hospital in Houston.

Live long and prosper

Hospitalized leeches

When 6-year-old Dusty Tillery of Weatherford nearly severed his ear in a farm accident in January 1993, he might have lived with the scar for the rest of his life. Fort Worth plastic surgeon Walter Sorokolit reattached the boy's ear during a two-hour operation at Cook-Fort Worth Children's Medical Center. But as so often happens in cases like Dusty's, circulation didn't return to the ear. However, Dr. Sorokolit didn't give up. He suggested treatment by *Hirudo medicinals*, a laboratory-bred strain of leeches. Three times each day, a pediatric postsurgical nurse and Dusty's mom picked up the five-inch-long, black invertebrates with forceps and placed them two at a time on Dusty's ear. The leeches created microscopic punctures with their sucker teeth and got the blood flowing through the damaged capillaries. Three days of leech therapy and about a month of healing repaired Dusty's ear.

Beak braces

Marianne Hayes despaired when Sydney was hatched with a deformed beak. The rare black palm cockatoo, valued at about $15,000, had an upper beak that scissored with the lower half. The deformity made it impossible for Sydney to crack the hard tropical nuts that are a staple in any black palm cockatoo's diet. Then Dr. Jim Roberts, an orthodontist in Denton, came to the rescue. Hayes, persuaded Roberts that the beak of the 2-month-old bird could somehow be repaired. Roberts fitted Sydney with plastic-and-steel braces. The appliance had to be reattached with epoxy every week. But in just two months, Sydney was consuming his favorite tropical nuts and impressing all the cockatoo chicks.

MEDICAL HISTORIES

Taking care of the children

❖ In 1913, nurse Mae Smith borrowed Red Cross tents and set up a "baby camp" for malnourished and sick infants in Dallas. She persuaded doctors and nurses to volunteer treatment and raised funds for a temporary building. In 1929, Smith appealed to businessman Tom Bradford, Sr., for funding of an official children's hospital. He donated $100,000 to the cause. The Bradford Memorial Hospital for Babies later became a part of Dallas' Children's Medical Center.

Other medical firsts

• *The Galveston Medical Journal*, published in 1866 by Dr. Greensville S. Dowell, was the first medical periodical published in Texas.
• On December 21, 1929, Baylor University Hospital in Dallas initiated the first-ever group hospital-insurance plan. The first group insured was the Dallas Public School teachers.
• The first Texas nursing school was organized at John Sealy Hospital in Galveston in 1890.
• The state's first class of professional nurses graduated from the Galveston's John Sealy Hospital in 1895.

A wagon ride to a hospital

❖ In 1869, three young French nuns rode a wagon from Galveston to San Antonio. Working under the guidance of Mother Madeleine Chollet, the Sisters of Charity of the Incarnate founded Santa Rosa Hospital, the largest Catholic hospital in the United States.

The cost of illness

❖ Doctors tended the sick during the years of the Texas Republic for about $5 per call during the day. After 9 P.M., the fee doubled to $10. A consultation for a malady cost $15. Midwifery ran between $30 and $40. Of course, not all payments were made in cash. Corn, cotton, pigs, horses, cows, and even land made acceptable trades for balances due.

Frontier doctor

Austrian-born Dr. Sofie Herzog arrived in Brazoria in 1893 and immediately caused the raising of Texas eyebrows. She was a widow with 14 children. She dressed in a split skirt to ride astride her horse as it galloped through the streets. Most unusual of all though, was the necklace she wore as a good luck charm. Her medical skills were most often put to use extracting bullets from gunshot victims involved in shoot-outs. As she removed the bullets, she strung them into a necklace. Dr. Sofie, as the townsfolk called her, died in 1925. At her request she was buried with her lucky strand of two dozen bullets.

A Texas child makes medical history

❖ Stormie Jones, the world's first heart-and-liver transplant patient, died at age 13 on November 11, 1990, nearly seven years after her historic operation. The West Texas girl was born with a rare liver disease that pushed her cholesterol level to ten times above normal. She was only six years old when she received the groundbreaking double transplant. By that time, she had suffered two heart attacks, undergone two triple bypass operations, and lived through valve-replacement surgery.

After a bout with hepatitis in early 1990, Stormie received her second liver transplant, but the new organ was damaged when the disease returned that summer. On November 11, she flew to Children's Hospital of Pittsburgh for treatment of flu-like symptoms. Her unexpected death came just a few hours later.

❖ Texas women helped move medical science along in Texas.
   •Dr. Molly Armstrong became the first woman optometrist in Texas and second in the nation in the early 1900s.
   •Minnie Fisher Cunningham became the first woman to receive a pharmacy degree from the University of Texas in 1902.
   •Dr. Daisy Emery Allen became one of the first two women to graduate from medical school in Texas in 1897. She practiced for almost 50 years in the Fort Worth area.

Firsts for women

CHECKING OUT LONE STAR LIBRARIES

❖ In 1918, the Library and Historical Commission chose Elizabeth Howard West as the Texas State Librarian. She became the first woman commissioned head of a department in Texas government. More importantly, she used her position to help establish the free public library system in Texas and to initiate state library services for the blind. West left state government in 1925, but she didn't stray from her library work. She became the first librarian at the new Texas Technological College in Lubbock. There she helped guide the construction of the first library building on the campus. West died in 1948.

First official bookworm

Getting a free read

The Texas Federation of Women's Clubs, organized in 1897, set a goal to start a free library in every Texas county. By 1907, the group had founded 65 free libraries, including libraries in major cities such as Dallas, Houston, San Antonio, and El Paso. Of all the Texas libraries organized before 1950, 85 percent were started by Women's Clubs.

Return to sender
The Wineburgh Philatelic Research Library, founded in 1976 at the University of Texas at Dallas, gets the stamp of approval as one of the top five philatelic libraries in the United States.

Celebrating a cellist

For 15 years, the music library at the University of North Texas in Denton was silent about a collection of classic tapes. The library holds the most complete—and possibly the only—set of broadcasts of *Toscanini: The Man Behind the Legend*, an NBC radio show that aired between 1963 and 1967. The 500 reel-to-reel tapes contain hundreds of hours of interviews and music from cellist Arturo Toscanini. Because of their tenuous condition, the library stored, but did not play, the tapes. In 1994, a Dallas nonprofit group came to the rescue. Young Virtuosos International donated $5,000 to have the tapes analyzed. A music expert found that the tapes could indeed be restored so that future musicians could hear and enjoy for themselves the music and the voice of "The Maestro."

The president's library

❖ On November 30, 1994, ground was broken at Texas A&M University in College Station for the $85-million complex that will be

home to the George Bush School of Government of Public Service and his presidential library. When completed in 1997, it will be the 10th presidential library in the nation and the second in Texas. The library will house 36 million pages of documents that chronicle such historic world events as the reunification of Germany and the collapse of the Soviet Union.

AWARDS AND HONORS

Lone Star Nobel laureates

❖ In 1977, French-born American physicist Roger C.L. Guillemin shared the Nobel Prize in physiology or medicine for discoveries about brain hormones that he made while working at the Texas Medical Center in Houston. Guillemin was the first Nobel laureate in Texas. Dr. Alfred G. Gilman, chairman of the University of Texas Southwestern Medical Center in Dallas, was the latest Texan to receive a Nobel for his work on G proteins in 1994. As key molecules in the inner workings of cells, G proteins help translate chemical signals into action. Defects in G proteins can cause cells to malfunction and lead to diseases as varied as cancer and cholera.

A Nobel three-peat

With Dr. Alfred G. Gilman's 1994 Nobel Prize in physiology or medicine (far right), the University of Texas Southwestern Medical Center at Dallas became the only medical school in the world with three Nobel Prizes awarded in less than a decade. In 1988, Dr. Johann Deisenhofer (standing) won the prize in chemistry for determining the three-dimensional structure of a cell membrane protein. In 1985, Dr. Michael S. Brown (far left) and Dr. Joseph Goldstein (second from left) shared the Nobel in physiology or medicine for their work in cholesterol metabolism.

❖ Since 1914, the National Association for the Advancement of Colored People (NAACP) has awarded the Spingarn Medal for the highest achievement by an African American. Three native Texans have been honored with the award.

Highest achievement

1975 – Dancer and choreographer Alvin Ailey of Rogers
1983 – Los Angeles Mayor Thomas Bradley of Calvert
1991 – Congresswoman/educator Barbara Jordan of Houston

SCIENCE AND TECHNOLOGY

❖ In 1889, a young graduate from Ohio State University was hired at Texas A&M University as an associate professor of veterinary science. The first assignment given Mark Francis was to find a cure for tick fever in cattle. The disease was killing 40 to 70 percent of the cattle imported to Texas. Francis worked for 10 years until he finally developed a serum. He inoculated disease-prone cattle against the deadly disease and also developed an economical dip that killed the disease-carrying ticks on cattle. His work opened the way for the safe importation of foreign cattle and the export of Texas cattle, earning him the title of the "father of the modern Texas cattle industry."

Saving Texas bovines

❖ In 1989, the federal government billed the superconducting supercollider as the world's largest atom smasher. It was meant to reveal the mysteries of the universe by crashing together sub-subatomic particles inside a 54-mile oval tunnel. The great smasher was to be located in the countryside of Ellis County around the city of Waxahachie, under land where cotton and cattle had been raised for decades. Dozens of Texas residents lost land that had been in their families for generations as the government bought up property for the gigantic collider. Then in 1992, the budget-cutting ax fell on the great scientific experiment. The $8.3-billion project was whittled down by a vote in the U.S. House of Representatives until it died. Texans were left with a big hole in the ground, still pondering the secrets of the universe and the workings of the federal government.

The big bang's gone

❖ Of the hundreds of meteorites that fall to Earth each year, one seemed to be just beginning its journey when it landed in Texas in 1903. George Duncan, age seven, discovered the unearthly object near Toyah in Reeves County. The meteorite then traveled to Balmorhea. It was displayed in a store for several years while souvenir hunters sliced off slivers of the space rock. When the meteorite moved to Fort Worth, it was mistakenly identified as a chunk of platinum. After 10 years of touring Texas, the 1,530-pound rock journeyed to Illinois as an acquisition of the Field Museum of Chicago. The meteorite rested there until 1987. When the Field Museum was remodeled, the cosmic chunk returned to Texas. Estimated at 4.5 billion years old, the space rock seems to have finally found a permanent home at the McDonald Observatory in the Davis Mountains of Texas.

The unusual travels of a meteorite

Trying to feed the world

In October 1994, the South Plains Food Bank unveiled an operation that is capable of drying enough carrots, potatoes, onions, and other vegetables to feed 40,000 people a day. The Breedlove Dehydration Plant in Lubbock was called the world's first such operation for charity. Private donations funded the $7.8-million plant that can process spoil-prone fresh produce into food that's easy to store and transport. Food-bank officials estimated the cost of a nutritious meal from the plant at only four cents.

Plenty of power

❖ According to *The Guinness Book of Records 1995*, the largest nuclear-power unit in the nation is at Bay City, Texas. The South Texas Number 1 unit packs a capability of 1,251 megawatts. The Number 2 unit has a capability of 1,250 megawatts.

THE BOLD AND THE BEAUTIFUL

A recognizable face

❖ For supermodel Bridget Hall, 1994 shaped up into a super year. Hall appeared on the March 1994 cover of *Allure*, the May 1994 cover of *Elle*, and the May 1994 cover of *Cosmopolitan*. She also turned 17 years old. Hall started modeling at age 10 in 1987. By 1992, she had put her high-school days on hold for a job that pays about $10,000 a day.

When she isn't posing for Guess ads or taking to the runway for Calvin Klein, Hall lives with her mom in Farmer's Branch.

Here she comes

Three Texas women have worn the Miss America crown.
- Jo-Caroll Dennison of Tyler in 1942
- Phyllis Ann George (below) of Denton in 1971
- Shirley Cothran of Fort Worth in 1975

Fashion fun from Texas

Todd Oldham's loud and chaotic fashions are easy to spot in a crowd. There's the tiger-striped plastic raincoat; the tie-dyed, snowflake-dotted gown; and the women's suits woven from strikingly colored ribbons. Oldham grew up in the north Texas town of Keller where his mother encouraged his interest and skill in sewing. After designing duds in Dallas during the oil boom of the 1980s, he left for New York in 1988. Today his multicultural styles are sold at Neiman's and Bergdorf's. He opened his own studio in Soho in September 1994. He's also the only designer to land a regular spot on MTV. The "Todd Time" segments on MTV's *House of Style* tout the Todd look that's more magical than practical.

Still kicking after all these years

In 1940, Gussie Nell Davis organized the Kilgore Rangerettes dancing troupe at Kilgore Junior College in East Texas. The long-legged, cowgirl-clad dancers changed football half-times forever and became an institution that represented the Lone Star State at festivities across the nation. Davis, who retired in 1979, once said of her young charges, "By the time I was through with them, they were scared to death to act like little heathens." To this day, every high-kicking Rangerette must be able to touch the brim of her white cowboy hat with her white cowboy boot.

ETCETERA

❖ At Carswell Air Force Base near Fort Worth, the *Lucky Lady II* departed on February 26, 1949, for the world's first nonstop flight around the world. Captain James Gallagher piloted the Boeing B-50 Superfortress that was refueled in midair by tanker planes. The flight took 94 hours and one minute.

First time around

The sacred gift of the longhorn

In 1859, construction of the Christ Church was underway on Texas Avenue in Houston. A cattleman driving his herd past the site stopped to ask a workman about the project. When the worker explained that a church was being built, the cowman lassoed one of the steers and presented the longhorn as his contribution to the church. That spontaneous gift is still remembered today. Since 1941, the horns of a longhorn have appeared on the official seal of the Episcopal Diocese of Texas.

❖ In 1974, the Texas Department of Agriculture initiated the Texas Family Land Heritage Program to honor the staying power and tradition of family farms and ranches. Each year the department searches for, finds, and registers land that has been in continuous agricultural production under one family for 100 years or more. The owner must live on the property and work the land or must manage the day-to-day operations. Even with these and other stringent restrictions, close to 2,500 farms and ranches have been registered in the program since its inception.

Legacies of the land

❖ The Center for the Study of the Vietnam Conflict at Texas Tech University in Lubbock probably holds more Vietnam War documents than any repository except the federal government. The center's first acquisition came in 1989 when Lubbock County resident Dan Siewert, a Navy medic who served in Vietnam in 1967, donated his letters to the collection. William E. Colby, director of the CIA in the mid-1970s, later donated his private papers. In 1994, ground was broken for a $9-million Special Collection Building to house the historic collection.

War records

❖ Between 1936 and 1939, brothers Elmo, Quentin, and Edison Schaefer constructed a 10-inch-diameter telescope because their father wanted to see the mountains on the moon. Edison and a neighbor ground the telescope's mirror on top of a 55-gallon barrel. The Schaefer Observatory went unused for decades until the Schaefer family donated it to the Schulenburg Independent School District in 1992. Money from the family and funds raised by civic groups renovated the old observatory. It consists of a galvanized-metal revolving dome, 12 feet in diameter and mounted on wooden supports 13 feet tall. It now houses a 14-inch telescope for use by student stargazers.

Studying the stars

TEXAS ONE DAY AT A TIME

If there is an asterisk (*) after an item, check the index for more information on the subject.

JANUARY

1   Author Larry L. King born in Putnam 1929*
    The Houston Oilers defeated the Los Angeles Chargers 24-16 in the American Football League's first championship game 1961*
    Jesse Holman Jones, civic leader, philanthropist, and political figure, died in Houston 1956

2   Cowboy singing and acting star Tex Ritter died in Nashville 1974*
    Country singer Roger Miller born in Fort Worth 1936

3   Rock musician Stephen Stills born in Dallas 1945
    Houston Oilers blew a 35-3 lead in the American Football Conference Wild Card game and lost to the Buffalo Bills 1993*
    Actor Dabney Coleman born in Austin 1932

5   Dancer-choreographer Alvin Ailey born in Rogers 1931*
    Rogers Hornsby, one of the best second basemen in baseball history, died 1963*

7   Humble Oil Field discovered 1905

8   The first State Supreme Court composed entirely of women was appointed 1925*
    Cleburne and Houston Heights high schools played to a scoreless tie in the first state championship 1921*
    Republican Edmund J. Davis took office as governor 1870

9   Anson Jones, the last president of the Republic of Texas, checked into the Capital Hotel in Houston, put a gun to his head, and killed himself 1858*

10 Spindletop, the great oil gusher near Beaumont, erupted 1901*

11 Gail Borden, Jr., inventor of condensed milk, died in Borden 1874*
    Golfer Ben Crenshaw born in Austin 1952

12 Cowboy singer and film actor Tex Ritter born in Murvaul 1907*
    James Farmer, civil rights leader, born in Marshall 1920
    Country singer Ray Price born in Perryville 1926
    Award-winning crime novelist Patricia Highsmith born in Fort Worth 1921

13 Jose Antonio Navarro, early Texas political figure and signer of the Texas Declaration of Independence, died of natural causes 1871
    Chemist Louis Weisberg, who helped develop the atomic bomb, born in Waco 1891

16 Dancer, singer, actress, and director Debbie Allen born in Houston 1950
    Anthony Joseph "A.J." Foyt, four-time Indianapolis 500 winner, born in Houston 1935*

18 The Securities and Exchange Commission filed a lawsuit alleging stock fraud against Houston developer Frank Sharp, and the Sharpstown scandal that ended the careers of dozens of state officials began 1971

19 Blues singer and rock artist Janis Joplin born in Port Arthur 1943

20 Miriam Amanda Ferguson took oath of office as Texas' first woman governor 1925*
    Lyndon Baines Johnson, the 36th president of the United States, retired after 36 years in national politics 1969*
    Anson Jones, the last president of the Republic of Texas, born in Barrington, Massachusetts 1798*

21 The first public library in Texas opened by the Galveston Chamber of Commerce 1871*
    Singer, songwriter Mac Davis born in Lubbock 1942
    Thomas Volney Munson, who helped save the French wine industry, died in Denison 1913*
    Ashbel Smith, the "father of Texas medicine," died 1886
    Actor Robby Benson born in Dallas 1956

22 George Foreman of Marshall defeated Smokin' Joe Frazier to become Heavyweight Champion of the World 1973*
    Lyndon Baines Johnson, 36th president of the United States, died 1973*

23 Molly Wright (married name Molly Armstrong), the first woman optometrist in Texas, born in Bell County 1875

25 Hall of Fame football wide receiver Don Maynard born in Crosbyton 1937
    Ground was broken for Texas Stadium in Irving 1969*
    The Third Congress of the Republic of Texas adopted the Lone Star flag 1839*

26 Audie Murphy became the most decorated American soldier in World War II for his actions on this day in 1945 near Kayserberg, France*
    In 1905, James Stephen Hogg, the first native-born governor of Texas, suffered injuries in a train wreck that led to his death*
    Children's author Margaret Cousins born Mundy 1905

27 Edward Higgins White II, America's first man to walk in space, was killed with crewmates Virgil Grissom and Roger Chaffee when a fire broke out in their *Apollo* spacecraft during a preflight ground test 1967*
    Sculptor Elisabet Ney, who moved to Texas in 1892, born in Germany 1833*

28   George Foreman, the oldest man ever to become a heavyweight boxing champion, born in Marshall 1948*

The Dallas Cowboys National League Football franchise was awarded to Clint Murchison, Jr., and Bedford Wynne 1960*

Astronaut John M. Fabian born in Goose Creek 1939*

29   The National All-Stars defeated the Texas All-Stars 3-2 in the first polo match played in the Astrodome 1966*

30   The first-ever two-way moving sidewalk started operation at Dallas' Love Field Air Terminal 1958*

Baylor and Rice Universities met on the court and played the first basketball game in the new Southwest Conference 1915

Samuel Taliaferro Rayburn, U.S. representative, born in Roane County, Tennessee 1882

31   The mockingbird was named the state bird 1927

Ernie Banks, the great baseball shortstop who won consecutive MVP honors in 1958 and 1959, born in Dallas 1931*

FEBRUARY

1   Joe Thomas Meador, who stole the Quedlinburg treasures during World War II, died 1980*

The Menger Hotel in San Antonio opened for business 1959

Baylor University was founded 1845*

2   The Treaty of Guadalupe Hidalgo, which ended the Mexican War and established the Rio Grande as the boundary between the United States and Mexico, signed 1848

Gossip columnist Liz Smith born in Fort Worth 1923*

Actress Farrah Fawcett born in Corpus Christi 1947

Professional football star Dexter Manley born in Houston 1959

Children's author Mary Blount Christian born in Houston 1933

3   Rock and roll star Buddy Holly and J.P. Richardson, The Big Bopper who was known for the song "Chantilly Lace," died in an airplane crash 1959*

Actress Morgan Fairchild born in Dallas 1950

Willie Shoemaker, horse racing's greatest jockey, retired 1990*

4   Billy Olson of Abilene became the first person to clear 19 feet in the pole vault 1983*

5   The Houston Symphony premiered composer-arranger David Guion's *Texas Suite* 1952*

Belle Starr, the Bandit Queen of Texas, born in Carthage, Missouri 1848

6   Actor Rip Torn born in Temple 1931

7   Fred Gipson, author of *Old Yeller*, born in Mason 1908*

8   Film director King Vidor born in Galveston 1894

The American Football League Dallas Texans announced the team was moving to Kansas City 1963

The coldest temperature ever recorded in Texas, –23°F, occurred in Seminole 1933*

9   Grand Ol' Opry star Ernest Tubb born in Ellis County 1914*

Mike Singletary, the legendary football linebacker, born in Houston 1958

10   Buffalo Bayou, the first railway in Texas, received its charter 1850

11   Lloyd Bentsen, long-time Texas Senator and Secretary of the Treasury under President Bill Clinton, born in Mission 1921

The crew of the *San Antonio* staged the first and only mutiny in the history of the Republic of Texas 1842

12   The coldest temperature ever recorded in Texas, –23°F, occurred in Tulia 1899*

13   The Texas Legislature named Joanna Troutman the creator of the first Lone Star flag 1913*

Stormie Jones, age six, was the first recipient of a heart-and-liver transplant 1984*

15   Cattle raisers formed the Stock-Raisers Association of North-West Texas 1877*

The last Constitution of the state of Texas was adopted 1876

17   H.L. Hunt, Texas oilman, born 1889

18   Frenchman Louis Paulhan performed the first public demonstration of an airplane flight in Texas 1910*

19   Anson Jones resigned as President of the Republic of Texas and J. Pickney Henderson took office as the state's first governor 1846

Anti-nuclear activist Karen Silkwood born in Longview 1946

20   Actress Sandy Duncan born in Henderson 1946

Chester W. Nimitz, who led the Allied forces to victory in the Pacific during World War II, died 1966*

21   Comanche Chief Quanah Parker died at age 64 1911*

Congresswoman and educator Barbara Jordan born in Houston 1936*

23   Musician Johnny Winter born in Beaumont 1944

Senator and presidential candidate Phil Gramm raised $4.1 million at a single fundraiser—the most of any political candidate ever 1995

24   Actor Zachary Scott born in Austin 1914

Chester W. Nimitz, who led the Allied forces to victory in the Pacific during World War II, born in Fredericksburg 1885*

25   Antonio López de Santa Anna born at Jalapa, Vera Cruz, 1794*

26 The first nonstop flight around the world departed from Carswell Air Force Base near Fort Worth 1949*

Warren "Rip" Collins, college football star and professional baseball player, born in Weatherford 1896*

27 Governor John Connally born in Floresville 1917*

Hall of Fame football end Raymond Berry born in Corpus Christi 1933

Jose Antonio Navarro, early Texas political figure and signer of the Texas Declaration of Independence, born in San Antonio 1795

28 Branch Davidian followers shot down four federal agents and wounded 16 in a gun battle at the cult compound in Waco 1993*

Tony award winner and Broadway star Tommy Tune born in Wichita Falls 1939*

Texas ratified the Prohibition Amendment 1918

Professional football star Charles Aaron "Bubba" Smith born in Orange 1945

MARCH

2 Texas Declaration of Independence signed at Washington-on-the-Brazos 1836*

In a biplane known as *Old No. 1*, Lt. Benjamin D. Foulois flew through the air for a little more than seven minutes at Fort Sam Houston in San Antonio. The event marked the beginning of the U.S. Air Force 1910

The legendary Sam Houston, a president of the Republic of Texas, born in Rockbridge County, Virginia 1793*

3 James Stephen Hogg, the first native-born governor of Texas, died from complications of an injury he received in a train wreck 1906*

4 Actress Paula Prentiss born in San Antonio 1939

6 The Alamo fell, leaving 187 Texans dead and 600 Mexican soldiers dead or wounded 1836*

7 The bluebonnet was designated the state flower 1901

8 Governor Preston Smith born in Corn Hill 1912

Historian and author Walter Prescott Webb died in an automobile accident 1963*

Actress Cyd Charisse born in Amarillo 1923

9 President George Bush designated the Flower Garden Banks as the 10th marine sanctuary in the U.S. 1992*

10 Professional golfer Sandra Jean Palmer born in Fort Worth 1941*

11 King Fisher and Ben Thompson killed in San Antonio 1884

Newsman Sam Donaldson born in El Paso 1934*

12 Three-time Indy 500 winner Johnny Rutherford born in Fort Worth 1938

14 Charles Lindbergh started pilot training at San Antonio's Brooks Field in 1845

14 Jack Ruby was sentenced to death in the electric chair on the charge "murder with malice" for killing John F. Kennedy's alleged assassin Lee Harvey Oswald 1964*

Screenwriter Horton Foote born in Wharton 1916*

15 Lightnin' Hopkins, blues musician, born in Centerville 1912

Astronaut Alan L. Bean, who made the second moon landing, born in Wheeler 1932*

16 Governor Jim Hogg gave John Wesley Hardin, the state's most infamous killer, a full pardon 1894*

17 Sammy Baugh, college and professional football star, born in Temple 1914*

18 Explosion of New London school left 293 students and faculty dead in 1937*

Jockey Willie Shoemaker made his first horse-racing ride 1949*

19 Minnie Fisher Cunningham, founder and first executive secretary of the League of Women Voters, born in New Waverly 1882

20 Governor Coke Stephenson born in Mason County 1888

Polykarp Kusch, the Nobel Prize winner in physics in 1955, died at age 82 in Dallas 1993

22 James Abercrombie invented the oil-well drilling blowout preventer 1922

23 Umphrey Lee, first chancellor of Southern Methodist University, born in Indiana 1893

Maynard Jackson, Jr., first African-American mayor of Atlanta, born in Dallas 1938

24 Actress Joan Crawford born in San Antonio 1908*

James Stephen Hogg, the first native-born governor of Texas, born near Rusk in Cherokee County 1851*

Cowboys on Panhandle ranches went on strike to get wages increased from a dollar a day 1883

26 Sandra Day O'Connor, first woman to sit on the U.S. Supreme Court, born in El Paso 1930*

27 The Goliad massacre occurred on Palm Sunday 1836*

28 Dwight D. Eisenhower died in Washington 1969*

Border bandit Antonio Zapata captured 1840

29 Earl Campbell, the great Houston Oiler running back, born in Tyler 1955*

Governor James Allred born in Bowie 1899

30 John Warnock Hinckley, Jr., of Highland Park attempted to assassinate President Ronald Reagan in Washington, D.C., 1981*

Dallas County created from parts of Robertson and Nacogdoches counties 1846

31 Jack Johnson, boxing's first African-American heavyweight champion, born in Galveston 1878*

Singer and songwriter Lefty Frizzell born in Corsicana 1928

Grammy-winning Mexican-American singer Selena Quintanilla Perez shot and killed 1995

31 Political activist Norman Mayer, who held Washington Monument hostage as a protest against nuclear weapons in December 1981, born in El Paso 1916

APRIL

1 Ragtime pianist and composer Scott Joplin died 1917*
Actress Debbie Reynolds born in El Paso 1932
Astronaut William F. Fisher born in Dallas 1946*
2 Bulldogger and cowboy entertainer Bill Pickett died 1932*
Clara Driscoll, philanthropist, author, and historic preservationist, born in St. Mary's on Copano Bay 1881*
Ralph Yarborough won a U.S. Senate seat in a special election and served for 13 years beginning 1957
3 Historian and author Walter Prescott Webb born in Panola County 1888*
Governor John Connally signed the act that made official the salute to the Texas flag 1965
Max Hirsch, famed thoroughbred horse trainer, died 1969*
4 Tris Speaker, Baseball Hall of Famer, born in Hubbard 1888*
Dr. Denton Arthur Cooley implanted the world's first entirely artificial heart into a human at Houston's Texas Heart Institute 1969*
5 Actress Gale Storm born in Bloomington 1922
Jesse Holman Jones, civic leader, philanthropist, political figure and builder of 30 Texas skyscrapers born in Robertson County, Tennessee 1874
7 The legendary Sarah Bernhardt gave her final American performance in *Camille* at Galveston's Grand Opera House 1911*
Sam Rayburn was sworn in as a member of the U.S. House of Representatives and served for 48 years 1913
9 Astrodome opened in Houston 1965*
Author Frances Sanger Mossiker born in Dallas 1906
Actor Dennis Quaid born in Houston 1954*
Astronaut Kenneth D. Cockrell born in Austin 1950*
10 Dallas Cowboys quarterback and sports announcer Don Meredith born in Mt. Vernon 1938
Major league baseball arrived in Texas with the Houston Colt 45's defeating the Chicago Cubs 11-2 1962
The worst single tornado in Texas history hit Wichita Falls killing 42, injuring 1,740, and destroying more than 3,000 homes 1979
Lyndon Baines Johnson was elected to the U.S. House of Representatives 1937*
11 The Ballpark in Arlington opened with a game between the Texas Rangers and the Milwaukee Brewers. The Brewers won 4-3, 1994*

12 Lucille Ann Collier, better known as actress and Broadway star Ann Miller, born in Chireno 1923*
Children's author and illustrator Hardie Gramatky (wrote classic *Little Toot*) born in Dallas 1907
14 Woody Guthrie wrote the classic song, "So Long, It's Been Good to Know You" in Pampa 1935*
Van Cliburn won the International Tchaikovsky Competition 1958*
16 The ship *Grandcamp* exploded in Texas City 1947*
Tejano music artist Selena Quintanilla Perez born in Lake Jackson 1971*
Hall of Fame football defensive back Dick "Night Train" Lane born in Austin 1928
17 The League of United Latin American Citizens (LULAC) founded in Corpus Christi 1929
19 The Branch Davidian cult compound in Waco went up in flames ending a 51-day siege 1993*
20 Jockey Willie Shoemaker, age 17, rode to his first win in horse racing 1949*
21 Texans won independence at the Battle of San Jacinto 1836*
Officials dedicated the San Jacinto Monument 1939*
22 Television producer Aaron Spelling born in Dallas 1925*
Randy Matson of Texas A&M was the first to toss a shot-put more than 71 feet 1967*
The city of Dallas honored long-time Dallas Cowboys coach Tom Landry with a parade through downtown after he was fired by the team's new owner Jerry Jones 1989
The first graduating class from the University of Texas Medical Branch in Galveston received diplomas 1892
23 The last remaining boundary marker between the Republic of Texas and the United States was set 1841*
24 Author William Goyen born in Trinity 1915
Musician Roy Orbison, who wrote the song "Oh, Pretty Woman," born in Wink 1935
26 Actress and comedienne Carol Burnett born in San Antonio 1936*
27 Rogers Hornsby, the "Magnificent Rajah" of baseball fame, born in Winters 1896*
28 Secretary of State James A. Baker III born in Houston 1930
Astronaut John O. Creighton born in Orange 1943*
29 Author Elmer Kelton born in Andrews County 1926
30 Texas country music legend Willie Hughes Nelson born in Abbott 1933*

MAY

1 Author Terry Southern born in Alvarado 1924
Texas Ranger pitcher Nolan Ryan threw his seventh career no-hitter, the most in baseball history, against the Toronto Blue Jays 1991*

1 Hall of Fame football halfback Ollie Matson born in Trinity 1930
Mark David Chapman, the man who murdered musician John Lennon, born in Fort Worth 1955
2 Country musician Larry Gatlin born in Seminole 1948
Henry Allen Bullock, the first African-American professor appointed to the University of Texas Arts and Sciences faculty, born in North Carolina 1906*
Dr. Denton Cooley performed the first successful U.S. heart transplant at the Texas Heart Institute in Houston 1968*
3 Singer, songwriter, and Grammy winner Christopher Cross born in San Antonio 1951
5 Country and western singer Michael Martin Murphy born in Austin 1938
McDonald Observatory inaugurated its original telescope, the 82-inch Otto Struve Memorial, in 1939*
7 Dwight David Eisenhower accepted the German surrender at Rheims 1945*
8 Randy Matson of Texas A&M was the first to toss a shot-put more than 70 feet 1965*
11 Actor Randy Quaid born in Houston 1950
A tornado touched down in Waco killing 114 and destroying 2,000 homes and offices 1953
12 The University of Texas Glee Club performed "The Eyes of Texas" for the first time 1903*
13 Bob Wills, fiddle player and creator of Western Swing music, died 1975*
The last battle of the Civil War took place at Palmito Ranch 1865*
14 Santa Anna signed two treaties at Velasco that ended the Texas Revolution 1836
15 Katherine Anne Porter, author and Pulitzer Prize winner, born in Indian Creek 1890*
Entertainer Trini Lopez born in Dallas 1937
Actor Lee Horsley born in Muleshoe 1955
Theodore Roosevelt arrived in San Antonio and assembled his Rough Riders 1898*
16 Jane, a slave, was the first woman legally hanged in Texas 1853*
Oveta Culp Hobby appointed the first director of the Women's Auxiliary Army Corps 1916*
19 Cynthia Ann Parker was captured by Comanche Indians during a raid on Fort Parker 1836*
20 The Western Hills Hotel in Fort Worth became the first hotel to establish a heliport 1953*
22 President Eisenhower signed the National Tidelands Bill 1953*
A multiple-vortex tornado struck Saragosa in Reeves County killing 30, injuring 121, and damaging 85 percent of the town's structures 1987
23 Frank Hamer and five other lawmen killed notorious outlaws Bonnie and Clyde 1934*
24 The first oil and gas magazine ever published was *Oil Investors' Journal* issued in 1902*

25 Bill Sharman, the only basketball coach ever to win championships in three different leagues, born in Abilene 1926*
Golf-ball-sized hail pelted Monahans and caused $8 million in damages 1982
Katie Currie Muse organized the first Texas chapter of the United Daughters of the Confederacy 1896
27 Country and western singer Don Williams born in Floydada 1939
Michael Francis "Pinky" Higgins born in 1909 in Red Oak. Higgins holds the world record for most consecutive baseball hits. He slammed 12 hits for the American League Boston Red Sox during a four-game span between June 19 and 21, 1938
28 Bullwinkle, Shell Offshore's 1,365-foot drill and production platform jacket, and the world's tallest offshore platform, was launched from Ingleside 1988
The Santa Rita No. 1 oil well gushed in and brought wealth to the University of Texas 1923*
Musician and songwriter T-Bone Walker born in Linden 1910
30 Author Leon Hale born in Stephenville 1921

JUNE

1 Texas A&M University initiated the Limited Coeducational Policy, which allowed the daughters and wives of students, employees, staff, and faculty to attend the all-male institution 1963*
Real estate developer Jesse Holman Jones died in Houston 1956
Actor Powers Boothe, who won an Emmy for portrayal of Rev. Jim Jones in TV movie *Guyana Tragedy: The Story of Jim Jones*, born in Snyder 1949
3 Pulitzer Prize-winning author Larry McMurtry born in Wichita Falls 1936*
Margo Jones' Theatre-in-the-Round opened in the Gulf Oil Building of the Texas State Fair 1947*
Edward Higgins White II of San Antonio became the first American to walk in space 1965*
4 Lone Star Gas Company filed a charter to become the first natural gas distributor in Texas 1909*
Country musician Freddy Fender born in San Benito 1942
Professional golfer Sandra Haynie born in Fort Worth 1943
Author Robert Fulghum born Waco 1937*
5 David Browning, Olympic diving champion from the University of Texas, born in Boston 1931*
6 Major Ripley Arnold established a fort on the Clear Fork of the Trinity River and named it Fort Worth 1849*
8 Pop singer Boz Scaggs born in Dallas 1944

8 A fire and explosion broke open the Norwegian supertanker *Mega Borg* in the Gulf of Mexico 1990*

9 The first commercial oil well in Texas came in at Corsicana 1894*

10 Jack Johnson, boxing's first African-American heavyweight champion, died 1946*

11 Author Robert E. Howard died 1936*

Lucy Holcombe Pickens, whose picture was imprinted on Confederate money, born in Marshall 1832

Henry Gabriel Cisneros, who became the first Hispanic mayor of a major U.S. city when he was elected in San Antonio in 1981, born in San Antonio 1947

12 Brian and Denise Welker of Sugar Land became the couple who rolled the highest bowling score ever 1994*

Henry Cohn, who helped immigrant Jewish families find homes in Texas, died 1952*

13 Miriam Amanda Wallace, better known as Texas Governor Ma Ferguson, born in Bell County 1875*

15 Musician Waylon Jennings born in Littlefield 1937

16 Race riots erupted in Beaumont 1943

Author/photographer John Howard Griffin, who wrote *Black Like Me*, born in Dallas 1920

17 The Bess Johnson-Adams & Hale Number 1 oil well roared in and produced the "world's richest acre" 1937

19 In Galveston, Major General Gordon Granger read the proclamation that freed an estimated 200,000 Texas slaves 1865*

Actress Phylicia Rashad born in Houston 1948

22 Singer and actor Kris Kristofferson born in Brownsville 1936*

Antonio López de Santa Anna died 1876

Basketball player Clyde "The Glide" Drexler born in Houston 1954

23 Grand Saline native Wiley Post took off in his airplane the *Winnie Mae* on a trip around the world 1931*

25 Businesswoman and former Miss America Phyllis George born in Denton 1949*

26 Babe Didrikson Zaharias, the greatest woman athlete in sports history, born in Port Arthur 1911*

27 Businessman and presidential candidate H. Ross Perot born in Texarkana 1930*

29 Actor Gary Busey born in Goose Creek 1944

Sculptor Elisabet Ney, who moved to Texas in 1892, died in Austin 1907*

30 The Flagship Hotel in Galveston, the first major hotel to be built over a pier, opened 1965*

JULY

2 Model Jerry Hall, who married Rolling Stone star Mick Jagger, born in Mesquite 1956

2 Children's author-editor Oren Arnold born in Minden 1900

3 Country blues singer Blind Lemon Jefferson born on a farm near Wortham 1897*

Actress and singer Betty Buckley born in Big Spring 1947*

Babe Didrikson Zaharias won the U.S. Women's Open by 12 strokes 1954*

4 The first Pecos Rodeo, billed as the first rodeo in the world, was held in 1883

5 John Henry Kirby chartered the Kirby Lumber Company 1901

6 Kearie Lee Berry, the Southwest Conference Heavyweight Wrestling Champion in 1915 and 1916, born in Denton 1893

7 Actress Shelley Duvall born in Houston 1949

Alphonso Steele, the last survivor of the Battle of San Jacinto, died 1911

8 The town of Post, founded by cereal king C.W. Post, became the seat of Garza County 1907*

10 Ima Hogg, civic leader and daughter of Governor James Stephen Hogg, born in Mineola 1882*

Richard King, founder of the King Ranch, born in New York 1824*

11 Author and illustrator Tom Lea born in El Paso 1907*

Beauford Jester became the first Texas governor to die in office 1949

13 Country and western singer Louise Mandrell born in Corpus Christi 1954

Professional basketball player Anthony Jerome "Spud" Webb born in Dallas 1963

14 Broadway star Jules Bledsoe died in Hollywood 1943*

16 Cherokee Chief Bowles killed in the last battle between Cherokee Indians and Anglos in Texas 1839*

17 Clara Driscoll, philanthropist, author, and historic preservationist, died in Corpus Christi 1945*

19 Billy Richard Olson, record-setting pole vaulter, born in Abilene 1958*

21 Notorious robber Sam Bass died at age 27 1878*

20 The first word ever spoken from the moon was "Houston" in 1969*

22 Don Henley, co-founder of the Eagles and later solo musician, born in Gilmer 1947

23 A special session of the Texas Legislature ratified the 19th amendment to the U.S. Constitution giving women the right to vote 1919*

The Texas Bankers' Association organized in Lampasas 1885*

Actor Woody Harrelson born in Midland 1961*

Writer Donald Barthelme, author of novella *Snow White*, died of cancer in Houston 1989

24 Stage actor, director, and producer Margo Jones died 1955*

25   Babe Didrikson Zaharias tossed a baseball 296 feet at Jersey City, New Jersey, to set a women's world record for the longest baseball throw 1931*

26   The legendary Sam Houston, a president of the Republic of Texas, died in Huntsville of pneumonia 1863*

Garland Roark, author of adventure stories, born in Groesbeck 1904

28   William E. Morris of Nueces County received the first cotton acreage reduction payment from the federal government for plowing under 47 acres of cotton 1933

29   Thomas Jefferson Rusk, aged 53, a leader of the Republic of Texas, committed suicide 1857

Oscar Fox, Hill Country native and prolific writer of cowboy songs, died 1961

30   The last public hanging in the Lone Star State took place in Waco 1923*

A fire and explosion killed 19 and injured 32 at the Shamrock Oil and Gas tank farm near Dumas 1956

31   Jim Reeves, Grand Ol' Opry star who grew up in Carthage, died in a plane crash 1964

AUGUST

1   Milton M. Holland, the first native Texan to be awarded the Medal of Honor, born 1844*

Charles Whitman killed and wounded dozens of people as he shot from the tower at the University of Texas in Austin 1966*

Jackie Joyner set a new world record in the heptathlon with 7,158 points in Houston 1986

2   Delta Air Lines Flight 191 crashed at Dallas/Fort Worth International Airport killing 132 passengers 1985*

The famous Chicken Ranch whorehouse near La Grange closed by Sheriff Jim Flournoy 1973

3   Hurricane Celia hit Corpus Christi with winds up to 180 miles per hour in 1970. Miraculously, only 11 people died 1970

Hall of Fame football wide receiver Lance Alworth born in Houston 1940

An 11-day siege at the Huntsville prison ended with the deaths of several hostages and prisoners 1974

6   Author John Graves born in Fort Worth 1920

Concert hall and honky-tonk Armadillo World Headquarters opened in Austin 1970*

7   Johnson Blair Cherry, winning football coach of the Amarillo Sandies and University of Texas Longhorns, born in Kerens 1907

Congressman Mickey Leland died in a plane crash over Gambela, Ethiopia 1989

9   William B. Travis, commander at the Alamo, born in South Carolina 1809

11   Actress Sharon Tate, born in Dallas in 1943, and four others were found murdered in Los Angeles. Charles Manson and several members of his cult were arrested 1968

12   Country and western singer Buck Owens born in Sherman 1929

Temple Houston, the son of Sam Houston, became the first child born in the Governor's Mansion 1860

The hottest temperature ever recorded in Texas, 120°F, occurred in Seymour 1936*

13   Golfer Ben Hogan born in Dublin, Texas 1912*

14   Actor and comedian Steve Martin born in Waco 1945

The Gulf Freeway between Galveston and Houston was dedicated 1952

15   The biggest crowd in National Football League history watched the Dallas Cowboys and the Houston Oilers compete at Azteca Stadium in Mexico City 1994*

Houston Mayor Kathy Whitmire born in Houston 1946*

Gene Upshaw, who was inducted into Football's Hall of Fame in 1987, born in Robstown 1945

Journalist Linda Ellerbee born in Bryan 1944

15-21   Hurricane Alicia, one of the costliest in the state's history, struck the Texas coast and spawned 22 tornadoes 1983

16   Lothar Witzke, the first German spy to receive a death sentence from American forces during World War I, arrived at Fort Sam Houston, was court-martialed, and sentenced to hang 1918*

Actor Fess Parker, star of television's "Davy Crockett," born in Fort Worth 1927

Mirabeau B. Lamar, third president of the Republic of Texas, born in Jefferson County, Georgia 1798*

18   Actor Patrick Swayze, star of the films *Ghost* and *Dirty Dancing*, born in Houston 1954*

Rafer Lewis Johnson, Olympic gold medalist, born in Hillsboro 1935*

19   Outlaw John Wesley Hardin killed in El Paso 1895*

William Lee Shoemaker, horse racing's greatest jockey, born in Fabens 1931*

Tom Connally, an influential U.S. congressman who served for 36 years, born near Hewitt 1877

Ima Hogg, civic leader and daughter of Governor James Stephen Hogg, died at 93 while on vacation in London 1975

20   Country and western singer Jim Reeves born in Panola County 1924*

Jack Teagarden, jazz trombonist who played with the Dorsey brothers and later formed his own band, born in Vernon 1905

21   Actor and singer Kenny Rogers born in Houston 1938

22   Dr. Denton Cooley born in Houston 1920*

22   Lamar Hunt, a Dallas businessman, formed and announced the new American Football League 1959*

23   The Camp Logan riots resulted in the death penalty for 13 African-American soldiers and life imprisonment for 41 in 1917

24   Tom C. Clark became an Associate Justice of the U.S. Supreme Court 1949*

The University of Texas announced that Herman Barnett of Lockhart would be the first African-American admitted to the UT Medical Branch in Galveston 1949

Composer and musician Mason Williams born in Abilene 1938

25   Governor James E. Ferguson impeached and removed from office 1917*

26   Brothers John and Augustus Allen of New York bought land along Buffalo Bayou and named the town Houston, after their hero at the Battle of San Jacinto 1836

Astronaut John E. Blaha born in San Antonio 1942*

27   Lyndon Baines Johnson, 36th president of the United States, born in Gillespie County 1908*

28   Lyndon Baines Johnson beat Coke Stevenson in a runoff for the U.S. Senate 1948*

29   Bob Beamon, the University of Texas at El Paso student who won an Olympic gold medal for the long jump in 1968, born in New York 1946*

Sam Colt received a patent on a new revolver, "The Walker," named after Texas Ranger Sam Walker 1839*

31   Governor James E. Ferguson born in Salado 1871

Baseball Hall of Fame outfielder Frank Robinson born in Beaumont 1935*

SEPTEMBER

1   Country and western singer Boxcar Willie born in Steratt 1931

2   Admiral Chester W. Nimitz signed the agreement of Japanese surrender on board the battleship *Missouri* in Tokyo Bay 1945*

Professional football running back Eric Dickerson born in Sealy 1960

Allen Stuart Drury, journalist/author of *Advise and Consent*, born in Houston 1918

3   Georgetown resident J.C. Johnson, 86, disturbed a hive of African "killer" bees while mowing his lawn and was stung 1,000 times before being rescued 1994*

Actress Valerie Perrine born in Galveston 1943

4   Actress Judith Ivey born in El Paso 1951

5   On the opening weekend of the 1992-1993 college football season, all Southwest Conference teams except Texas A&M went down in defeat signaling the end of the SWC 1992*

6   Claire Lee Chennault, who organized "The Flying Tigers" during World War I, born in Commerce 1890*

7   A fire in Houston's Gulf Hotel killed 55 people 1943

8   A hurricane slammed into Galveston Island, took 6,000 to 8,000 lives, and became known as the worst natural disaster in U.S. history*

Presidents Richard Nixon and Gustavo Díaz Ordaz dedicated the 6-mile-long Amistad Dam bordering the United States and Mexico 1969*

Naturalist Euell Gibbons born in Clarksville 1911

Actor Henry Thomas born in San Antonio 1982*

9   Thrall recorded 38.2 inches of rain, a state record 1921*

Author/photographer John Howard Griffin (*Black Like Me*) died in 1980 Fort Worth

10   Hurricane Carla struck the upper Texas coast 1961

11   The University of Tulsa defeated the University of Houston 14-0 in the first football game played in the Astrodome 1965*

Astronaut Robert L. Crippen born in Beaumont 1937*

12   Texas Instruments of Dallas successfully tested the first integrated circuit 1958*

Country and western singer George Jones born in Saratoga 1931*

Singer and songwriter Barry White born in Galveston 1944

13   Carlysle Graham Raht, who helped develop the atomic bomb, born in Cooke County 1880

15   Two locomotives made history with a staged, head-on collision 1896*

Texas State Networks gave its first radio broadcast 1938*

Actor Tommy Lee Jones born in San Saba 1946*

16   A hurricane slammed into the city of Indianola and demolished most of the town in 1875. When another hurricane struck the following August, the city ceased to exist forever 1876

17   Andrew "Rube" Foster, the "father of black Baseball," born in Calvert 1879*

18   Author J. Frank Dobie died 1964*

The Beatles played a concert at Dallas Memorial Auditorium 1964*

Leon Jaworski, special prosecutor during Watergate, born in Waco 1905*

18-23   Hurricane Beulah blew into Brownsville and spawned 115 tornadoes, the most ever produced by a single hurricane 1967*

20   Actress Crystal Bernard of television's "Wings" born in Garland 1964

Billie Jean King beat Bobby Riggs in a tennis "Battle of the Sexes" in Houston 1973

21   Actor Larry Hagman born in Fort Worth 1931*

23   John A. Lomax, the non-musician who preserved Texas folk music, born in Mississippi 1867*

24 *The Daily Texan* at the University of Texas became the first daily college newspaper in the South 1913

Joe Greene, who was inducted into Football's Hall of Fame in 1987, born in Temple 1946

25 Sandra Day O'Connor became the first female Associate Justice in the history of the U.S. Supreme Court 1981*

Oliver Loving, who blazed cattle trails with Charles Goodnight, died in New Mexico 1867

26 J. Frank Dobie, the "father of Texas literature," born in Live Oak County 1888*

27 Musician and actor Meat Loaf born in Dallas 1947

Hall of Fame golfer Kathrynne Ann Whitworth born in Monahans 1939*

Babe Didrikson Zaharias, America's greatest female athlete, died in Galveston 1956*

29 Singing cowboy Gene Autry born in Tioga 1907*

OCTOBER

1 The Texas State Penitentiary at Huntsville received its first prisoner 1849*

The Dallas Morning News published its first edition 1885*

2 Actor George Emmett (Spanky) McFarland of *Our Gang* comedy films born in Fort Worth 1928

Critic Rex Reed born in Fort Worth 1939*

Civil rights leader Bobby G. Seale born in Dallas 1936

3 Daisy Bradford No. 3 blew in near Henderson and the East Texas Oil Field was discovered 1930*

4 Texas A&M University opened its campus in Bryan 1876

Blues singer Janis Joplin, 27, died of a heroine overdose at Hollywood's Landmark Hotel 1970*

5 Musician Steve Miller born Dallas 1943

The Dallas Stars national hockey team played its first game 1993

Joshua Logan, broadway producer and director who won the Pulitzer Prize along with Richard Rodgers and Oscar Hammerstein II for *South Pacific* in 1950, born in Texarkana 1908

6 The University of Texas defeated Notre Dame 7-6 in a season home opener in South Bend, Indiana, and finally gave the Southwest Conference national credibility 1934*

HemisFair, the first international exposition ever held in the South, closed in San Antonio 1968

7 The Western Hills Hotel in Fort Worth officially opened 1951*

Political figure Lieutenant Colonel Oliver North born in San Antonio 1943

10 Outlaw Wild Bill Longley put to death by hanging in Giddings 1878*

Country singer Tanya Tucker born in Seminole 1958

10 Dr. Alfred G. Gilman, chairman of the University of Texas Southwestern Medical Center in Dallas, won the Nobel Prize in physiology or medicine 1994*

11 President Gerald R. Ford signed legislation to create the Big Thicket National Preserve 1974*

Comanche Chief Satanta committed suicide by jumping from a second-story window while in prison 1874*

14 Apache War Chief Victorio shot to death in the Candelaria Mountains of Mexico 1880*

Dwight David Eisenhower, the 34th president of the United States, born in Denison 1890*

Jessica McClure slipped down a well in Midland and remained trapped for 58 hours before being rescued 1987*

15 President Franklin D. Roosevelt proclaimed the establishment of four national forests in Texas 1936*

Laredo native Orlando Canizales made boxing history when he won his 16th straight International Boxing Federation bantam-weight title 1994*

16 Balcones Canyonlands National Wildlife Refuge created 1992*

George Jo Hennard rammed his pickup truck into a crowded Luby's cafeteria in Killeen and shot to death 23 people 1991*

The Rice University Owls beat the University of Texas Longhorns in the first Sunday football game ever played in Southwest Conference history 1994*

Famed trick shooter Adolph Topperwein born in Boerne 1902*

18 Mesquite-based AT&T Power Systems became the first U.S. manufacturer to ever win Japan's prestigious Deming Prize for quality 1994*

Joe Routt, the first Aggie to be named a Consensus All-American, born in Chappell Hill 1914

19 Country singer Jeannie C. Riley born in Anson 1945

Democratic Party leader Robert Strauss born in Lockhart 1918

21 Soviet dancer Andrei Ustinov left the touring Moscow Ballet in Dallas and was granted political asylum 1987*

22 Eugene C. Barker, preeminent Texas historian, died 1956

24 Actor Murray Abraham born in El Paso 1940

Musician J.P. Richardson, also known as The Big Bopper, born in Sabine Pass 1930

Hall of Fame football quarterback Y.A. Tittle born in Marshall 1926

25 Comedienne Minnie Pearl born in Centerville 1912

26 Actress Jaclyn Smith born in Houston 1948

George Foreman won the Olympic gold medal in heavyweight boxing 1968*

William B. Travis, Alamo hero, married Rosanna Cato, one of his former students, in Alabama 1828

27 The first piling was driven at the foot of Fifteenth Street in Galveston to start the great seawall 1902

28 Tom Connally, an influential U.S. congressman who served for 36 years, died 1963

30 George Foreman lost his heavyweight champion boxing title to Muhammad Ali 1974*

31 Newsman Dan Rather born in Wharton 1931

Actress, singer, and cowgirl Dale Evans born in Uvalde 1912

Outlaw Black Jack Ketchum born in San Saba County 1863

NOVEMBER

1 Country singer and Grammy winner Lyle Lovett born in Klein 1956

The last cattle were sold off the famous XIT ranch 1912*

Actor Robert Foxworth born in Houston 1941

3 Stephen Fuller Austin, the "father of Texas," born in Virginia 1793*

4 Author A.C. Greene born in Abilene 1923

5 George Foreman knocked out Michael Moorer and became the oldest man ever to win boxing's heavyweight championship title 1994*

6 Doug Sahm, leader of the Sir Douglas Quintet and founder of the Texas Tornadoes, born in San Antonio 1941

7 Texas Hereford Association founded in San Antonio 1889

Texas Rangers arrested Johnny Ringo and George Glidden to end the bloody "Hoodoo War" in Mason County 1876

9 Gail Borden, inventor of condensed milk who moved to Texas in 1829, born in Norwich, New York 1801*

10 Ten Texas Rangers and 50 Native Americans died in an Archer County battle 1837

Hall of Fame football center Clyde "Bulldog" Turner born in Sweetwater 1919

Eugene C. Barker, preeminent Texas historian, born near Riverside in Walker County 1874

David Stockman, architect of President Reagan's economic policies, born in Camp Hood 1946

11 Hartley Edwards of Denison blew "Taps" in the forest of Compiègne, France, to signal the end of World War I 1918*

Stormie Jones, age 13, the West Texas girl who became the world's first heart-and-liver transplant patient, died 1990*

Author Irmengarde Eberle (Allyn Allen; Phyllis Ann Carter, pseudonyms) born in San Antonio 1898

14 Fort Phantom Hill established north of Abilene 1851

Astronaut Edward H. White II, America's first man to walk in space, born in San Antonio 1930*

15 Lorenzo de Zavala, signer of the Texas Declaration of Independence and a vice president of the Republic of Texas, died in San Antonio 1836

16 Sam Rayburn, Speaker of the Texas House for 21 years, died at age 79 in Bonham 1961

Dallas Cowboys football great Harvey Martin born in Dallas 1950

Women's tennis star Zina Garrison born in Houston 1963

17 The cornerstone for the first building at the University of Texas was laid 1882

18 Nina Vance opened The Alley Theatre in Houston 1947

20 Howard R. Hughes, Sr., applied for a patent for the Hughes Rock Bit that changed oil drilling history 1908

22 President John F. Kennedy assassinated in Dallas 1963*

Lyndon Baines Johnson became the 36th president of the United States 1963*

John Nance Garner, vice president under Franklin D. Roosevelt, born in northeastern Texas 1868*

23 James Henderson became governor and served only 28 days 1853*

The University of Texas longhorn mascot got its name—Bevo—after a prank by Texas A&M University students 1915*

24 Jack Ruby shot and killed President John F. Kennedy's alleged assassin Lee Harvey Oswald 1963*

Ragtime pianist and composer Scott Joplin born in Texarkana 1868*

Hall of Fame football defensive back Yale Lary born in Fort Worth 1930

25 The first play-by-play radio broadcast of a football game was made in College Station 1920*

The Texas Navy was created 1850

26 Cartoonist Ben Sargent born in Amarillo 1948

Legendary Indian fighter Colonel Kit Carson fought his last battle at Adobe Walls 1864

27 Two-time chairman of the Congressional Black Caucus Mickey (George Thomas) Leland born in Lubbock 1944

29 Billionaire H.L. Hunt died at age 85 in Dallas 1974

30 Texas revolutionary scout and fighter Erastus "Deaf" Smith died 1837

Ground was broken at Texas A&M University in College Station for the $85-million complex that will be home to the George Bush School of Government of Public Service and his presidential library 1994*

DECEMBER

1 Mary Martin, star of Broadway's *Peter Pan* and *South Pacific*, born in Weatherford 1913

1   Professional golfer Lee Buck Trevino born in Dallas 1939*

Bobby Morrow won his third gold medal in track and field at the Olympic Games in Melbourne, Australia, 1956*

Actor Dan Blocker, who played Hoss on TV's "Bonanza," born in Bowie 1932

Country singer Johnny Rodriquez born in Sabinal 1952

5   Thomas Jefferson Rusk, a leader of the Republic of Texas, born in South Carolina 1803

6   Blues musician Huddie "Leadbelly" Ledbetter, 64, died 1949*

All-American football star Ben Lee Boynton born in Waco 1898*

8   The state Capitol in Austin was officially transferred to the citizens of Texas in 1888*

Tris Speaker, baseball great, died 1958*

L. Theo Bellmont, athletic director at the University of Texas, made the Southwest Conference official 1914*

9   Houston attorney Leon Jaworski, the man who served as special prosecutor during the Watergate scandal, died 1982*

Andrew "Rube" Foster, the "father of black Baseball," died in Kankakee, Illinois 1903*

Anson Jones, last president of the Republic of Texas, took the oath of office 1844*

Golfer Tom Kite born in Austin 1949*

10   The first official flag of the Republic of Texas, known as the David G. Burnet flag, adopted 1836*

11   Amon Carter, Fort Worth businessman and philanthropist, born in Crafton 1879*

13   A railroad disaster in Humble resulted in 22 deaths 1922

Houston's Sam Houston High School beat Comanche in the first state football finals, but the game wasn't recognized by the University Interscholastic League 1913*

14   Randall Duell, creator of Six Flags Over Texas, died 1992

15   The tracks of the Texas Pacific and the Southern Pacific railroads were joined in Sierra Blanca to create the second transcontinental railroad 1881*

18   U.S. Attorney General Ramsey Clark born in Dallas 1927

19   Hall of Fame football quarterback Bobby Layne born in Santa Anna 1926

Mirabeau B. Lamar, the third president of the Republic of Texas, died of a heart attack 1859*

Texan Walter Williams, the last surviving soldier of the American Civil War, died at age 117 and was buried at Mount Pleasant Cemetery 1959

21   Edith Wilmans, the first woman ever elected to the Texas House of Representatives, born 1882*

Baylor University Hospital in Dallas initiated the first-ever group hospital-insurance plan 1929*

22   Claudia Alta Taylor, better known as Lady Bird Johnson, born in Karnack 1912*

Political leader and longtime Speaker of the House Jim Wright born in Fort Worth 1922*

24   Panna Maria, the nation's oldest continuous Polish settlement, established by 800 Polish immigrants 1854*

25   Actress Sissy Spacek born in Quitman 1949

Country and western singer Barbara Mandrell born in Houston 1948

27   Stephen Fuller Austin, the "father of Texas," died 1836*

28   Dallas Cowboys wide receiver Drew Pearson made the famous "Hail Mary" catch to win the game against the Minnesota Vikings 1975*

Musician Edgar Winter born in Beaumont 1946

29   Texas became 28th state in the United States 1845*

The Texas Folklore Society chartered 1909*

Former Los Angeles Mayor Thomas Bradley born in Calvert 1917*

30   Homer Norton, football coach at Texas A&M during the winning streaks of the 1940s, born in Alabama 1896

Hall of Fame football player Mel Renfro born in Houston 1941

The worst ice storm in 30 years hit northeast Texas killing four and causing $14 million in damages 1978

31   The Austin concert hall and honky-tonk Armadillo World Headquarters closed 1980*

Northern Texas Map

These maps shows the main cities of the state and most places mentioned in the book. If you cannot find a specific place on one of these maps, it may be found on one of the special supplementary maps found throughout the book. Every effort has been made to include everything; however, in some cases we were not able to list every entry because of space limitations. If the place you seek is not listed, we apologize.

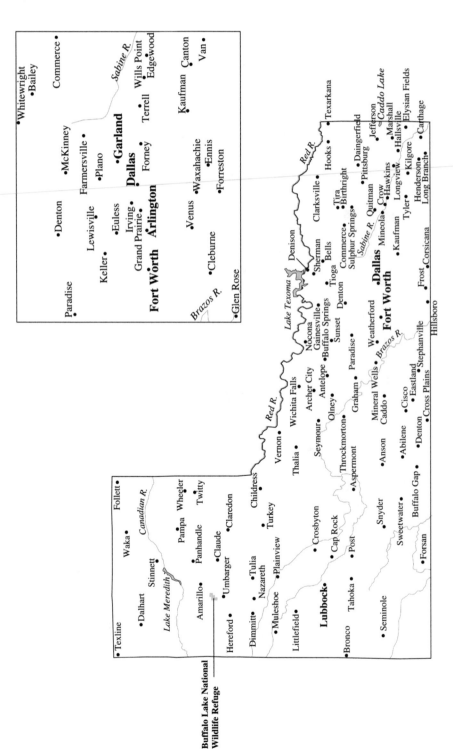

Buffalo Lake National Wildlife Refuge

Legend

- State Capitol
- City or town

Bold type indicates National Park or Land

Italic type indicates body of water or island

Sothwestern Texas Map

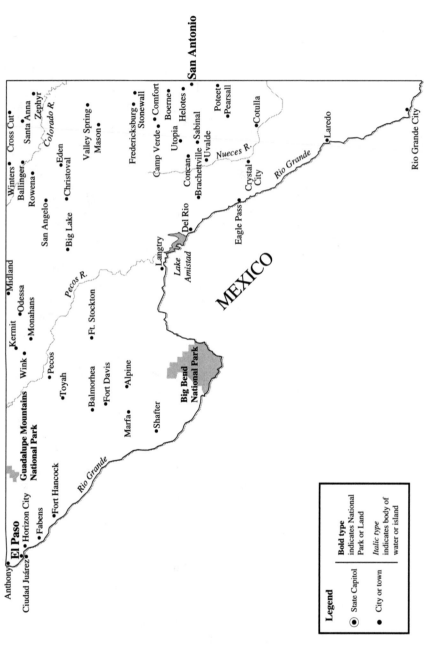

Legend

⊙ State Capitol

• City or town

Bold type
indicates National
Park or Land

Italic type
indicates body of
water or island

Southeastern Texas Map

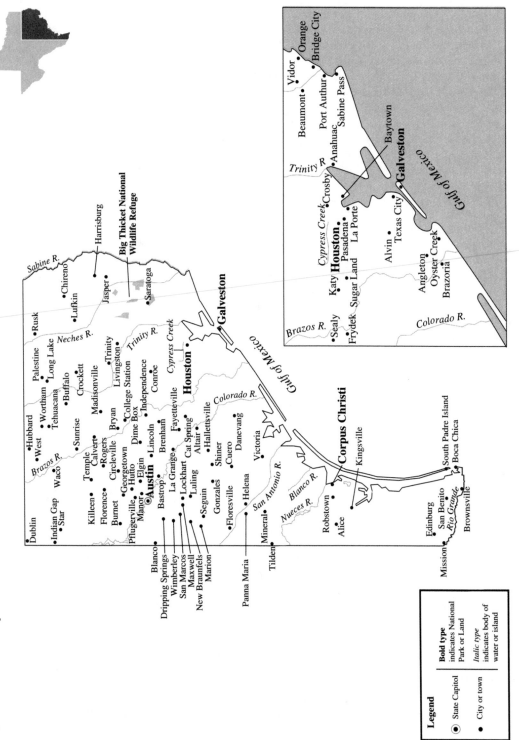

Legend

Bold type indicates National Park or Land

Italic type indicates body of water or island

◉ State Capitol

• City or town

SELECTED REFERENCES

Francis Edward Abernethy, ed. *Legendary Ladies of Texas,* Dallas: Texas Folklore Society, E-Heart Press, 1981.

America's Wildlife Hideaway. National Wildlife Federation, 1989.

George Bomar. *Texas Weather.* Austin: University of Texas Press, 1983.

Paul Burka, ed. *Texas, Our Texas.* Austin: Texas Monthly Press, 1986.

Anne Dingus. *Book of Texas Lists!* Austin: Texas Monthly Press, 1982.

T.R. Fehrenback. *Lone Star: A History of Texas and the Texans.* New York: American Legacy Press, 1983.

James L. Haley. *Texas: From Spindletop Through World War II.* New York: St. Martin's Press, 1993.

Mike Kingston, ed. *1994-95 Texas Almanac and State Industrial Guide.* Dallas: *The Dallas Morning News*, 1993.

James Ward Lee. *Classics of Texas Fiction.* Dallas: E-Heart Press, 1987.

Peter Matthews, ed. *Guinness Book of Records, 1994.* New York: Facts-on-File, 1993.

David G. McComb. *Texas: A Modern History.* Austin: University of Texas Press, 1989.

Jay Robert Nash. *Darkest Hours.* New York: Nelson-Hall, 1976.

Richard Phelan. *Texas Wild: The Land, Plants, and Animals of the Lone Star State.* New York: E.P. Dutton & Co., Inc., 1976.

Rupert N. Richardson. *Texas: The Lone Star State.* Englewood Cliffs, N.J.: Prentice-Hall, Inc., 1943.

Mary Beth Rogers. *Texas Women: A Celebration of History.* Austin: Texas Foundation for Women's Resources, 1981.

Lawrence W. Speck. *Landmarks of Texas Architecture.* Austin: University of Texas Press, 1986.

A. Ray Stephens and William M. Holmes. *Historical Atlas of Texas.* Norman, Okla.: University of Oklahoma Press, 1989.

Ron Stone. *The Book of Texas Days.* Fredericksburg, Tex.: Shearer Publishing, 1984.

Deborah Stratton, ed. *The Texas 500: 1994-1995.* Austin: The Reference Press, 1993.

Fred Tarpley. *1001 Texas Place Names.* Austin: University of Texas Press, 1980.

John Edward Weems. *"If You Don't Like The Weather..."*. Austin: Texas Monthly Press, 1986.

The author used various issues of *Texas Highways, Texas Monthly, Texas Parks and Wildlife,* and the *Dallas Morning News.*

PHOTO CREDITS

Adrian Photography: 71
Austin Convention and Visitors Bureau: 15
Austin Historical Center/Austin Public Library: 124
Barakaat Holdings Limited: 139 right
Bob Barry: 118, 120
Beaumont Convention and Visitors Bureau: 142
Big Thicket National Preserve: 24
BMG Distribution: 119
©Tim Boole, 1992: 85
Photo provided by Borden, Inc.: 77
George Bush Library: 176 top
Cal Farley's Boys Ranch: 144
©1994 CBS Inc.: 166
©1994 Dallas Cowboy Cheerleaders: 135
Dallas Cowboys: 134 both
Dallas Maveriks: 139 left
Dallas Museum of Art: 96
Steve Delafield: 173
Dewall Pollei & Cowley Advertising and Design: 72
Dwight D. Eisenhower: 57, 101
El Paso Mission Trail Association: 61
Fiesta Texas: 63
Flagship Hotel: 90
Fort Worth Convention and Visitors Bureau: 68, 104
Chris Haston ©1995 The Lyons Group: 84

C.W. Hayes, 189/ U.S. Geological Survey: 49
Ken Hoge/Texas Heart Institute: 172
Photo by Image Projections: 146
Irving Convention and Visitors Bureau: 97
Junior League of El Paso: 103
John F. Kennedy Library: 159 bottom
LBJ Library Collection: 54 middle
Kentucky State Library: 178
Library of Congress: 54 right
Los Angelas RAMS: 131 left
Courtesy of the Movie Studio at Los Colinas: 112
Larry Murphy: 168, 169
NASA: 170
National Archives and Record Administration: 53, 160, 161
National Cowgirl Hall of Fame: 129
National Park Service/D.O. Hambly: 26
National Park Service/Fred Mang, Jr.: 23
National Wildflower Research Center: 37
Randee St. Nicholas 2/93D: 123
P.G.A. Tour: 140
©Paine Bridges: 69
Perot Services Company: 82
Pittsburgh Steelers: 131 right
Professional Cowboy Association: 128
Ronald Reagan Library: 154
San Antonio Convention and Visitors Bureau/Al Rendon: 4

San Antonio Missions National Historic Park: 43
Southwest Airlines: 87
Pete Spudich: 137
Stanley Marsh 3: 105
Statuary Hall: 9, 98
The Supreme Court Historical Society: 51
Texas Department of Commerce: 29
Texas Department of Transportation: 13, 60
Texas Fiddlers Hall of Fame: 126
Texas Medical Center: 171
Texas Ranger Hall of Fame & Museum: 157, 158, 159 top
Texas Rangers: 138
Archives Division, Texas State Library: 41, 45 both, 50 left, 50 middle, 52, 114, 153, 156
©Merlin D. Tuttle: 32
U.S. Fish and Wildlife Service photo by Wyman Meinzer: 33
University of Texas at El Paso: 99
UT Southwestern Medical Center at Dallas: 176 bottom
Wisconsin Center for Film and Theater Research: 108, 110, 115

INDEX